THE HISTORY OF PROVIDENCE,
AS MANIFESTED IN SCRIPTURE

THE HISTORY OF PROVIDENCE, AS MANIFESTED IN SCRIPTURE

Alexander Carson

THE BANNER OF TRUTH TRUST

THE BANNER OF TRUTH TRUST
3 Murrayfield Road, Edinburgh EH12 6EL, UK
P.O. Box 621, Carlisle, PA 17013, USA

*

First published in 1840
First Banner of Truth Trust Edition 2012
© The Banner of Truth Trust 2012

ISBN: 978 1 84871 175 4

*

Typeset in 10/14 Sabon Oldstyle Figures at
the Banner of Truth Trust, Edinburgh

Printed in the USA by
Versa Press, Inc.,
East Peoria, IL

Contents

Biographical Sketch of the Author

ALEXANDER CARSON, Baptist minister, was born in Anna-
hone near Stewartstown, Co. Tyrone, about 1776. His parents
were Scottish Presbyterians, settled in Ireland, who consecrated
their son to the ministry at an early age. He was sent to a classical
school run by a certain Mr Peebles in the village of Tullyhogue near
Cookstown, and afterwards to the University of Glasgow, where,
through disciplined study he became a good Greek scholar — 'the
first scholar of his time', according to Robert Haldane. He proceeded B.A. and M.A. In 1798 at the age of twenty-two, he was
ordained pastor of the Presbyterian congregation at Tubbermore
(Tobermore) in Co. Londonderry. His evangelical Calvinism caused
a disagreement with not a few of his hearers who inclined to the
Arian heresy that had become so widespread among the Presbyterians in Ireland. A few years later Carson resigned the pastorate,
shook off the shackles of Presbyterianism, and published his 'Reasons for Separating from the Synod of Ulster' in 1804. Part of his
congregation followed him. For some years he preached in barns
and in the open air. In 1814 a small meeting-house was built in
which he devotedly laboured for thirty years. In the intervals of his
ministry he employed his pen in contending earnestly for the faith,
and published books on such disputed subjects as the Inspiration
and Interpretation of Scripture, Transubstantiation, the Trinity, etc.
In 1827 he had a sharp controversy with Samuel Lee, Professor of
Hebrew at Cambridge, and published a book entitled *The Incom-
petency of Prof. Lee for translating the Holy Scriptures*, followed
by a reply to Lee's answer. In attempting to refute Haldane's *New
Views of Baptism* he was himself converted to Baptist principles,

and afterwards published (1831) his best-known book, *Baptism, Its Mode and Subjects*. Of this he printed an enlarged edition in 1844; it was subscribed for by four hundred Baptist ministers. The whole impression was rapidly disposed of, and a new edition of ten thousand copies called for.

By his writings and the publication of his books Carson became widely known; and so much were they esteemed in America that two universities simultaneously bestowed upon him the honorary degree of LL.D. He also became well known nearer home by travelling through most of the English counties, preaching as he went on behalf of Baptist missions. Returning from his last tour in 1844, while waiting at Liverpool for the steamer to Belfast, he fell over the edge of the quay, dislocated his shoulder, and was nearly drowned. He was rescued and taken to the steamer; but on his arrival at Belfast he was unable to proceed further, and after eight days he died, on August 24, 1844, in the sixty-eighth year of his age. His remains were removed to 'Solitude', his house near Tubbermore, and buried near the meeting-house where he had preached, and where six months before he had buried his wife.

A collection of Carson's works was posthumously published in Dublin in six stout volumes. At the end of the sixth volume there is a copious collection of extracts from sixteen different notices of Carson and his writings, in which he is said to be a second Jonathan Edwards, and the first biblical critic of the nineteenth century.

Preface

THE Providence of God in his government of the world is a subject of the deepest interest to the Christian. By proper views of
it he will see God in the daily works of his hands. Philosophy, falsely
so called, and the depravity of the human heart, make a veil of the
physical laws by which God usually conducts his government, which
hides God in his own works. But truth and Scripture represent all
physical laws as having their effect from the immediate agency of
Almighty Power, and view God as working in his Providence as
truly as he wrought in his works of creation. Christians themselves,
though they recognize the doctrine, are prone to overlook it in practice, and consequently to be deprived, in a great measure, of that
advantage which a constant and deep impression of this truth is
calculated to give. An exhibition, then, of the scriptural evidence of
the Providence of God must be of great importance to the stability
and comfort of all true believers.

There is nothing that grieves the Christian more sensibly than the
introduction and progress of error in religion. Against this he ought
to contend earnestly at every risk. He ought not to be ashamed of
any part of the divine testimony with the knowledge of which God
has honoured him, nor to seek the praise of men by concealing or
modifying God's truth. But in doing this he will be greatly supported, if he considers that it is the will of God that heresies shall
enter and pervert many. When he has nailed his colours to the mast,
and sinks with his ship, he can have the satisfaction of knowing
that his commander will ultimately have the victory; and that even
the partial damage which the enemy has been enabled to inflict was

a part of the purpose of his Sovereign Lord and Master. Without this view of Divine Providence, I cannot see any consolation for the Christian on considering the ravages of error. Philosophy combines with fanaticism, superstition with idolatry, to oppose the Lord's Anointed. One only comfort is, that the Omnipotent Lord reigneth, and even by opposers does his pleasure. 'He that sitteth in the heavens shall laugh: the Lord shall have them in derision.' He will be honoured even in the wrath of his enemies.

Nothing has a greater effect in leading Christians into error than its success. Men in general judge of a cause by its success; and Christians, though they do not recognize it as evidence, yet are often greatly influenced by it. Opinions spread by infection, rather than by a thorough investigation of the evidence. An accurate acquaintance with the ways of Providence, as manifested in Scripture, is calculated to deliver from this prejudice. In the Bible we see that God has often granted much success to his enemies. By this they are hardened in their rebellion. Mere success is no proof of truth; and the want of it is no proof of error.

A proper acquaintance with the doctrine of Providence would also be of importance to guard us from having recourse to artifice and craft in the propagation of truth. The apostle Paul, with all his zeal for the gospel, disclaims all worldly wisdom in his attempts to advance its progress. He commended the truth to every man's conscience in the sight of God. Let us use the means which God has appointed. But if Christianity was in danger of being banished from the earth, let us not attempt to assist it by fraud, craft, or means that are dishonourable. Let us fight the battles of the Lord with the weapons which he has put into our hands, but let us never support truth with sophistry. Leave the event of success to the General. All the ingenuity of all the wise men of the world could not extend the gospel one inch beyond the limits assigned by God.

It is often afflicting to the Christian to consider the signs of the times in which he lives. Hitherto the affairs of this world have been under the dominion of the prince of darkness. But in the subject of

Providence we have consolation. We know that the very opposition made to the kingdom of Christ is a part of the plan of divine wisdom; and will be overruled for the glory of God and of our Immanuel. God has given the world into the dominion of Satan, but not in such a sense as to exclude himself from the government. The wrath of Satan, as well as the wrath of man, will be obliged to praise God; and any device of it, which has not this tendency, Jehovah will restrain, and not suffer to be manifested.

I

Abraham driven by famine into Egypt

Genesis 12:10

PLENTY and scarcity are equally from the Lord; and though famine is one of the scourges with which he afflicts his enemies, his own people also are the objects of his designs in such visitations. The famine with which the land of Canaan was visited on this occasion appears evidently to be intended by Providence to bring his servant Abraham into trial. Abraham was obliged for subsistence to go down into Egypt; and in Egypt he was tried in a peculiar manner, by the fear of losing his life, on account of the beauty of Sarah his wife. This had a very wise and important purpose. It afforded an opportunity of proving that the strength of the faith which Abraham afterwards displayed, was not from any peculiar vigour of mind, or any natural fortitude which he possessed superior to other men. On the contrary, there never was an instance of greater pusillanimity than that which Abraham manifested on this occasion. From fear of losing his life, he exposed the honour of himself and of his wife, in a manner that the least courageous person, possessed of any delicacy of feeling, would not imitate. No danger could excuse him. The certainty of death would not justify such conduct. It was still worse when the event showed that his fears were groundless; and his suspicions were not only dishonourable to his God, but injurious to the court of Egypt. His sin and cowardice were the greater, as he endeavoured to prevent danger by the aid of falsehood. He taught his wife to represent herself as his sister, in a way that led to the conviction that she was not his wife. — 'And there was a famine in the land: and Abram went down into Egypt to sojourn there; for the famine was grievous in the land. And it came to pass, when he was come near to enter into Egypt, that he said unto Sarai his wife, Behold now, I know that thou art a fair woman to look upon: Therefore it shall come to pass, when the Egyptians shall see thee, that they shall say, This is his wife: and they will kill me, but they will save thee alive. Say, I pray thee, thou art my sister: that it may be well with me for thy sake; and my soul shall live because of thee. And it came to pass, that, when Abram was come into Egypt, the Egyptians beheld the woman that she was very fair.' Gen. 12:10-14.

And is this Abraham? Is this the mighty man of faith? Is this the man who, from the strength of his faith in the divine testimony, is constituted the father of the faithful to the end of the world? Is this the man who had strength of nerve to lay his only son on the altar, and grasp the knife to sacrifice him to the Lord? Then let us learn that faith is the gift of God; that the strength of it depends not on the vigour of the human mind, but on the Spirit of the Lord who bestows and upholds it.

How useful is this instance of weakness in this mighty man of faith! Had Abraham always supported his character for unconquerable faith, men would have represented it as owing to peculiar nobility of mind, and as naturally the product of his own virtue. Indeed, after all the instances of Abraham's weakness when left to himself, many are in the habit of representing Abraham's great faith as worthy of justification from its own intrinsic excellence. But all such representations are proved utterly false, not only by the express declarations of Scripture, but also in a pointed manner, by Abraham's utter want of faith whenever God left him to himself. Let those who are in the habit of giving glory to Abraham on account of the faith by which he was justified, attend to this disgraceful instance of cowardice and total want of trust in the Divine protector. If Abraham discovered the strongest instance of faith, he also manifested the most pusillanimous example of distrust. There is nothing that is good in man. 'Not unto us, not unto us, but unto thy name, O Lord, be the glory.' 'In me,' says Paul, 'that is, in my flesh, dwelleth no good thing.'

This instance of weakness in Abraham is also of great importance for the encouragement of timid believers. In prospect of great trial, they may deprive themselves of the encouragement afforded in Abraham's faith, by considering him as utterly beyond the reach of imitators. Abraham, they may say, was strong; we are nothing but weakness. And what was Abraham but weakness when left to himself? And when God was with him his strength was unconquerable. In like manner, whatever may be the greatness of the trial to which God calls the weakest of his people, they have encouragement to trust in his strength. He will not suffer them to be tempted above that they are able to bear, but will, with the temptation, make a way to escape, that they may be able to bear it. He perfects strength in their weakness. If God would call the weakest of his people to a trial as great as that of Abraham, he is able to uphold him as he did the father of the faithful.

The Providence of God, in directing the circumstances that here brought Abraham into trial, is seen also in the fact that Sarah happened to be seen by Pharaoh's princes. Not only did 'the Egyptians behold the woman that she was very fair, the princes also of Pharaoh saw her, and commended her before Pharaoh.' She might have been long in the country without being seen by any of the court. Indeed, had precaution been used, she might have been little seen even by the common people of Egypt. And it is strange that Abraham's fears did not lead him to keep his wife in retirement. The manners of the time also were favourable to this. Sarah had a tent of her own, and might have remained secluded from common observation. But it was the Lord's design that Abraham should be, in this affair, brought into trial, and all circumstances open the way to the trial. Except the Lord keep the city, the watchman watch in vain. Sarah is seen by those who had constant and immediate access to the king: they commend her beauty to him, and she is brought into his house to be one of his wives. Such is the unsearchable wisdom of God, that he performs his purposes through the means of the counsels and actions of men. Human intellect cannot fathom this; but it is presented to our view in the Scriptures in almost every page.

How consoling is this exhibition of Divine Providence! God often delivers his people from the injurious consequences of the indulgence of their wisdom. Abraham sinfully brought himself into the danger of dishonouring himself and his wife: God permitted the plan to operate to the very brink of fulfilment. But then he mercifully counteracted it: By his Providence Pharaoh was prevented from fulfilling his purpose. 'And the Lord plagued Pharaoh and his house with great plagues, because of Sarai Abram's wife.' And no doubt disease and afflictive accidents are often employed by God to keep the wicked from injuring his people; and to keep his people from fulfilling sinful or hurtful purposes. Men of God ought to take evil as well as good as coming from the Lord. Not only did Pharaoh, through this interference of Providence, abstain from taking Sarah to be his wife—'He commanded his men concerning him; and they sent him away, and his wife, and all that he had.' By this means he prevented all further occasion of evil. But while Abraham is dismissed, he is not spoiled. He had received great riches from Pharaoh, and he is allowed to carry all with him. This was the direction of the affair by Divine Providence. Had it been God's will, Pharaoh might have sent Abraham away stripped of all his goods. No doubt, also, the Providence of God directed the dismissal of Abraham, that he might go back and sojourn in the land of promise. He was to go about from place to place as a stranger and pilgrim in that country, as a father of all believers, who are strangers and pilgrims on earth. Abraham was not to be put in possession of the land of Canaan, but he is to live in it; and for this purpose Divine Providence, when the object of his residence in Egypt was fulfilled, sent him back to reside in the typical land of promise.

2

Abraham's victory over Chedorlaomer

Genesis 14:20

THE race is not to the swift, nor is the battle to the strong. It is God who giveth the victory. The most numerous and the best disciplined armies are no security for success. Divine Providence disposes the event according to sovereign pleasure. Even without any miraculous interference, the most powerful armies are often defeated by a small number. So was it on this occasion. The household of Abraham, with a few confederates, obtained an easy victory over the forces of four powerful kings.

Yet this does not imply that the strongest means in our power are not to be employed, and every exertion made to gain the purpose. Abraham armed his trained servants, and availed himself of the assistance of his confederates. He divided his band, attacked the enemy by night, and used every precaution, as if he depended for success solely on his own wisdom and power. He fought, he conquered; but God gave victory. 'Blessed be the Most High God,' says Melchizedek, 'who hath delivered thine enemies into thine hand.' God is the author of the victory obtained through the means of Abraham's little army, as truly as if the enemy had been defeated by the artillery of heaven, while Abraham and his men had been reposing on their beds. In all things let the people of the Lord trust in him with the greatest confidence; in all things let them with the utmost earnestness and vigour use the means that God puts in their power. This is the will of God with respect both to things temporal and things spiritual. Men are prone to separate what God has joined together. They either depend on means, or neglect them.

In this affair we see also the Providence of God in bringing his people into danger, that he may try their faith, exercise their patience, and manifest himself as their deliverer. The rebellion of the king's subject to Chedorlaomer, his expedition against them, and his victory over them, were all necessary to show God as the author of victory to his servant Abraham. By this means Lot was made a captive, and Abraham obliged to attempt his deliverance. We ought not to expose ourselves to danger unnecessarily; but when the Providence of God brings dangers around us, we need not fear deliverance by Providence. He will either save us from ruin, or glorify himself and us in our sufferings.

3

Providence manifested in the fulfilment of prophecy. Every step in the accomplishment of the prediction, with respect to the condition of the Israelites in Egypt, was conducted by the hand of an overruling Providence.

Genesis 15:13

IT WAS necessary, in the Divine wisdom, that the posterity of Abraham by Isaac should for a long period sojourn in the land of Egypt. God declared this most particularly to the patriarch— Gen. 15:13-16—'And he said unto Abram, Know of a surety that thy seed shall be a stranger in a land that is not theirs, and shall serve them; and they shall afflict them four hundred years; and also that nation, whom they shall serve, will I judge: and afterward shall they come out with great substance. And thou shalt go to thy fathers in peace; thou shalt be buried in a good old age. But in the fourth generation they shall come hither again: for the iniquity of the Amorites is not yet full.' How wonderfully did all circumstances in Providence lead to the fulfilment of this prediction! The whole history of Joseph was a preliminary to it. At the proper time for the removal of Jacob's family into the land of their future slavery, a famine forced them into Egypt. They were obliged to look abroad for provisions, and God had furnished them unto Pharaoh through the means of Joseph. Here then we have them translated to the destined place by the working of an all-wise Providence. By like providential circumstances they were brought into a state of the utmost degradation and misery. They were at first in the highest favour. This was natural and to be expected. The mighty obligations that Pharaoh was under to Joseph were calculated to procure favour to all his kindred. But when it was God's time to reverse the situation of his people, his Providence opened a way to bring them into oppression and slavery. Another king arose, who knew not Joseph, and who was ungenerously and unjustly influenced by fear, jealousy, and ambition—Exod. 1:8-14—'Now there arose up a new king over Egypt, which knew not Joseph. And he said unto his people, Behold, the people of the children of Israel are more and mightier than we: Come on, let us deal wisely with them; lest they multiply, and it come to pass, that, when there falleth out any war, they join also unto our enemies, and fight against us, and so get them out of the land. Therefore they did set over them taskmasters to afflict them with their burdens. And they built for Pharaoh treasure cities, Pithom and Raamses. But the more they afflicted them, the more they multiplied and grew. And they were grieved because of the children of Israel. And the Egyptians made the children of Israel to serve with rigour: And they made their lives bitter with hard bondage, in mortar, and in brick, and in all manner of service in the field: all their service, wherein they made them serve, was with rigour.' It was very natural and not unreasonable that the king of Egypt should guard against the growing power of the children of Israel. But why did he not either dismiss them from his kingdom, or treat them justly as subjects? We see how different is the conduct of this monarch from that of Abimelech with respect to Isaac. He is apprehensive of danger from the prosperity of the patriarch, and he mildly and not unjustly commands him to depart out of his kingdom—Gen. 26:13-17. How different was the conduct of Abimelech from that of Pharaoh! They both acted freely, yet they both acted in accordance with the divine appointment, without knowing it. God had no purpose to serve by oppressing Isaac through Abimelech, and God does not afflict his people without useful purpose. Therefore, he so ordered it by an inscrutable Providence, that Abimelech acted kindly in guarding against the power of Isaac. God had a purpose to serve by the afflictions of the children of Israel in Egypt, though, by a like inscrutable Providence, Pharaoh, instead of dismissing them from his country, desires to enslave them, and retain them in a state of the most abject bondage.

But the same Providence that brought the Israelites into the most miserable slavery, at the same time, through the very means of Pharaoh's tyranny, raised up a deliverer for Israel, and educated him in the very court, and even in the very family, of the oppressor. Moses was exposed, and by a wonderful Providence was made the son of Pharaoh's daughter, in order that he might be the better fitted to become a deliverer to the house of Abraham from bondage in Egypt. How wonderful! How deep are the counsels of Jehovah! We ought to search for them in his word, examine them with the utmost diligence; but not attempt to fathom them, or account for them in agreement with our own wisdom. We ought to behold and bow with the most profound submission. It is as great a proof of weakness as of wickedness to attempt to grasp the plans of Jehovah with the feeble intellect of man. He charges the very angels with folly.

4

Abraham sitting in the door of his tent

Genesis 18:1

A T A CERTAIN time, Abraham chanced, as men speak, to sit in his tent door in the cool of the day. What could be more natural? What apparently could be more accidental? Yet it was evidently providential. It was divinely ordered that, at the moment in which the heavenly messengers approached Abraham's dwelling, as travellers seeming to pass on another errand, the patriarch was found sitting at the door of his tent, that he might espy and arrest them with his hospitality. In no circumstances, it is true, could the heavenly visitants have been at a loss to find him. But it is usually God's way to bring about his purposes in a providential manner, and to guide events by an unseen hand. In his dealings his own people may discover him; but from the world he lies hid. Men in general see nothing but chance and nature, and second causes in the things that take place on the earth. The Christian may see God in every thing. It is in him we live, and move, and have our being. Abraham, then, at the moment of the arrival of his heavenly guests, was sitting at the tent door in order to be ready to behold and receive them. They were not obliged to seek him, or introduce themselves. A heaven-directed accident gave room for the hospitality of the patriarch to invite the strangers without a discovery of their quality or their errand. 'And the Lord appeared unto him on the plains of Mamre; and he sat in the tent door in the heat of the day. And he lifted up his eyes and looked, and lo, three men stood by him; and when he saw them, he ran to meet them from the tent door, and bowed himself toward the ground.'

A like providential arrangement placed Lot in the gate of Sodom to receive the angels on their arrival at that city. 'And there came two angels to Sodom at even; and Lot sat at the gate of Sodom: and

Lot seeing them, rose up to meet them; and he bowed himself to the ground.'—Gen. 19:1.

By this providential method of reception, there was an opportunity afforded to the men of Sodom to behold the strangers in the appearance of men, and to manifest a specimen of that wickedness on account of which the Lord was about to bring destruction on the cities of the plain. The angels might have come with an angelic appearance, or they might have come as men by night, and unseen by the men of Sodom. But coming in either of these ways, an occasion would not have been given to the men of Sodom to manifest the abominations of their hearts. The strangers, therefore, by this appointment of Providence, were seen by the men of the city, and a scene of revolting wickedness was acted immediately before the pouring out of vengeance. 'But before they lay down, the men of the city, even the men of Sodom, compassed the house round, both old and young, all the people from every quarter.'

Here we have an instance of the sovereignty of God in his Providence. He here acts in a manner which it would be wicked in any mortal to imitate. He does not tempt any man to sin, but he brings them into situations that manifest what is in them. He adopted a method by which the guilt of Sodom was proved and aggravated. He might have adopted a method by which this would have been avoided. Now, this it would be utterly unlawful for men to do. As far as in our power we should avoid every thing that we think calculated to be the occasion of leading men into sin. We should on no account attempt to prove a man to be a hypocrite by presenting him with a temptation, which we judge would manifest him. This is the province of a sovereign God only. We should give no occasion of stumbling either to Jew or Gentile, or to the church of God.

By this method of the angelic appearance, there was also, both to Abraham and Lot, an opportunity given to manifest hospitality. That it had this design, as well as to be an excitement to hospitality in the people of God, is evident from the use made of the fact by the

Epistle to the Hebrews: 'Be not forgetful to entertain strangers; for thereby some have entertained angels unawares.'—Heb. 13:2.

5

Providential restraints from evil

Genesis 20:6

AS GOD by his Providence sometimes opens a way to manifest the evil that is in the hearts of men, and even of his own people; so he also sometimes restrains them from committing the evil which they purpose, or which they would commit if occasion was presented. A providential interference often prevents men from rashly doing what they would have done, if no such interference had taken place, and which would have been irremediably injurious to themselves or others. A remarkable instance we have of this in the withholding of Abimelech from taking to wife Sarah, the wife of Abraham. He had taken her into his house, but God, by the restraints of his Providence, withheld him from accomplishing his purpose, and from the dishonour of Abraham. 'I also,' says God, 'withheld thee from sinning against me: therefore suffered I thee not to touch her.' By his overruling Providence God prevented the accomplishment of so great an evil. Had this deed been accomplished, it might have been forgiven; but the evil of it could never have been repaired. Had Abimelech given the injured husband his kingdom, it would have been a compensation utterly unequivalent. God then prevented an injury that could never have been repaired. His Providence then threw an obstacle in the way of the accomplishment of the foul deed.

By a like pusillanimity, Isaac exposed the honour of his wife Rebekah, and by a like providential restraint, God preserved her

ıgh the men of Gerar had asked Isaac about his
said that she was his sister, yet he was long in the
..ıjury to his wife's honour. And at last, by a provi-
...ı event, Abimelech discovered that Rebekah was the wife of
Isaac, Gen. 26:8-9, 'And it came to pass when he had been there a
long time, that Abimelech, king of the Philistines, looked out at a
window, and saw, and, behold, Isaac was sporting with Rebekah his
wife. And Abimelech called Isaac, and said, Behold, of a surety she
is thy wife: and how saidst thou she is my sister?'

How beautifully, how wonderfully, does the Providence of God
co-operate with his purposes of grace! God rules as absolutely on
earth as he does in heaven. Nothing takes place but what he has
ordained for his own glory, and for the good of his own people.
Believers are in the world in the midst of their enemies, who have all
earthly power in their hands, yet the Lord preserves them uninjured
in every instance in which it is not for his own glory and their good
that they should suffer.

6

The ram caught by the horns in the thicket

Genesis 22:13

THIS was a very extraordinary occasion; and, as the nature of
the case did not allow Abraham to be provided with a beast
for a sacrifice, we might have expected that God would provide
one for him by miracle. He could as easily have caused a ram to
come of himself from any part of the adjacent country, as he had
formerly brought the animals to Noah in the ark. But not so; he did
not choose to do the thing by miracle. He furnished the sacrifice
by his Providence. 'And Abraham lifted up his eyes, and looked,

and, behold, behind him a ram caught in a thicket by his horns: and Abraham went out, took the ram, and offered him up for a burnt-offering in the stead of his son.' What could be more purely accidental than this? Was there any thing wonderful that a ram should happen to be entangled in the brambles where he was feeding? What could be more natural? Why should it be thought that Providence was concerned in the matter? It is, indeed, a very trifling thing, and a fact easily to be accounted for. But why did it happen on this occasion? Why was not the ram caught yesterday? Or why did it happen before to-morrow? Why was it on this day—in this hour—in this minute? A day sooner, or a day later, would not have answered the purpose. The ram must be caught, and held inextricably fast, at the moment that Abraham needed him. Why was the ram caught here? Had it been at a distance, or out of the view of Abraham, it might as well not have been caught at all. It is caught at this moment, at this very spot where it is needed. Why was the caught beast a ram, and not a deer, or some other horned animal? Because such an animal would not have answered for the sacrifice that was to be offered. Why was it not a he-goat? Because, though such an animal was a suitable sacrifice in some circumstances, a ram was most suitable on the present occasion. Why was it a male, and not a female? Because, though in some circumstances female animals were employed in sacrifice, yet a male is that usually employed for a good typical purpose. This, then, is the work of God, as much as even the creation of the world. It is a miracle of Providence, and shows us how to read the book of Providence. We ought to see the hand of God in the most trifling things. Nothing is too great for his Providence to effect, nothing is so small as to be below his attention. This fact teaches us also that what God requires from us for his worship, he will supply to us by his Providence.

7

Expulsion of Hagar from the house of Abraham

Genesis 21:10

IN HER design of expelling Hagar from the house of Abraham,
Sarah was excited and influenced by her own private feelings
and interests alone. She uttered her own sentiments in her own language. Yet she uttered the truth of God, in God's words, in a figure.
What she said with respect to Hagar, Ishmael, Isaac, and herself,
was all providentially adapted to express the gospel in an allegory.
The Spirit of God by Paul, in the Epistle to the Galatians, expounds
this transaction in this sense. The words of Sarah, with respect to
her own private affairs, are quoted as the words of inspiration with
respect to the nature of the gospel. 'Nevertheless,' says the apostle,
'what saith the Scripture? Cast out the bondwoman and her son:
for the son of the bondwoman shall not be heir with the son of the
freewoman.' Gal. 4:30. Here the words of Sarah are expounded as
referring to the gospel, as fully as if they had no primary reference. It
is not said, 'What saith Sarah?' but 'What saith the Scripture?' The
words employed providentially by Sarah in her own affairs are, in
another point of view, the words of Scripture with reference to the
way of salvation. In the inscrutable wisdom of God, the words are
the words of Sarah and of God—of Sarah, in her own sense, of the
Spirit, as a symbolical expression of the gospel. Men who receive
the truth of God no further than they can comprehend the nature of
the thing testified, cannot believe that the allegorical meaning taken
out of the expression by Paul, was really in the design of the Holy
Spirit when the words were used by Sarah, and recorded by Moses.
They view the historical document as merely casually adapted to
illustrate the point in hand, and, as such, ingeniously employed by
the apostle. But these men wrest the Scriptures, and deny the palpa-
ble testimony of the Holy Spirit. Paul does not use the historical fact

as casually adapted to illustrate the gospel, but expressly expounds
it as the testimony of the Spirit in the ancient Scriptures. 'What
saith the Scripture?' It is used as an argument to convince, and not
as an illustration to explain. 'Tell me,' says he, 'ye that desire to
be under the law, do you not hear the law?' Is not this proof from
the law? After this introduction he proceeds to relate the history
in its allegorical meaning. 'For it is written, Rejoice, thou barren
that bearest not; break forth and cry, thou that bearest not: for the
desolate hath many more children than she which hath an husband.
Now we, brethren, as Isaac was, are the children of promise. But,
as then, he that was born after the flesh persecuted him that was
born after the Spirit, even so it is now. Nevertheless, what saith the
Scripture? Cast out the bondwoman and her son: for the son of
the bondwoman shall not be heir with the son of the freewoman.
So, then, brethren, we are not the children of the bondwoman, but
of the free.' What a wonderful combination of providential events
was necessary to fit this history to the shadowing of the gospel!
Abraham must have a wife a freewoman; he must have also a wife
who was a slave. He must have a son by this slave, and a son in a
peculiar manner by his wife. The slave and her son must be cast out;
and not only excluded from the inheritance, but from a residence in
the family. The wife must express, with regard to her own affairs, in
her own language, language that the Holy Spirit adapts to an allegorical declaration of the gospel. This surely is Divine wisdom. And
this both illustrates and proves the inspiration of the Scriptures.
The very words of Scripture, with respect to historical details and
circumstances which, in themselves, have no direct concern with
the gospel, are adapted, in the most wonderful manner, to express a
secondary meaning, known at the time only to the Holy Spirit. The
unfeeling demand of Sarah, with regard to her domestic concerns,
is, in another point of view, the language of the Spirit figuratively
expressing the nature of the gospel.

8

Isaac mocked by Ishmael

Genesis 21:9

NOTHING could be more natural to the situation than the conduct of Ishmael, in mocking the pretensions and prospects of Isaac, on the occasion of the feast of weaning. He was the first-born, and would, of course, expect that he should have the pre-eminence. He would feel a sense not only of injury but of insult. His haughty soul could not bear that such honours should be conferred on his younger brother. He saw himself degraded, and stripped of what he considered his just honours in his father's house. He vented his feelings in mocking the pretensions of the favourite son.

The matter, however, was directed by Providence. Ishmael's mocking of Isaac was necessary as a type of the carnal son mocking the spiritual seed. In this light it is viewed by Paul in the Epistle to the Galatians. 'But as then he that was born after the flesh persecuted him that was born after the Spirit, even so it is now.' The Providence of God provided an emblem of the persecution of his spiritual children by those who depend on carnal descent; and the Spirit of inspiration treasured it up in the divine records, to be expounded in due time by an apostle of Christ. This shows the necessity of inspiration, even in the most trifling historical events. What could less need inspiration than the record of Ishmael's mocking? The wisdom of this world would ask, what need of inspiration in recording such a fact? But an uninspired historian might have omitted the fact altogether, while it was necessary as a shadow of a peculiarity in the kingdom of Christ. Man is no competent judge with respect to what is necessary to be recorded in Scripture. This can be known only to the wisdom of God.

This mocking was necessary, also, to give occasion to the excitement and demand of Sarah. If Sarah's demand was necessary as a figure of the gospel, that which occasioned her demand must also have been equally necessary. And, if the mocking by Ishmael, and the demand of expulsion by Sarah, were necessary, so also must have been the weaning-feast which gave occasion to all. There is here a chain, every link of which is of Providence.

Yet Ishmael's mocking was his own sin, in which Providence had no share. The fact is obvious; the explanation of it is beyond the power of human intellect. It is our duty to recognise the ways of God as far as he has manifested them; it is as vain as it is impious to attempt to explain what the unsearchable wisdom of God has concealed.

9

The Providence of God prospering the affairs of Abraham

Genesis 21:22

W E OFTEN read that God blessed Abraham and Isaac in reference to the prosperity of their temporal affairs. Yet it was through industry and attention to business, as in the case of other men, that their wealth increased. From this let us learn two things. Let us look to God for every thing; and let us ascribe to him the smallest as well as the greatest of the things which we possess. Let us at the same time expect every blessing from God through the appointed means. There are on this subject two extremes, equally injurious. Some look not sufficiently to the necessity of the divine blessing on the labour and exertion employed to procure the necessaries and comforts of life. When they succeed, they are unthankful to God: when they fail, overlooking the true cause, they neglect the proper remedy. In temporal things, as well as in spiritual, we should seek all things from God, through the use of the means which he has appointed. We have as much need for God in the concerns of this world, as we have with respect to the world to come. In him we live, and move, and have our being. He is the author of every good and perfect gift.

How shameful is it that many, called Christians, overlook that Providence that was so fully recognised by Abimelech, king of Gerar, in the land of the Philistines! He saw the uncommon prosperity of Abraham, and he ascribed it to the blessing of God on his labours. 'And it came to pass at that time, that Abimelech and Phicol, the chief captain of his host, spake unto Abraham, saying, God is with thee in all that thou doest.' Our blind philosophers cannot see what was so clearly discovered by this king of the Philistines. Their indolent god rules only by general laws. God is excluded by them from all immediate concern in the affairs of men.

10
Abraham informed about the family of his brother Nahor

Genesis 22:20

IT WAS necessary that the typical kingdom of Israel should be unmixed with the nations of Canaan. Isaac, therefore, must not take a wife of the inhabitants of the country in which he resided. His wife must be of his own kindred. But how is this to be brought about? Abraham, as far as we know, remained without any intelligence from his relations, till after the time when he was commanded to sacrifice his son Isaac. Some time after this, we learn that he received tidings with respect to his relations, in which it is mentioned that Rebekah was born to Bethuel. In this way there was timely notice to the Patriarch to plan with respect to the marriage of his son; and on this was founded the commission given to his servant to go to the kindred of his master for a wife to Isaac, Gen. 22:20-23 — 'And it came to pass after these things, that it was told Abraham, saying, Behold, Milcah, she hath also born children unto thy brother Nahor; Huz his first-born, and Buz his brother, and Kemuel the father of Aram, and Chesed, and Hazo, and Pildash, and Jidlaph, and Bethuel. And Bethuel begat Rebekah: these eight Milcah did bear to Nahor, Abraham's brother.'

How many things, apparently accidental, are necessary to open a way to the acquaintance of those who are afterwards to be married to each other! Husbands and wives may be born for each other, as much as Eve was formed for Adam, while their marriage depends on the most trifling accident.

11

Abraham's purchase of the cave of Machpelah for a burying-ground

Genesis 23

WHY was Abraham so solicitous to have a burying-place in Canaan by purchase? Was not the country all his own by promise? Why does he not bury in it, as he had lived in it, relying on the word of the Most High? Did he fear that, without purchase, the bones of his relatives would be disinterred? Did he trust the Lord with respect to the possession of the whole country by his posterity; and fear with respect to the spot where he and his wife should lie? Why did he not at least accept the generous offer of the people, and bury in some one of the chief of their sepulchres? If this was not sufficient, why did he not accept the offer of Ephron, and take the field as a gift? Did not Ephron propose to give it legally, in full right, for nothing? Was it the pride of independence that prevented him from receiving the possession as a gift? This would have been unworthy of Abraham; and at other times he freely received what was bestowed. He scrupled not to receive the gifts of Abimelech, king of Gerar. Yet all the politeness and noble generosity of the son of Heth could not prevail with the Patriarch, nor induce him to depart from his resolution. Purchase, purchase, purchase; nothing but purchase. He still insists on giving what the thing is worth, in the current money of the merchant. I cannot say what was in the mind of Abraham; but I have no doubt as to what was the intention of Providence, who overruled in this matter. The heavenly Canaan is, to the heirs of promise, most entirely a free gift, yet it cost the Saviour full price. A figure of this, then, the Spirit of inspiration gives us in this affair. Abraham received the land of Canaan by promise; yet, to show that our salvation cost the Saviour full price, the Patriarch, in Divine Providence, is led to the possession of a burying-place in Canaan by purchase. Abraham would not accept the ground on any other terms than paying the full amount of its value. Some persons, under a profession of Christianity, are now beginning to discover that the death of Christ was not truly a price. Such a sentiment finds no support, either in the doctrines of the New Testament, or in the types of the Old. Redeemed sinners have in Christ paid all that justice could demand.

12

Success of Abraham's servant in seeking a wife for his master's son

Genesis 24

A WIFE must be found for Isaac from the house of the brethren of his father; and the Providence of God suggests and prospers every step in the process of seeking her. The servant, before swearing, very prudently suggests, that the person sought might not be willing to come. It is a very trying thing to leave country and kindred for ever. Abraham's trust is, that the Lord his God would send his angel before the commissioner, and prosper his journey. No means were neglected; every argument was employed to effect the purpose. But it was through the interference of Divine Providence that all these means were to be blessed. Accordingly, the servant sets out on his journey, with every preparation that he thought calculated to be useful in effecting his purpose; but he trusts only in the blessing of the God of his master to prosper his errand. When he arrived at the city of Nahor, he looked to the Lord to direct him by his Providence; and Providence blessed him with a most wonderful success. 'And he arose and went into the city of Nahor.' — 'And the servant took ten camels of the camels of his master, and departed; for all the goods of his master were in his hand: and he arose, and went to Mesopotamia, unto the city of Nahor. And he made his camels to kneel down without the city by a well of water at the time of the evening, even the time that women go out to draw water. And he said, O Lord God of my master Abraham, I pray thee, send me good speed this day, and show kindness unto my master Abraham. Behold, I stand here by the well of water; and the daughters of the men of the city come out to draw water. And let it come to pass, that the damsel to whom I shall say, Let down thy pitcher, I pray thee, that I may drink; and she shall say, Drink, and I will give thy camels drink also: let the same be she that thou hast appointed for thy servant Isaac; and thereby shall I know that thou hast showed kindness unto my master. And it came to pass, before he had done speaking, that, behold, Rebekah came out, who was born to Bethuel, son of Milcah, the wife of Nahor, Abraham's brother, with her pitcher upon her shoulder. And the damsel was very fair to look upon, a virgin, neither had any man known her: and she went down to the well, and filled her pitcher, and came up. And the servant ran to meet her, and said, Let me, I pray thee, drink a little water of thy pitcher. And she said, Drink, my lord: and she hasted, and let down her pitcher upon her hand, and gave him drink. And when she had done giving him drink, she said, I will draw water for thy camels also, until they have done drinking. And she hasted, and emptied her pitcher into the trough, and ran again unto the well to draw water, and drew for all his camels. And the man wondering at her held his peace, to wit whether the Lord had made his journey prosperous or not.' It was to the Lord that he looked for good speed. He knew that all the wealth of his master, and all his own prudent management of the affair, might fail. But he knew that the God of Abraham could give success to the means which he employed. And the Lord prospered him in a most remarkable manner. All is natural, but all is providential; and the combination of all the links in the chain is a miracle of Providence. The time of his arrival was providential—in the evening, at the time when women go out to draw water. He was not obliged to make inquiries, or loiter about the suburbs for a length of time. He comes in the very moment that ensured the immediate meeting with Rebekah. What put it into his mind to make such a strange request to God, with respect to the daughters of the men of the city who should come out at that time to draw water? And what power made the answer so wonderfully correspond to the prayer? Could one out of a million of chances secure such a coincidence, without an overruling Providence? What brought out Rebekah at that very moment? Why Rebekah, more than any other of the daughters of the men of the city? Rebekah came—she came even before he had done speaking. God often answers the prayers of his people, even while the word is in their mouth. Let Christians who seek a wife, ask one from the Lord. He can give what is suitable—he can remove all difficulties. Abraham's servant, as far as we see, made the request from the suggestion of his own mind. There was no direct revelation given to him on the matter. He himself plans what he was to ask from the female who should come to the well; and also what she should answer. And, in giving him an answer, Rebekah speaks not by revelation, but from the impulse of her own mind, conscious of nothing but kindness to a stranger. Yet the correspondence between his request to God, and her answer to him, could be effected by nothing but by Divine Providence. They both spoke from themselves: they both spoke from the Lord.

In the prayer of Abraham's servant, we have a full recognition of the important truth that the Providence of God overrules and directs the free resolves and very words of men. Had not this been his belief, he would not have requested that the damsel applied to for water should not only comply with his request, but form her answer in the very words which he dictated for her. What a puzzling question would this be to the authors of theories of inspiration? Their silly philosophy would strive in vain to solve this difficulty. But Abraham's servant, without respect to any theory, looked to God for an answer from the mouth of one with whom he had no acquaintance, in the very words which he himself chose to dictate. In one point of view, she gave her own answer in her own words; in another point of view, she gave that answer from God, or words which God providentially put into her mouth. The most unlettered of the people of God often know about God, what the presumptuous philosophy of the wise will not suffer them to see.

On receiving Rebekah's reply to his request, in the very words which himself had dictated in his prayer to God, Abraham's servant was astonished and overwhelmed with wonder and gratitude; and he refers all to the presence of the Lord with him. 'And he said,

Blessed be the Lord God of my master Abraham, who hath not left destitute my master of his mercy and his truth: I being in the way, the Lord led me to the house of my master's brother.' He knew the city in which Abraham's kindred resided, and, doubtless, he would make all proper inquiries on his journey. But, after all, it was the Lord who led him to the place, and who prospered his message. In all our success, after all the exertions of our minds and bodies in effecting our purposes, we should give all the glory to the Lord. We should see God in all the events of our lives, and walk before him ever on earth.

Abraham was very rich, yet the obtaining a suitable wife for his son was a matter of great importance in the eyes of this man of God, his servant; for which he expresses thankfulness with the deepest humiliation. 'And I bowed down my head,' said he, 'and worshipped the Lord, and blessed the Lord God of my master Abraham, which had led me in the right way, to take my master's brother's daughter unto his son.'

Such was the success of Abraham's servant hitherto. But, had the Providence of the Lord ceased to direct the event, the issue might still have been otherwise. Notwithstanding the wealth of Abraham, and all the favourable circumstances in which his servant made his entrance into the house of Bethuel, the suit might still have been unsuccessful. The destiny of Rebekah was, by this marriage, much beyond any prospects which she could have had in her own country. But on unbelief these prospects would have little influence. Abraham was now a stranger and a pilgrim in the country where he lived; and, to unbelief, his future possession of the land would be utterly incredible. Prejudice, also, against his singularity in religion might have had more weight with Rebekah and her father's house than all the riches of her suitor. A thousand whims might have prevented the marriage. But, in the Providence of God, the suit was agreeable to both Rebekah and her family. 'Then Laban and Bethuel answered and said, The thing proceedeth from the Lord; we cannot speak good or bad.' 'And they called Rebekah, and said unto her,

Wilt thou go with this man? And she answered and said, I will go.'
Divine Providence secured the consent of all who had a right to
interfere.

Marriage is the most important relation in life. Nothing so much
concerns happiness in this world and the service of God as a proper
choice. It is strange that Christians in general look so little to the
Lord in this matter.

13

The arrival of Rebekah at the time when Isaac was engaged in communion with God by meditation and prayer

Genesis 24:63

I T IS but a slight circumstance, but as an instance of providential wisdom, it is worthy of observation, that, at the moment of
Rebekah's arrival at the residence of her future husband, he was
engaged in meditation and prayer. This may be in man's view an
accidental coincidence, but it is the arrangement of the Providence
of God. The trifling fact is recorded by the wisdom of inspiration; and there is nothing recorded which is not calculated in one
way or other to give us instruction. The believer ought to see him
who is invisible, and to commune with him as his confidential and
Almighty friend. The nearer he lives to God, the happier will he be.
Yet strange, the corrupt heart of man, even in the believer, is prone
to seek happiness by departing from God. It is only when he is kept
by the power of God, and as far as he is kept, that he finds his happiness in God's favour. To encourage his people to constant fellowship
with him, he increases their happiness, as they increase in a desire to
enjoy his presence. He is the hearer of their prayers, and they never

seek him in vain. If he gives them not the very thing which they ask, he will give them what is better for them; and he will give them what they ask when it is good for them. Here he honours prayer by putting Isaac in possession of his highest earthly blessing, while he was engaged in meditation and prayer.—'And Isaac went out to meditate in the field at the eventide: and he lifted up his eyes, and saw, and, behold, the camels were coming.'—Gen. 24:63.

14

The fulfilment of the promise of God to Abraham with respect to Ishmael

Genesis 17:20, 25:16

'AND as for Ishmael, I have heard thee,' says God to Abraham; 'behold, I have blessed him, and will make him fruitful, and will multiply him exceedingly: twelve princes shall he beget; and I will make him a great nation.' This promise was in a great measure fulfilled, even while Isaac, the heir of the promises, was a stranger and a pilgrim in Canaan. 'These are the sons of Ishmael, and these are their names, by their towns, and by their castles; twelve princes according to their nations.'—Gen. 25:16. And how did the Lord fulfil this promise? Altogether in a way of Providence. He did every thing with an unseen hand, exactly as he still does every thing in all the kingdoms of the earth. His own people can trace his steps, and recognise the marks of his presence. But he lies hid from the observation of the world. It is delightfully instructive to the believer to trace the history of the descendants of Ishmael; and behold how wonderfully God has fulfilled his promise to Abraham with respect to them. And in this ought we not to see the Providence of God in the affairs of all nations, of all ages? Who is it that raises up nations to prosperity, or casts them down and destroys them? Who is it that bestows empires, and upholds the thrones of kings? Who is it that sends the sword, and gives conquest to the ambitious? Who is it that regulates all the affairs of earth, and sends war or peace, prosperity or adversity, victory or defeat, at his pleasure? It is the God who made, and who fulfils this promise with respect to the son of Abraham.

15
Jacob's purchase of the birthright
Genesis 25:29

CAN any man approve of the conduct of Jacob? It was base, it was ungenerous, it was hypocritical, it was unjust. Yet the God of Providence gives it success, while he does not sanction it. He does more than this. He makes conduct, of which he disapproves, the very means of effecting his eternal purpose. And was he at a loss for means to accomplish his purpose, that he chose to fulfil his will by an act of the foulest treachery? No, he has his choice of means to effect the events which he designs to bring about. And this means was the best suited to answer the ends of his sovereign wisdom. It was in every part suited to his design. Had any part of it been otherwise, it would never have existed.

The sovereignty of Providence meets us here at the very threshold. Could any thing have been easier for Providence to effect, than to cause that Jacob should have been the first-born of the twins? This would have taken away all occasion for the existence of this disgraceful conduct in Jacob. But instead of making Jacob the first-born, Providence undoubtedly constitutes Esau the first-born for a specific purpose. God designedly gives occasion to the scheme of Jacob and his mother. In the very birth of the children, Divine Providence points out the future history by Jacob taking hold of Esau's heel.

The different dispositions, habits, and manner of life of the two brothers, were calculated to co-operate in bringing about the event here related. 'Esau was a cunning hunter, a man of the field; and Jacob was a plain man, dwelling in tents.' This circumstance was the occasion of exposing Esau to the hunger, through the temptation of which he was induced to sell his birthright, while it afforded to Jacob an opportunity of supplying his brother's want at the moment.

The sinful partiality of the parents, each for a different child, had also a distinguished share in bringing about the event. The ground of Isaac's peculiar love to Esau was utterly unwarrantable; and it is not said that Rebekah's preference of Jacob was grounded on his character. At all events, she loved Jacob peculiarly, and by this means the birthright was transferred from Esau to his younger brother. Had Esau been the favourite of his mother, or of both his parents, this scheme would not have been contrived to deprive him of his birthright. Every link in the chain is inserted by the hand of Providence.

The answer of God to Rebekah, declaring that 'the elder shall serve the younger,' no doubt makes Isaac guilty of rashness at least, in conferring the birthright, without farther consulting the Lord. He acted evidently out of preference to Esau. But this is another feature of the Sovereignty of Providence in this matter. God could easily have made Jacob the favourite of his father as well as of his mother. Had he done so, no occasion could have been given to this crime in Jacob. His father would have given him the blessing by consulting the mind of the Lord. This providential circumstance shows us also that God can effect his purposes through the means of persons who intend to thwart them, as well as by those who intend to give them effect. He made Isaac transfer the birthright to Jacob, in the very act by which he intended to give it to Esau; and thus to derange the appointment of God. It may alleviate the guilt of Rebekah in this matter, that she knew the divine appointment. But it is not said that she acted on this principle. She loved Jacob, and therefore contrived to give him the birthright. There is no intimation that, from honouring the divine intentions, she endeavoured to fulfil them. Even had this been true, it would not justify her. She should have left to the Lord the means of effecting his own sovereign purposes. David knew that he was to be king in the place of Saul, yet David would not on that account destroy or injure the Lord's anointed even when he was in his power, and when his own life was in the greatest danger from the king of Israel.

Many persons think that the account of this transaction is irrational and incredible. How could Esau be at the point of death by hunger in his father's residence? But this objection is grounded on a supposition that is not true. It is not in evidence, and therefore need not be believed, that the two brothers were now in their father's usual place of abode. On the contrary, there is sufficient evidence that this was not the case. Jacob, we are told, was a plain man, dwelling in tents. This implies that he had his residence at different places, as his business of a shepherd required. Like the sons of Jacob, who were living at a distance from their father, when he sent Joseph to visit them, Jacob himself, in the same occupation, was obliged to live at a distance from his father. Esau, wherever he usually resided, was out in the chase, and, on his return, called at the tent of his brother Jacob. This circumstance occasioned the temptation by which Esau lost his birthright, and Jacob forfeited his integrity; but by which God fulfilled his sovereign will.

Were this a mere possibility, it is sufficient to answer the objection, but that it is a fact is in evidence from the passage itself. When Esau had finished eating and drinking, he 'rose up and went his way.' Does not this imply, that his usual place of residence was elsewhere? Rashness and incredulity often start objections, which, instead of manifesting uncommon perspicacity, owe their origin to ignorance and want of attention.

16

The annoyances of the man of God by the world, under the control of Providence

Genesis 26:22

IN ALL ages and in all countries God's people are strangers and pilgrims, and will be subject to ill treatment under the very best forms of government. There are innumerable ways in which they may be annoyed by their enemies, beyond redress from the best system of laws under the best administrators. Their comfort is, that Divine Providence overrules and regulates the extent of mischief which his wisdom may see meet to permit their enemies to inflict on them. The wrath of man he will make to praise him; and whatever of this wrath is not for his glory and the good of his people, he will restrain. He suffered the herdsmen of Gerar to strive with the servants of Isaac for the wells which the latter had dug. They did so repeatedly. This was necessary in the typical people, and it served to manifest the peaceable character of Isaac. But, though there is no end to the unreasonableness of men, there is a limit to the extent in which Divine Providence will suffer it to manifest itself against his people. At the digging of the third well, the Philistines ceased to strive. And that this was not accidental, or unrelated to Providence, we know from the pious acknowledgement of Isaac on the occasion. 'And he called the name of it Rehoboth; and he said, For now the Lord hath made room for us.' A man of the world—a philosopher, would see nothing here but mere accident, without any connection with Providence. But the man of God ascribes the ceasing of the annoyance of his enemies to the overruling power of the Ruler of the world. What a consolation to the Christian to reflect on this fact! He is in safety while he is on all sides encircled by those who hate him. He lies down in the midst of bears and lions, yet he rises in tranquillity and peace. Were it not for Divine Providence, the people of God, who, compared with the world, are but a handful, would be extirpated utterly from the earth. They are like the family of Abraham and Isaac sojourning as strangers among the inhabitants of Canaan. But Abraham and Isaac were as safe, when they sojourned in Cannan as strangers, as were Solomon and David when they ruled over all the nations as far as the river Euphrates. God's Providence is the inheritance of his people

17
Transference of the blessing of Jacob

HOW many providential circumstances are linked into one chain, to confer the blessing of his father on Jacob? Among these we may recognize the blindness of Isaac. Had he not been afflicted with great dimness of sight, the scheme by which Jacob succeeded could never have taken place. We have no account of any such blindness in Abraham, when he had arrived at a much greater age. Why did not God prevent Jacob's sin, by continuing strength of eye-sight to his father? Why did a Sovereign Providence make way for this scheme, by inflicting blindness on Isaac? God did not approve this scheme, and yet in his sovereignty it fulfilled his purpose. Who can comprehend this mystery? Who can fathom the depth of this wisdom? Silence, ye prating philosophers! You cannot by searching find out God. Your line cannot measure his conduct.

Another providential circumstance in this matter is, that Isaac, though eminently a man of God, and, by divine revelation, sufficiently informed of God's preference of Jacob, yet attended not to this intimation, so as to ask consent of the Lord before he acted. He either remained ignorant of what he might have known, or from partiality neglected to attend to it. The ignorance of the Lord's people often fulfils the purposes of his will, as well as their knowledge. Yet, in all such cases, it is to their guilt and injury. Isaac did not add to his own happiness, or to that of his family, by his inattention to the revelation of the divine will with respect to his two sons. It would have been much better for all parties that he had asked counsel at the mouth of the Lord, before he had attempted to transfer the blessing. His intention did not succeed, and he added to the guilt of Esau, by laying before him the occasion of intentional murder.

The coupling of the eating of the savoury meat with the conveying of the blessing, whether it was whim or wisdom, is another providential circumstance that was necessary as a foundation for the scheme of Jacob's mother. Had Isaac given the blessing without this previous step, the artifice of Rebekah could have had no place.

Another link in this chain is, that Rebekah overheard Isaac when he addressed Esau about bringing him the savoury meat from the field. Had she not heard this, her plot could not have been formed. What placed her within hearing at that particular time? Why did not Isaac use precaution, and whisper the matter to his son? The thing must be heard by Rebekah. The accident that placed her within hearing was a link in Providence.

As was observed before, in order to transfer the blessing to Jacob, it was necessary that he should be the favourite son of his mother. This is another link in the chain.

To the formation of this scheme, by which the blessing was transferred to Jacob, it was necessary that Rebekah and her son, both of whom were true servants of God, should be ignorant, or regardless of their duty in an astonishing degree. Every feature of the plot is vile and wicked. Yet this mother, this servant of the Lord, invents that hypocritical device, which her son, so eminent a man of God, was base enough to execute. How is it that they combined to practise so shameful a deception? This conduct was not influenced by the faith of Abraham, but was the result of unbelief. Not relying on the power and wisdom of God to give effect to his own purposes,

THE HISTORY OF PROVIDENCE

they foolishly, as well as impiously, took the accomplishment of the divine counsels into their own hands, and brought about the divine appointment by sinful means. Here we see that God can fulfil his will through the means even of the sins of his own people. Here is sovereignty. Here is the depth of divine wisdom. The result of the conduct of Jacob and his mother was a fulfilment of God's eternal purpose; yet their conduct is not the less sinful. A child may see the justness of this observation; but can an angel of God fathom this abyss? Be silent, proud Philosophy; and thou, vain Theology, who lovest to lisp in the phraseology of science. Can ye show the harmony of these two apparently opposite truths? God ordains what men's sin effects. Yet man is guilty, and God is just!

The sovereignty of God, with respect to Jacob and Esau, is so offensive to the human mind, that it is not unusual, on this subject, to take revenge on the divine conduct, under the colour of lashing the misconduct of this favourite. A comparison of Esau with Jacob is made at great length, and greatly to the advantage of the elder brother. Esau is a plain, blunt, honest man, of great virtue and integrity; while Jacob is a deep, designing hypocrite. God says, 'Jacob have I loved, and Esau have I hated;' but the language of their heart is, 'Esau have I loved, and Jacob have I hated.' And why do they love Esau; why do they hate Jacob? Just because they hate that divine Sovereignty which preferred the younger to the elder. There is no reason to hide, or palliate, the sins of Jacob in this matter. By his misconduct, we see that it is not on account of works of our own righteousness that God chooses or saves us. The ground of God's preference of his people is his own free and sovereign goodwill. We should not hide this, by endeavouring to justify or excuse any thing that is wrong in Jacob. But nothing but disaffection to God will prefer the character of Esau to that of Jacob. With all his faults, Jacob was a man of God; with all that the most partial affection can claim for Esau, he was a man who profanely undervalued his birthright. He was a carnal man, who had all his happiness in this world. When he was roused, he showed what was in his heart.

He purposed to take revenge by murdering his brother. This is the virtue of the reprobate, who is so great a favourite with the enemies of God. With all the ingenuity of Rebekah, her scheme would have been frustrated, had it not been assisted by an addition from the prudence of Jacob. The savoury meat might have been brought to Isaac by Jacob in the room of Esau; but though the blindness of the Patriarch might not have been able to detect the imposture, his hand would have discovered the deceit. Here, then, there is another link added to the chain which connects Jacob with the blessing. Jacob thinks of the danger of detection, and his mother, by another contrivance, guards effectually against it. She covered his hands and his neck with the skins of the kids, and the smooth Jacob passes for the hairy Esau.

But, after all, what a hair's breadth escape from detection? Though Isaac was so dim of sight that he could not discover the difference between his sons by their external appearance, yet his ear is not so deficient but that it still recognises the difference between their voices. 'The voice is Jacob's voice, but the hands are the hands of Esau.' What prevents the whole plot from now being broken up? What makes Isaac, the guarded, suspicious Isaac, overlook this symptom? Why did he not put the matter to a farther proof? Was any thing more easy? Why did he not demand that both his sons should come into his presence? But the blessing is to be transferred to Jacob. This was God's eternal, unchangeable purpose. Isaac, then, with all his wariness, overcomes his well-founded suspicions, and boldly confers the blessing, when both affection and prudence cried out for delay. Men's wisdom and men's weakness both equally fulfil God's purposes. Here is wisdom. Let those who are truly wise study and admire it. The language in which Isaac conferred the blessing was, no doubt, the immediate dictation of the Holy Spirit; and, therefore, we cannot properly speak of this as a providential circumstance. But in this, inspiration is quite in keeping with the Providence exhibited in this matter. In conferring the blessing the Holy Spirit puts nothing into the mouth of the Patriarch by which he could see that Jacob was the person to whom he was speaking. The blessing was conferred in language so general, that there is no allusion whatever to any thing peculiar in Jacob. Here is the wisdom of the manner of inspiration. It speaks suitably to the character and situations of the persons by whom it speaks. This fact, instead of being discovered by human wisdom, is so little understood by many Christians, that they have been led by it to invent theories of inspiration, which make the Scriptures in a great measure the mere word of men, and virtually divest them of inspiration.

After all the preparations of hypocrisy and prudence, after all his hardy falsehoods and acting, with his venison and kids' skins, and garments of Esau, Jacob was on the very point of being detected in time to disappoint him of the blessing. What a wonderful, what a providential escape! Jacob is scarcely gone out with the blessing when Esau comes in to receive it. 'And it came to pass, as soon as Isaac had made an end of blessing Jacob, and Jacob was yet scarce gone out from the presence of Isaac his father, that Esau his brother came in from his hunting.' Who is so blind as not to see the hand of Providence here? Had Esau been a few minutes sooner, Jacob's scheme would have been frustrated. The sovereign God in his Providence prospers the plan which was to fulfil his purposes, while his holy law utterly disclaims that plan. Every link in this chain is inserted by an overruling Providence, while Jacob and his mother are solely the authors of their guilty conduct.

The transaction is finished; Jacob is blessed, and blessed he must be. But the Lord of Providence must continually protect him, and preserve him for the promised blessing. That Providence is immediately at work to watch over him, and defend him from his brother's malice. 'And Esau hated Jacob because of the blessing wherewith his father blessed him: and Esau said in his heart, The days of mourning for my father are at hand, then will I slay my brother Jacob.' What can prevent him from executing his wicked purpose? What then becomes of the blessing? When Esau made this purpose, why did he not keep it to himself? He said this in his heart: Why did he not keep it there? Why did he put it in words? Why did he make a confidant, or speak so as to be overheard? Yet he did so. Some person was made aware of Esau's intention; and that person discovered the intention to Esau's mother. Was he entrusted with it by Esau? Why then was he not true to his trust? Did he merely learn the intention of Esau by overhearing him speaking to himself? In every light the thing is overruled by Providence. What a consolation does this afford to the Lord's people, when they are threatened in life or property. God by his Providence discovered and disappointed the murderous intention of Esau, even though the conduct of Israel, in provoking the wrath of his brother, was greatly to be blamed. Shall not the Lord be the protector of his people, when by obedience to his will they subject themselves and fortunes to danger? The wicked are not permitted to execute the thousandth part of the mischief which they design against the Lord's people. His Providence watches over his children, and in due season manifests the plots of their enemies, or in one way or other prevents their execution.

In this wicked purpose of Esau, we see the hand of Divine Providence also, in sending Israel to the land of his fathers, where God had provided for him a wife; and where his life, in the house of Laban, might afford a fit emblem of Jesus, of whom this man of sorrows was an eminent type. Afflictive dispensations of Providence are designed for the good to the Lord's people, as well as events that are direct blessings. All things work together for good to them who love God, and are called according to his purpose.

18

Jacob's immediate meeting with Rachel on his approach to Haran

Genesis 29

JACOB was a distinguished type of Christ, and many points of resemblance present themselves to our view in his history. Among these the following are striking:—He was sent by his father to a distant country to seek a wife. 'And Isaac called Jacob, and blessed him, and charged him, and said unto him, Thou shalt not take a wife of the daughters of Canaan. Arise, go to Padanaram, to the house of Bethuel, thy mother's father, and take thee a wife from thence of the daughters of Laban, thy mother's brother.' And Jesus came from heaven to espouse his bride—the Lamb's wife—bone of his bone, and flesh of his flesh. On his journey, Jacob slept in the open air, and made the stones of Bethel his pillow. And Jesus, who was Lord of the universe, appeared on earth in the most destitute circumstances. While the foxes had holes, and the birds of the air had nests, the Son of man had not where to lay his head. All these points of resemblance were providential, resulting naturally from the situation in which Jacob was placed. The wisdom of man could discover in them no designed illustration of future events. But the Ruler of the world can direct the most trifling and seemingly fortuitous events, to serve his own glorious purposes. Jacob was as truly adapted to shadow the Saviour in the lowliest parts of his humiliation, as Solomon was in the highest glory of his exaltation.

The Providence of God directing the journey of Jacob is strikingly impressed on our notice, on his approach to Haran. By what compass he steered through the deserts that lay in his way, by what information he arrived in the neighbourhood of Haran, we are not told. But, however he was directed, one thing we see—he did not miss his way. Without any difficulty he lights at once on the people whom he sought. 'Then Jacob went on his journey, and came into the land of the people of the east. And he looked, and, behold, a well in the field, and, lo, there were three flocks of sheep lying by it; for out of that well they watered the flocks.' Here he is led by Providence to the point of destination as directly as were the wise men of the east by the star which pointed to the house in Bethlehem in which the Saviour was born. At the moment of his arrival, there were three flocks of sheep lying by the well. This was providential, for had he arrived at a time when all the flocks were at pasture, he would have missed the shepherds of Haran. Throughout all the hours of the light of day, why was it that he happened to come to this spot at the time when the flocks were lying by the well? The thing appears to be marked still more particularly as a fact in Providence. By what Jacob afterwards says to the shepherds (verse 7), it appears that it was rather early for the flocks to come to water, and Rachel's flock had not then arrived. Divine Providence sent some of the flocks sooner than usual, in order that the shepherds might be in waiting to receive Jacob.

And now comes Rachel, the future wife of this eminent Patriarch; and the Providence of the Lord presented to his view that person whom at random he was seeking, and in whom so much of his earthly happiness was centred. The people of the Lord should see his hand in leading them throughout all their earthly pilgrimage. In all their ways they should acknowledge him. If they have a prosperous journey, they should give the praise to him who led Jacob to the well of Haran. Nothing is so little as to be below the attention of his Providence: nothing is so great as to be beyond the power of his Providence to accomplish.

19

Jacob's prosperity in the service of Laban

Genesis 30

JACOB had a hard service and a rigorous master. If he is to grow rich, it will not be from a great dowry, nor the generosity of Laban. He can have nothing but what he earns. Yet God did not forsake him; and his Providence made him wealthy in the land of his servitude. And it is remarkable, that even in the extraordinary way in which he was enriched, every thing was done not by immediate miracle, but in the way of Providence. God took the possessions of Laban, and gave them to Jacob; but he did it indirectly, and by the use of certain means to which his Providence gave effect. God could have commanded Laban to give Jacob what he saw fit. He could have given Jacob wealth without touching or diminishing the property of Laban. But in a way of Providence he transferred a considerable proportion of the property of Laban to Jacob as wages for service. And may we not see here a shadow of the kingdom given to Christ by his Father, on account of his hard service? And what was Jacob's was also the property of his wives and children. In like manner, believers are heirs of God, and joint-heirs with Christ.

This fact affords us a key to open to us the Providence of God, in conferring wealth, or in diminishing possessions. Whatever may be the means by which prosperity and adversity are brought about, they are in all instances the work of Providence. Divine Providence, indeed, is as much concerned in the prosperity of the wicked as in that of the righteous; and in every instance in which it occurs, the God of Providence has a design in it. In like manner, the poverty or adversity of the people of God is as much overruled by the hand of Providence as is their prosperity. Men of God ought to see his hand in their gains and in their losses; in their prosperity and in their adversity.

20

Jacob's return to Canaan

Genesis 31

A S LONG as it pleased God that Jacob should serve Laban, his Providence made his lot tolerable. But as soon as the moment arrived in which he purposed to send him back to his father's house, all things contributed to force him out of Syria. The sons of Laban began to murmur; and they complained that the substance of their father was transferred to Jacob. 'And he heard the words of Laban's sons, saying, Jacob hath taken away all that was our father's; and of that which was our father's hath he gotten all this glory.' Laban himself was now disaffected to him, in such a manner that he could not conceal his displeasure. There was no longer any peace for the stranger. God has served his purpose with him in servitude; and he must now go home. 'And Jacob beheld the countenance of Laban, and, behold, it was not toward him as before.'

In this situation he sends for his wives, and lays before them all his affairs. Do they side with their father? Do they still cling to their kindred and their country? Do they use all their efforts to induce Jacob to relinquish his purpose? Do they, as was natural, try every effort to soften their relatives, and reconcile the parties? No. Instantly they take part with their husband—both of them are equally decided and zealous. They are as ready to set out for Canaan as was Jacob himself. 'And Rachel and Leah answered and said unto him, Is there yet any portion or inheritance for us in our father's house? Are we not counted of him strangers? For he hath sold us, and hath quite devoured also our money. For all the riches which God hath taken from our father, that is ours, and our children's: now then, whatsoever God hath said unto thee, do.'—Gen. 31:14-16.

Here we see that what God ordains his Providence effects. All things conspire to fulfil his pleasure; and every obstacle that is calculated to oppose it is removed.

Here also we may perceive a shadow of divine things. The spouse of Christ is made willing to leave her parents, her relatives, and her country, and set out with her husband for the heavenly Canaan. There is a willing people in the day of power.

Jacob, however, does not arrive at Canaan without his difficulties. Providentially Laban was not informed of the departure of his son-in-law till the next day; and, therefore, Jacob was far advanced on his journey before he could be overtaken. This was greatly in favour of his escape. But Laban was informed of the flight, not only in time to attempt, but in time to accomplish, the overtaking of the fugitives. God frequently brings his people into imminent danger, to show his power and Providence in working their deliverance. Laban pursues for seven days, and at last overtakes his prey on the mount of Gilead. What now is to be done? Where now is an escape? Why, when the ordinary ways of Providence are not fitted to deliver the Lord's people out of danger, he takes extraordinary means to effect his purpose. The Lord appears to Laban in a dream, and forbids him to injure Jacob. There is no fear that the Lord will desert his people. In one way or other he will send relief.

But Divine Providence is seen even in this extraordinary deliverance. By the Divine warning the resolution of Laban was changed; and instead of attempting to injure them, he sent them away with his blessing. Thus all the people of God are hunted and pursued by their spiritual adversaries, as soon as they set out for the heavenly Canaan. But no efforts can disappoint them; and by the Providence of God, many who may at first have attempted to arrest and detain them, will in the end dismiss them with their blessing.

21

Jacob's meeting his brother Esau on his return from Syria

Genesis 32

NOTWITHSTANDING that Esau was determined on the murder of his brother, on account of the great provocations he had received from him, yet the eternal purposes of God secured his safety, as much as if he had been in heaven, under the throne of the Most High. But how does God preserve him? By his Providence alone, in the use of ordinary means, in which the eye of human wisdom would see nothing of divine interference at all. No miracle appears in altering the purpose of the intended murderer. All is natural. Providence works through the prudence of his servant. Jacob proposes to meet his brother, and disarm his wrath by the most consummate human wisdom. He avails himself of a deep knowledge of human nature; and connects such a series of conciliating circumstances, that the stubborn soul of Esau is broken down to child-like tenderness. The Patriarch sent messengers before him to apprize his brother of his approach; and charges them, in the first place, to inform him of his wonderful prosperity and riches. This itself is a conciliating circumstance. Prosperity creates friends. But in the case of these brothers, this was calculated to have a peculiar effect. Length of time might have cooled the passion of the discontented brother, but his interest still equally demands the murder. This alone can restore the inheritance, and disappoint the subtlety of Jacob. Nothing was so well calculated to allay the suspicions of evil from Jacob, as the fact of his uncommon wealth. Esau had no respect for the spiritual promises; and the great prosperity of Jacob would tend to convince him that he was in no danger of the machinations of his brother to deprive him of the wealth of Isaac.

The messengers are instructed also to recognise, in Jacob's name, the superiority of his elder brother. He uses the most honourable forms of address to Esau, recognising his lordship over him, and the most humiliating expressions with regard to himself. This was well calculated to soothe the pride of Esau, and soften his rugged heart.

In the answer of the messengers on their return from Esau, we may see a remarkable instance of Providence. 'And the messengers returned to Jacob, saying, We came to thy brother Esau, and also he cometh to meet thee, and four hundred men with him.' That this was with hostile intentions is most apparent. Jacob himself understood the matter in this light. 'Then Jacob was greatly afraid and distressed.' It was not to honour his brother that Esau would take such an escort to meet him. Yet there was no threatening. Not a word in reply, either good or bad. There is great cause for apprehension: there is some room for hope.

Here we see that Divine Providence brings his people into danger, and surrounds them with circumstances that create alarm, and keeps them for a time in suspense, in order to try and exercise their faith and patience. Providence might have instantly relieved Jacob from apprehensions on the return of the messengers. Esau might have been moved instantly to mercy, and to use language that would relieve his brother from his anxiety. Why did he not do so? Does God take pleasure in the pain of his people? No; but it was in wisdom that Jacob was not instantly relieved. Had he got a favourable answer, he would not have had room to exhibit the admirable combination of faith and works which is now presented to our view. His suspense was good for him; it is good for us. For a like reason, Jesus did not instantly relieve the woman of Syro-Phoenicia. Let the Lord's people, then, in their distresses think of this. Let them hope against hope; and let them never cease to trust in God, and use the means that they may judge most prudent to avert any threatened evil, or obtain any wished-for good. The dark clouds that thicken over their heads may burst in blessings. Providence may bring them to the brink of ruin, and keep them trembling over the precipice; but he can prevent them from falling over, and can draw them back when he pleases.

On the return of the messengers Jacob was greatly alarmed; but he did not despair. He used every precaution of prudence, while he looked to the Lord for deliverance. It is plain that he expected deliverance only from the interposition of Providence; and it is equally plain that be expected this interposition in the use of means. Indeed, though Jacob took the most effectual means to soften Esau, yet all these means would have been utterly ineffectual without the interposition of Providence. Jacob, therefore, while he was planning and employing these means, still says, 'Deliver me, I pray thee, from the hand of my brother.' Means succeed by Providence, not without it. After all the preparations of Jacob, Esau might have remained obstinate and relentless.

Human wisdom will say, 'If God delivers, then leave it to him. Why use means?' 'If God says he will save, throw yourself into the river.' So said Satan: 'Cast thyself down, for it is written.' But Christ replies, 'It is written again, Thou shalt not tempt the Lord thy God.' The means are appointed by God as well as the end. God commanded Jacob to return, and promised to be with him. But in returning Jacob is in great danger, both from Laban and from Esau; and he uses the means of defence that God put in his power. In the use of these means God delivered him out of the hand of his enemies. Jacob, in faith, reminds God, of his command and promise: 'Return unto thy country, and to thy kindred, and I will deal well with thee.' But while he looks to God for deliverance, he plans and executes a most consummate scheme of wisdom. He divides his flocks into two bands, that if the one should be taken the other might have a chance of escape. Then he selected a present for his brother from his flocks and herds, and divided them into several bands, that the effect on his brother's mind might be the greater; with orders to his servants how to express themselves on the occasion. All these things were well calculated to effect his purpose, and appease the wrath of Esau. But when Jacob had planned and put in train all that his prudence could contrive to appease his incensed brother, he trusts not to his preparation. His confidence was in the God of his fathers, Abraham and Isaac. He spent the night in prayer, and his God gave efficiency to the means which his servant had employed.

How interesting is the meeting of the brothers! Jacob's only hope of safety is in God, for as yet he sees no instance nor symptom of reconciliation in his brother. He approaches him whom he had so greatly offended. 'He bowed himself to the ground seven times, until he came near to his brother.' The God who has the hearts of all men in his hands was not forgetful of his servant. Esau is overcome. Not only does he not injure, but natural affection bursts in tears from his eyes. 'And Esau ran to meet him, and embraced him, and fell on his neck, and kissed him: and they wept.' How glorious does the Providence of God appear in this interesting scene!

22

Cruelty of the sons of Jacob to the Shechemites

Genesis 34

WHEN we do not attend to the design of God with respect to the family of Jacob, we are inclined not only to blame the guilty conduct of two of the sons of Jacob, with respect to the Shechemites, but to regret the result of that nefarious doing. To human wisdom a fair prospect was opened of extending the knowledge and worship of God. Why, then, did the hand of Providence interpose and entirely break off this happy alliance? To those acquainted with the typical character of Israel, a moment's consideration will show that it was necessary to prevent the union of the accursed nations of Canaan with the family of Jacob. The nations of Canaan are in time to be expelled, and no union must be formed that will prevent this. As the kingdom of Christ is distinguished

45

from the kingdom of Satan, so the nation of Israel, the type of Christ's kingdom, must be distinct from the nations of Canaan, the types of God's enemies in every age.

Besides, a religious accession of the Shechemites to the house of Jacob, from the political motives on which they were about to act, was more likely to draw the worshippers of God into idolatry, than to draw idolaters into the service of God. The union proposed would most likely have ended in the rapid apostasy of the children of Israel. The union, then, must be prevented, and the guilty conduct of the sons of Jacob was overruled by God to prevent the union. The thing was of God, though all the guilt of it was with man. A sovereign Providence knew how to execute his purposes by the hands of wicked men.

Divine Providence could have prevented this union in many ways. He had, no doubt, a sufficient reason for that way which he actually did employ. It affords a striking emblem of the wisdom of the world in adopting a profession of Christianity from worldly motives, and of the folly of such wisdom. However wise the men of this world may think themselves in their conduct with respect to the religion of Christ from political motives, in the end, certain, and dreadful, and sudden will be their destruction. How many thousands, called Christians, are influenced in religion by no higher motives than those employed by Hamor and Shechem to persuade their subjects to embrace the religion of the house of Jacob? The wisdom of this world is foolishness with God.

23

Jacob's escape from the vengeance of the Canaanites, on the murder of the Shechemites by his sons

Genesis 35:5

BUT were the sons of Jacob blind through revenge? If their thirst of blood had been ever so great, might we not expect that they would still have respect to their own safety? If they should succeed, by their abominable hypocrisy, in cutting off the people of Shechem, could they expect to escape the vengeance of the neighbouring nations? Shall a single family undertake a quarrel against a multitude of nations, among whom they reside as strangers? Had they reflected, what could they expect but destruction to themselves and to the whole house of their father? It is evident that they could not have trusted for deliverance to the God of Israel, for they who believe and trust in him also obey him. Could they thus expect safety in this enormous violation of the law of God? It is evident they thought of nothing but of gratifying their revenge. They were blinded by the fury of their wrath.

But, notwithstanding this, God did not forget his servant Jacob. Divine Providence casts a shield over him and his guilty sons. But what was the means that God saw fit to make use of on this occasion for the deliverance of Jacob? Did he order Jacob to face his adversaries in the field, promising him the victory? Often he did so with the house of Israel. But not so here. This would have had an appearance of compromising the character of the Ruler of the world. He would have appeared to be like the gods of the Greeks and Trojans, without respect to right and wrong. God, therefore, employs not the children of Israel to defend themselves on this occasion. Here his wisdom sees fit to act without human means. Instead of delivering through the hands of men, he acts, by his Providence, on the minds of the affected nations, and fills them with the fear of the family of Jacob. The family of Jacob were but a handful of people, yet the Sovereign Lord made them a terror to powerful nations. 'And the terror of God was upon the cities that were round about them, and they did not pursue after the sons of Jacob.'

It is in this way that God defends and delivers his people, who are in the world as sheep in the midst of wolves. The enemies of God's people may rule, but God rules the rulers. His enemies may sit on the bench of judgment, but God presides in the court and directs the judgment. The wicked hate the righteous, but the terror of God often prevents the effects of their malice. It is this sovereign power of the Ruler of the world over the hearts of the children of men that makes man capable of civil rule. Were it not for this, no government could exist for a single month. God has appointed civil government, and his Providence supports it. All the numbers, and wisdom, and combination of men against existing powers, are generally of no avail. In one way or other, God, in his Providence, disappoints their purposes. When he sees fit to effect a revolution, the sons of Belial are always ready unconsciously to be the instruments. God does not employ his children in this vile work.

What consolation does this afford to the true children of God! It would indeed be a melancholy thing, if God would place them help-less in the power of the wicked, without himself directing and over-ruling the determinations and conduct of the enemies of Israel. But though the people of God are, in all things in which the authority of their Master does not interfere, to obey the rulers of this world under whom Divine Providence has placed them, yet they are, in the smallest matters as well as the greatest, under the sovereign care of him who rules the world.

24

Reuben's sin

Genesis 35:22

'AND Israel heard it.' Yes, the foul deed did not remain covered; although no doubt, every means of secrecy was employed. The Providence of God takes care to bring to light the works of darkness in his people. The case of David, and many others, fully confirm this. God sees in darkness as in the light, and when his people, in their departure from his laws, seek to hide themselves from him and from the world, he will publish their shame in the face of day. This ought to be an additional guard on the conduct of the people of God; and they ought to do nothing that will not bear the light. What is said in the ear or the closet will be proclaimed on the housetops. It is a grievous thing to bring a reproach on the cause of God, and by one's conduct stumble others, so as to prevent them from entering the kingdom of heaven. In this peculiarity of his Providence the wisdom of God is characteristic, and distinguished from that of men. Every man would hide the disgrace of those whom he loves. God makes it manifest. Christians are commanded to cover one another's faults; but God is not under law; and though he loves us infinitely beyond our love to one another, yet he puts his people to open shame, when they sin in secret.

25

The removal of Esau to Mount Seir

Genesis 36:6

THE removal of Esau with his family and possessions to Mount Seir, is evidently the effect of a peculiar Providence. The brothers were living in harmony. Why, then, did they not both continue to reside in the land of Canaan? The residence of Esau could not interfere with the right of Jacob to the ultimate inheritance of the land of promise. Let Esau reside where he might, Jacob must go down into Egypt, and others must possess the land of Canaan for a long period. Why, then, not disinherit Esau? If one of the brothers must give place, why did not Jacob? This would be more consistent with his former conduct on his return. He always gave the preference to Esau. The reason obviously is, had Esau continued to live in Canaan, his posterity must be ejected on the return of Israel from Egypt. God gave Mount Seir as an inheritance to the posterity of Esau, and he takes this way to put them in possession. The prosperity of the brothers made it impossible for them both to reside in the same neighbourhood; and God, who rules in the hearts of all men, even of those who know him not, directed that Esau should of himself resolve to leave the country of his birth. 'And Esau took his wives, and his sons, and his daughters, and all the persons of his house, and his cattle, and all his beasts, and all his substance, which he had got in the land of Canaan; and went into the country from the face of his brother Jacob. For their riches were more than that they might dwell together; and the land wherein they were strangers could not bear them because of their cattle. Thus dwelt Esau in Mount Seir: Esau is Edom.'—Gen. 36:6-8. How wonderful are the ways of Providence! God performs his purposes by the voluntary resolves of the most capricious tyrant, as easily as he guides the heavenly bodies by the laws of motion. Such wisdom is too wonderful for us.

26

Judah's secret sin manifested by Providence

Genesis 38:17

WHEN the people of the Lord, overcome by temptation, fall into the hands of Satan, and think to indulge in secrecy, without forfeiting their characters, they are generally disappointed. The works of darkness, in the children of this world, the Lord may reveal only when he comes to judgment, to bring to light the hidden things of darkness. But, when his own people forsake him secretly, he often puts them to public shame. The very plans of worldly wisdom, by which they continue to hide their sins, he can make the means of detection and discovery. So was it here with Judah. He was taken in a net, and what he thought to keep secret was laid open not only to those who knew him, but blazoned in the word of God before all generations. Let not the Lord's people, then, sin in secret with the hope of remaining covered. What they do in the secret closet, God can proclaim from the housetops.

How foolish and absurd is it to be more afraid of the eye of man than of God! We ought to look on God as being present with us continually, as much as if we saw him with our bodily eyes. 'Thou God seest me,' ought to be written, as it were, on the palms of our hands. We cannot by our subtlety hide ourselves from his penetrating eye. And he is a God who hateth iniquity.

27

The history of Joseph

Genesis 37

THE history of Joseph is a series of miracles of Providence. In it the hand of God, in the ruling of the world, is admirably revealed. God does his will through the voluntary actions of men, and effects his purpose as well by his enemies as by his friends; and through the disobedience and ignorance of his people, as well as through their obedience and knowledge. To account for this is beyond the reach of human intellect. Proud man tries to fathom the abyss, and when he fails, he relieves himself by denying its existence. He will not receive both parts of the truth, but, according to his humour, will modify one of them so as to suit the other, that he may glory that he can discover the deep things of the unsearchable God. What he cannot comprehend, with him cannot be true. Will vain man never cease to strive with the Almighty? Will he never learn that the ways of the Lord are inscrutable? 'O the depth of the riches both of the wisdom and knowledge of God! How unsearchable are his judgments, and his ways past finding out.'

Joseph was selected by God as one of the persons who were to be types of Christ; and the peculiarity of his typical resemblance required every fact in his history. Jesus was envied and hated by his brethren the Jews: Joseph, as his type in this respect, must be hated by his father's sons. To effect this, Joseph must be the darling of his father. Was it wise, was it just, in Jacob to show so marked a preference to his son Joseph? The best child should certainly be the most esteemed; but the preference of Joseph was because he was the son of the old age of his father. Some have struggled to relieve the Patriarch from this reprehension, but in vain. And there is no need to strain the word of God, to excuse or justify Jacob in the preference. It was still more foolish to distinguish the favourite by the singularity of his dress. This could have no other tendency than to provoke the jealousy of his brethren. Yet this imprudent expression of the partiality of his father might be divinely directed as a shadow of what happened to him who was typified by Joseph, when his robe was stripped off, and when he himself was truly rent in pieces by the wild beasts of the forest on Mount Calvary. What Jacob believed about his darling son, was true with respect to the well beloved Son of God. 'Without doubt he was torn in pieces.'

Joseph's dreams finished what Jacob's imprudence had first excited. But why did he tell his dreams? Had he not, though younger, as much sagacity to interpret his own dreams as had his brethren? If he did understand them, why did not his prudence conceal them? If their meaning was concealed from him, why was it concealed? Still more strange! When he told his first dream, did he not see that his brethren understood its import? Why, then, did he childishly tell the second? Here this son of prudence, wise in youth, providentially acts in the most unguarded manner, evidently that a way might be opened for his future history.

When the moment approached which God had appointed to send Joseph to Egypt, his Providence opened the way, and put the means in train. The sons of Jacob were feeding their flocks at a distance, and it occurs to Jacob to send Joseph to visit them. Why had the sons of Jacob removed to such a distance from Hebron? Why at this particular time? Because this opened a way to fulfil the Lord's purposes. Now all things concur to bring about the predestined event. All the lines meet in this centre. As soon as his brethren discovered him at the greatest distance, it instantly occurred to them to rid themselves of the object of their envy. 'And when they saw him afar off, even before he came near unto them, they conspired against him to slay him.' Yes, to slay him, and he who was typified by Joseph was truly slain; but it was not God's design to give effect to this conspiracy of murder, and, therefore, his Providence disappointed this part of the scheme. The heart of Reuben relented so far as to wish to prevent the death of the young man. How often are the intended deeds of blood prevented by a similar Providence! Some of the conspirators incline to mercy, and God uses their sympathy to prevent the execution. Jesus was to be buried in the heart of the earth: Joseph, his type, was cast into a pit; and the voice of prophecy speaks of the sufferings of Jesus as a sinking into a miry pit. But Jesus was to rise from the dead soon after his burial, and Joseph was drawn alive out of the pit in which he was placed by the cruelty of his brethren.

Jesus was to be sold: Joseph must be sold to represent him in this part of his sufferings. Jesus was to be sold by Judas, one of his brethren, one of his disciples; Joseph must then be sold by Judas, one of his brethren. Jesus was to be carried into Egypt, the typical house of bondage, because he took on him the sins of the Israel of God: Joseph, therefore, must be carried as a slave into Egypt.

But how is he to go to Egypt? Divine Providence has a conveyance in readiness, and a messenger waiting to receive the exile. Just as his brethren had let down Joseph into the pit, and had sat down to eat and drink, they 'lifted up their eyes, and looked, and, behold, a company of Ishmaelites came from Gilead with their camels, bearing spicery, and balm, and myrrh, going to carry it down to Egypt.' What brought them at this critical moment? And why were they Ishmaelites? As Ishmael himself mocked Isaac; and this is by the Apostle Paul interpreted as typifying the children of the flesh of Abraham persecuting his children by promise; so, here, the Ishmaelites, for a like reason, are the persons who sold Joseph to the Egyptians. The Jews, the carnal seed of Abraham, delivered Jesus to the Gentiles to be crucified. 'And Joseph was brought down into Egypt: and Potiphar, an officer of Pharaoh, captain of the guard, an Egyptian, bought him of the hands of the Ishmaelites, which had brought him down thither.'

In the person who bought Joseph we see the direction of Providence. Joseph might have come into Egypt, and remained in it through life, without an opportunity of rising to his destined dignity. How many thousands might have been his purchasers? How did it happen that an officer of the king of Egypt, even the officer of the guard, was the purchaser of Joseph? How many chances, in the language of man, were against this? Yet Joseph comes immediately into the house of Potiphar.

In the house of Potiphar the Providence of the Lord protected Joseph, and obtained for him the unbounded confidence of his master. But this prosperity must be interrupted. Joseph must go to prison, and from prison to court. To bring this to pass, Divine Providence employed the wickedness of his mistress. In prison he found favour; and that prison, providentially, was the one in which the king's prisoners were bound. This circumstance was the occasion of his deliverance and exaltation. After Joseph was imprisoned, it happened that two of Pharaoh's servants, that served about his person, were cast into the same prison. What a chance! The whole matter is of the Lord. This made Joseph known, at the proper time, to the king of Egypt. Jesus died between two malefactors, one of whom he saved, the other he suffered to perish in his sins. Joseph was imprisoned with two criminals, one of whom, by his interpretation of dreams, he saved, the other he hanged. Mark the providential circumstance in the forgetfulness of the chief butler. Joseph requested him to remember him before his master. But for two full years the chief butler forgot Joseph. Why was this? Had he made immediate application, and delivered him, Joseph would not now be at hand to interpret Pharaoh's dream, and accomplish all that the Lord had appointed for him. Joseph, without doubt, would have returned to his country. The chief butler, by the overruling Providence of God, forgot Joseph; but now the case is providentially brought to his mind, at the time when it served the purposes of God.

Jesus, after the suffering of death, was exalted, as Ruler over all worlds; Joseph, as a figure of this, was exalted over all Egypt. Joseph provided bread for Israel in their extremity: Jesus was the bread of life to the true Israel of God.

The children of Israel must be slaves in Egypt, to represent the natural slavery in which all the children of God are from the fall of Adam; and this is the means that God appointed to bring them there. The famine obliged them to seek food in Egypt; and this was the means of bringing them into the land of bondage. God, by his Providence, guides the affairs of this world, and in all things effects his eternal purposes. And all things work together for good to them who love God, and are called according to his purpose. Their very afflictions are sent in love and in mercy.

From the history of Joseph we may see that the same thing may be from man, in one point of view, and from God, in another; and that what man may do sinfully to the injury of the people of God, God may effect through them for the good of his people. It is man's work, yet it is, in another view, God's work. How it is God's work the ingenuity of man cannot point out, the intellect of man cannot discover. But that the same thing is of man and of God, the Divine testimony forbids us to doubt. 'But as for you,' says Joseph to his brethren, 'ye thought evil against me; but God meant it unto good, to bring to pass, as it is this day, to save much people alive.'

28
Prosperity of Joseph in bondage
Genesis 39:2

CAN any thing more clearly prove the continual and immediate agency of Providence in the affairs of this world, than this account of the prosperity of the house of Potiphar for the sake of Joseph? 'And the Lord was with Joseph, and he was a prosperous man; and he was in the house of his master the Egyptian.' The security and comfort of the man of God were not left to the operation of general laws. But 'the Lord was with Joseph.' And what was the consequence of the Lord's being with Joseph? Is not the prosperity of Joseph directly ascribed to this? — 'and he was a prosperous man.' The prosperity of Joseph is not left to the influence of mere foresight and arrangement in Providence, but is the immediate effect of the Lord's presence with him. Why, then, will the philosopher cruelly attempt to banish God from his people, and supply his place by certain fixed laws? Whether God acts by means of his usual laws, or contrary to them, his presence is equally necessary to produce the effect.

Here we are taught to consider worldly prosperity as the effect of Divine Providence. It is so in every instance, whether it respects his people or his enemies. Means are generally employed, but these means are of Providence as well as the event. Prosperity and adversity come both from God, though, in another respect, they may be the fruits of men's own doings.

But though God usually gives success to means, this is not universally the case. He sometimes shows that his own personal presence is necessary to the result. 'Except the Lord build the house,' says the Psalmist, 'they labour in vain that build it: except the Lord keep the city, the watchman waketh but in vain. It is vain for you to rise up early, to sit up late, to eat the bread of sorrows: for so he giveth his beloved sleep.'

The agency of Providence was so visible in the affairs in which Joseph was concerned, that it was recognised even by his heathen master. 'And his master saw that the Lord was with him, and that the Lord made all things that he did to prosper in his hands.' Here an ignorant pagan sees what blind philosophers, calling themselves Christians, cannot see. They see no need for God's immediate presence and operations: all things can be effected by foresight and arrangement. This is as absurd as it is wicked. Can foresight do any thing? Can mere arrangement act? Is not an agent necessary to give effect to design?

Here we see, also, the reason why Providence gives prosperity to his enemies. It is to fulfil some of his purposes. God prospered the affairs of Potiphar in the hands of Joseph, that Joseph might find favour with his master, as one of the steps in the process of bringing this type of Christ into prison, and then into glory. When God prospers the wicked, he has always some wise design in it. The fact neither proves that God does not conduct the affairs of men, nor that he prospers his enemies, and gives adversity to his people, out of caprice. All is done in wisdom.

This fact shows us, also, that God considers his Providence as sufficient evidence of his existence and agency. He acted in this providential way in order to produce a certain effect on Potiphar. And we see that Potiphar did understand the lesson. He saw that God was with Joseph. If so, all men will be held accountable for all that God hath done in his works of Providence, as well as of creation.

In like manner, when Joseph went to prison, the Lord was with him, and found favour for him in the sight of the keeper of the prison. In the case of the favour of Potiphar, we are informed of the way in which God wrought on the heart of a man who knew him not. He gave prosperity to Potiphar through the management of Joseph. But in the case of the governor of the prison, we have no information of any means employed to excite a favourable sentiment towards the prisoner. The Lord can work without means as well as with means. 'But the Lord was with Joseph, and showed him mercy, and gave him favour in the sight of the keeper of the prison. And the keeper of the prison committed to Joseph's hand all the prisoners that were in the prison; and whatsoever they did there, he was the doer of it. The keeper of the prison looked not to any thing that was under his hand; because the Lord was with him, and that which he did, the Lord made it to prosper.' Whatever was the occasion of exciting the compassion of the keeper of the prison at first, the hand of Providence was soon visible in the management of Joseph; and in the prosperity of the affairs under his direction, the agency of God was recognised.

Let all Christians, in places of trust, act like Joseph; and from the lowest situations they may in the end be brought to the highest. Let them, on all occasions, not only act with the strictest fidelity, but let them discover an earnestness in the service of their employers. The most ungodly men will soon perceive that to have such persons in their employment is commonly for their advantage.

29
Joseph's beauty
Genesis 39:6

THE comeliness of Joseph was a link in the chain of Providence that was essentially necessary to bring about the destined end. It was this that drew the attention of his mistress, and was the occasion of his being sent to prison. Accordingly, it is stated in this view by the inspired historian. Immediately before the account of her infamous attempt, it is said, 'And Joseph was a goodly person, and well-favoured.' Here we see not only that a Divine Providence was immediately engaged in bringing about the imprisonment of Joseph, but that it was in the view of God even in the formation of Joseph. This comeliness was given him for the very purpose. Had Joseph been an ordinary man, he would not have been sent to prison. Had he not been a remarkably handsome man, his virtue would not have been put to the test. Beauty, and wealth, and honour, and health, are all blessings of Providence, for which they ought to be thankful who possess them. But they are all the occasions of trial; and without divine strength to resist temptation may be the occasion of fall and ruin. Let every Christian, then, watch and guard against the temptation to which his providential gift may expose him. A victory over temptation, like that of Joseph, is never to be expected, except in the strength of the faith of the God of Abraham.

30

Character of Joseph taken away by false accusation

Genesis 39:13

IT MIGHT be supposed, that if Providence overrules and directs all things, the interests, and especially the characters of God's people, would always be safe and unassailed. Would any parent allow slander to exist even for a moment, or even to originate against his beloved children, if he were able to prevent it? But God's ways are not as our ways. Here we see, that instead of keeping his people from injury and the tongue of slander, it is by the means of false accusation that Providence brings Joseph to prison. The man of God is aspersed with calumny, and charged with sins which he had resisted under temptation of the strongest kind. That part of his character which is the admiration of every age, was the very part in which he suffered. A character was fixed on him, remarkable for crimes of which he was not only innocent, but to which he possessed the contrary virtues in a degree beyond any instances on record. And this false accusation had a plausibility that imposed on integrity, and prevailed, without any thing for a long time to counteract it, keeping him in the bondage of a prison. There is no security, then, to the people of God, that their lives, their property, and their characters, may not be taken away unjustly. There may be occasions when Providence will open a door for any, or for all, of these calamities. But this will never be the case, except it shall be for the glory of God, and for the good of the suffering individual. And, when in prison, Joseph was rendered comfortable by providential interference. If his character was unjustly taken away, it was restored in the fullest manner; and the virtues of his illustrious character are a perpetual record to his honour.

31

Circumstances may be misinterpreted, as well as facts may be forged

Genesis 39:12

IT IS usually considered that circumstances are the strongest evidences, and that, when facts may be forged, circumstances are expelled. Facts, supported by circumstances, are no doubt evidence beyond just question. But circumstances should not be admitted as decisive without a full consideration of their bearing. Here was a circumstance apparently so strong against Joseph, that at first view it is useless for counsel to attempt to extricate him. He leaves his cloak behind him. Can there be better evidence of the fact alleged, and of his guilt? Yet, when the thing is considered for a moment in a dispassionate manner, the circumstance is not quite so conclusive. No wonder Potiphar had not the coolness to weigh evidence on this occasion; but we may do it for him. Why, wife of Potiphar, did you on that occasion act so courageous a part, instead of flying for refuge to some more secure part of the house? Were you more intent to secure the culprit as a prisoner than to protect yourself from his insult? What need was there that you should seize him? Could your slave escape you? Or would your husband be so incredulous as not to believe you? Joseph, you are the injured man; and this is a vile woman. She is not urged by a sense of duty to punish you, but, instigated by revenge, to ruin you, an innocent man. And I have known, on occasions of accusations, some upright and impartial men ready, from a false interpretation of circumstances, to condemn the innocent, on the evidence of false accusers. It is remarkable, that, notwithstanding the leaning of modern times to the side of mercy, there are still occasionally some instances in which the innocent suffer, from a false interpretation of circumstances. When Providence, in any instance, has ordained this issue, vigilance is some way unaccountably asleep, and a strong disposition to punish flagrant injustice leads away from a cool consideration of the necessary import of circumstances. Joseph was ordered on this occasion to go to prison, therefore the deficiency in the evidence of circumstances did not occur to those who judged. No wonder that Potiphar should not be very suspicious to observe the flaw in the testimony. It is not either guilt or innocence, strictly speaking, that determines the fate of the accused at human tribunals. Innocence may be overwhelmed with calumny, and guilt may escape the keen eye of the most rigorous justice, and the most conclusive evidence. The lot of the prisoner is decided by Providence, whether he unjustly suffers, or is unjustly cleared.

32

Imprisonment of the chief butler and chief baker

Genesis 40:1

WHY was Pharaoh on this occasion displeased with two of his attendants? Why did he at this particular time send them to prison? We know nothing of the matter. But we know that, whatever was the offence of his officers, and whatever induced him to send them to prison, the thing was of God, that Joseph might be introduced to Pharaoh. How wonderful is the Providence of God! It overrules in the crimes of subjects and in the caprices of despots. These two men must come to prison at this time, whether it was through their own crimes, or through false suspicions on the part of their lord. This is the way to make Joseph acquainted with majesty.

But it was not enough to bring them to prison, to introduce them to the acquaintance of Joseph; there must be something to be a means of bringing Joseph to the acquaintance of Pharaoh. What then must this be? Kindness, perhaps, on the part of Joseph, to the prisoners. This will not serve. This might liberate Joseph, but it will not raise him to the second place in Egypt. What then are we to have? Why, the dream—the dream is the thing. For this connects with the future dreams of Pharaoh, and brings Joseph to interpret them. The dreams of the officers of Pharaoh are the counterpart of the dreams of Pharaoh: and they are designed by the same counsel. The letter and the type do not correspond more exactly than the dreams of the servants correspond to the future dreams of the master. Joseph's interpretation of the dreams of the chief butler and chief baker was necessary to bring him to interpret the dreams of the king. Nothing, then, but a dream suits the purpose, and dreams we have.

33
The chief butler remembered not Joseph
Genesis 40:23

'YET did not the chief butler remember Joseph, but forgat him.' Ungrateful man! Would not a word to your master procure the liberation of a man whom you knew to be innocent, and a man your greatest benefactor? Well, we may scold, but whatever was the cause of the forgetfulness of this officer, it was of God. He forgot for a time; but at the moment when it served the purpose of Divine Providence, all was brought to his mind, with a conviction of his ingratitude. 'I do remember my faults this day.' How providential was this forgetfulness! Had the chief butler remembered Joseph's application, it would have cost him only a word to his lord to open the prison to Joseph, and free him from his bondage to his master. But had this been done at the time, where would we find Joseph now, when we have need of him as an interpreter of dreams? Joseph, when liberated, would, without doubt, have hastened to his own country, and by this time he would have been safe in the house of Jacob. Where, then, would have been his exaltation as a saviour of Israel, and a type of Christ? Joseph, then, must be overlooked at the present, and remain quietly in prison till the moment of Pharaoh's dream. Then, like the lightning of heaven, the recollection of Joseph must strike the mind of the chief butler. He must no longer be forgetful. Divine Providence calls all to his recollection. He tells his unvarnished story to his lord. This is the very man that suits Pharaoh; and now the great character of Joseph must be manifested. Joseph was the son of a wealthy father; but he came to be sold as a slave into Egypt. He comes even into prison and to fetters. But now he comes to save Israel by procuring bread for them in Egypt. Now he comes to his glory. In like manner, Jesus, who thought it not robbery to be equal with God, was made a servant, and was imprisoned in the grave for the sins of men. But he is now exalted, and he reigns over all worlds in that nature in which he suffered. And we should look unto 'Jesus, the author and finisher of our faith; who, for the joy that was set before him, endured the cross, despising the shame, and is set down at the right hand of the throne of God.'

34
The same action ascribed to God in one sense, while in another it is the act of man
Genesis 45:7

THE sending of Joseph to Egypt was the guilty deed of his cruel and unnatural brothers. They are accountable for the whole transaction. Yet there is a sense in which God did this thing. The Scriptures assert both: both must be true. 'And God sent me before you,' says Joseph to his brethren, 'to preserve you a posterity in the earth, and to save your lives by a great deliverance. Lo, now it was not you that sent me hither, but God.' Not only, then, is it true, that God did this, but it is denied that his brethren did it. They did it in one sense: God did it in another. And the sense in which God did it, is so much more important than that in which they did it, that in that sense Joseph denies that they did it at all. Can human intellect descry the line that bounds the human and the divine agency in this matter? How did God do the thing that was wickedly done by men? Human arrogance may attempt to explain and distinguish, but it can never satisfy any sound mind. It may speak of divine permission as all that is meant by agency. But will simple permission warrant us to ascribe agency in such a sense as to deny agency to those who were, in the obvious sense, the agents? It is wisdom to submit to God, and prostrate ourselves before him in the dust. Who is man, that he should pretend to comprehend the ways of the unsearchable Jehovah?

35
The policy of the king of Egypt to retain the children of Israel, the means of his losing them

Exodus 1

THE Providence of God frequently makes the means which men wickedly employ to effect their purposes, the very means of thwarting them. So was it with the king of Egypt on this occasion. Alarmed with the increase of the children of Israel, yet not willing to lose them out of his dominions, he resolved to retain them in safety by oppression. Rulers may justly take precautions against any in their dominions from whom danger is apprehended. But it never can be just to oppress wantonly and without necessity. 'And the children of Israel were fruitful, and increased abundantly, and multiplied, and waxed exceeding mighty; and the land was filled with them. Now there arose up a new king over Egypt, which knew not Joseph. And he said unto his people, Behold the people of the children of Israel are more and mightier than we: Come on, let us deal wisely with them; lest they multiply, and it come to pass, that, when there falleth out any war, they join also unto our enemies, and fight against us, and so get them up out of the land.' This gave rise to a most cruel persecution, and ended in the deliverance of Israel out of Egypt. Had Pharaoh treated them with kindness, generosity, and justice, they never, humanly speaking, would have consented to leave Egypt for the promised land. After all that they had suffered, they were sometimes willing to go back to the land of bondage. All their oppressions and sufferings were necessary to make them willing to return to Canaan.

Let the people of God learn from this that they ought patiently to submit to the tyranny and oppression of civil rulers, if it is the will of Providence to cast their lot under such. They ought to take their afflictions as coming from the hand of God, in one point of view, as well as from the hand of man, in another. Cruel and oppressive treatment from their rulers may be necessary to urge them on to make progress in their journey to the heavenly Canaan. An oppressive law, by which they are excluded from office, honours, or emoluments, is very sinful in the authors, but may be very useful to the oppressed. If the world would know us, we would be inclined to know the world. It is better for the Christian when men cast out his name as evil, than when they celebrate it with the loudest praises.

36

Moses raised up by Providence as a deliverer to Israel

Exodus 2

B Y THE faith of his parents, Moses was not destroyed at his birth, and by a providential scheme he was brought up in the court of Pharaoh. What put it into the mind of his mother to form such a wish of saving him? Why is it suggested to her to make an ark of bulrushes, and put her children into it on the Nile? How many things, in such a situation, were more likely to destroy him than to save him? Why did Pharaoh's daughter come down so seasonably to the river to bathe? Why did she think of mercy, contrary to her father's orders? Why did she think of mercy to this child more than to the thousands that were perishing? And if compassion now touched her heart, why is she not contented with simply saving the child? Why does she adopt it as her own? Must compassion make her a mother? This might be whim or fancy, but it was the Lord's doing, and it is wondrous in our eyes. Moses must be educated in all the wisdom of the Egyptians: he must be brought up in the house of Pharaoh. The daughter of Pharaoh, then, must not only save the life of the child, but must adopt him as her own son.

But it is not enough that Moses should be adopted by the daughter of Pharaoh. It must be in circumstances that will preserve to Moses the knowledge of his descent. The child, then, was by Providence put into the hands of his own mother as his nurse.

Moses must be put to his work as the deliverer of Israel. The people of God must be delivered, not by interest at court, but by the strong hand of the Almighty. Moses, then, must be first brought out of the house of Pharaoh. Behold the circumstance which led to this event. 'And it came to pass in those days, when Moses was grown, that he went out unto his brethren, and looked on their burdens:

and he spied an Egyptian smiting an Hebrew, one of his brethren. And he looked this way and that way, and when he saw that there was no man, he slew the Egyptian, and hid him in the sand. And when he went out the second day, behold, two men of the Hebrews strove together: and he said to him that did the wrong, Wherefore smitest thou thy fellow? And he said, Who made thee a prince and a judge over us? intendest thou to kill me, as thou killedst the Egyptian? And Moses feared, and said, Surely this thing is known. Now when Pharaoh heard this thing, he sought to slay Moses. But Moses fled from the face of Pharaoh, and dwelt in the land of Midian: and he sat down by a well.'—Exod. 2:11-15. What a happy chance! What a wise Providence! Moses is providentially excited to visit his brethren. Why at that time more than any other time? At that time an Egyptian was smiting an Israelite. Moses *chanced* to see it: Providence placed it before him. He slew the Egyptian. Why did he act so imprudently? It was of God. He was a wise, and a meek man, yet he here acted rashly, and in anger. He took every precaution to conceal the matter, yet it was known. Man cannot hide what God would reveal.

But Moses must find out that this affair is not secret. Providence, then, ordered it that he went out a second time, and that, on that occasion, two Hebrews should be contending, and that he should behold them. He reproves the injurious person, and, instead of thankful submission, he is reminded of the death of the Egyptian. Pharaoh is in wrath: Moses flies, and remains in Midian, till the time that the Lord should call him to his work. How wonderfully does Providence overrule in all the accidents, and in all the occurrences in the lives of his people!

37

Plagues of Egypt

THE plagues brought on Egypt by the hand of Moses were a miraculous interposition of Almighty power. But from the nature of them, we may learn to see Providence in similar punishments of the world. The things brought by God on the Egyptians are things that occur providentially in other countries in all times. When, then, any nation or district is visited with similar calamities, it should be taken as a punishment inflicted by God on account of sin. Pestilential diseases, with respect to men or cattle, are not without Providence. Even when they are most successfully traced to natural causes, they should still be received as from God; for God is the author of nature, as well as he is the moral ruler of the world. He can make what are called the works of nature execute his judgments on account of sin. Now, if this is the case, even where calamities can be traced to certain causes, how much more so, when all the ingenuity, when all the philosophy of the wise, cannot satisfactorily account for the occurrence! Cases frequently occur that baffle every effort to account for them, without reference to the invisible hand of God. Whatever the children of this world may do in the time of calamity, it becomes the people of God to recognise his hand, and cast themselves in the dust before him. Let them acknowledge him in the time of judgment; and he who kept the Israelites safe, when he brought mourning on the Egyptians, can show that he is able to preserve in the midst of ruin.

38

Qualification of Bezaleel and Aholiab for making the tabernacle

Exodus 31

IN EGYPT the children of Israel were the most degraded slaves, and employed in the most laborious occupations. Their minds were not cultivated by education, nor were they instructed even in the useful or ornamental arts of life. The making of the tabernacle and its furniture required the most perfect skill in different arts and trades. How, then, were persons to be found for the execution of the work? God provided in this emergency, and gave the qualifications which were necessary for his own work. 'See, I have called Bezaleel by name, the son of Uri, the son of Hur, of the tribe of Judah: And I have filled him with the spirit of God, in wisdom, and in understanding, and in knowledge, and in all manner of workmanship, to devise cunning works, to work in gold, and in silver, and in brass, and in cutting of stones, to set them, and in carving of timber, to work in all manner of workmanship. And I, behold, I have given with him Aholiab, the son of Ahisamach, of the tribe of Dan: and in the hearts of all that are wise hearted I have put wisdom, that they may make all that I have commanded thee.'

These endowments, it is true, were immediately from the Lord, without any use of ordinary means, but they are such as are often witnessed in men of rare genius, whom Providence raises up to make discoveries and improvements even in arts and sciences. And in the qualifications conferred on those who made the typical house of God, we see that God provides the qualifications in those of his people whom he employs to do his work, in building up the spiritual house, his church. Whether these qualifications are the immediate gifts of God in their constitution of mind and body, or are the result of education, they are equally of God. But, in one way or other, the Lord will always qualify men for doing the work which he has appointed them to do. His work will never remain undone for want of qualified instruments. At the time he needs workmen, his Providence will supply them. The harvest may be plenteous, and the labourers may be few; but it is only the Lord of the harvest who can send labourers to reap. And when he intends to reap, labourers he will qualify, labourers he will send into his field, and the work will be done. When the cause of God needs the support of learning, he has it at his command. When he intends to humble the pride of learning, he may permit the learned to use their efforts to pull down the walls of his house, and can build them by men, on whom he confers gifts by nature, without the culture of education. Many of the most learned theologians are mere cumberers of the ground. Many of the most effectual workmen in raising the walls of the temple are mighty men of God, stored wholly with mental culture. This, however, does not imply that learning is useless. It is the gift of God as well as natural abilities; and there are things which without it cannot be done. No mental powers, without learning, could enable a man to translate the Scriptures; and no man can have the most authoritative source of evidence of the meaning of Scripture, who cannot reason from the original. Yet the most successful builders in Zion may be utterly unqualified as translators.

39

Readiness of the people to contribute for the making of the tabernacle

Exodus 35

A S THE Lord qualified men to perform the work of the tabernacle, so his Providence ordered it that the people were ready

to contribute every thing necessary for the work. 'And all the congregation of the children of Israel departed from the presence of Moses. And they came, everyone whose heart stirred him up, and everyone whom his spirit made willing, and they brought the Lord's offering to the work of the tabernacle of the congregation, and for all his service, and for the holy garments. And they came, both men and women, as many as were willing hearted, and brought bracelets, and earrings, and rings, and tablets, all jewels of gold; and every man that offered offered an offering of gold unto the Lord. And every man, with whom was found blue, and purple, and scarlet, and fine linen, and goats' hair, and red skins of rams, and badgers' skins, brought them. Everyone that did offer an offering of silver and brass brought the Lord's offering: and every man, with whom was found shittim wood for any work of the service, brought it. And all the women that were wise hearted did spin with their hands, and brought that which they had spun, both of blue, and of purple, and of scarlet, and of fine linen. And all the women whose heart stirred them up in wisdom spun goats' hair. And the rulers brought onyx stones, and stones to be set, for the ephod, and for the breastplate; and spice, and oil for the light, and for the anointing oil, and for the sweet incense. The children of Israel brought a willing offering unto the Lord, every man and woman, whose heart made them willing to bring for all manner of work, which the Lord had commanded to be made by the hand of Moses.'

In like manner, when the Lord has work to do, he can furnish workmen or find means. He makes his people willing to expend their substance in his service, as well as he raises up workmen. This is the greatest encouragement to the Lord's people, that he will never desert his cause, or suffer it to fail, when it is his purpose to establish it. The silver and the gold are his, and when his cause needs their aid, he can bring it into the treasury, even by the hand of those who were formerly his greatest enemies. But this does not imply that we may be careless about the Lord's cause, as if it may be wholly left to himself. He works through his people; and even when it is not his purpose to spread his gospel, it is the sin of his people that they neglect efforts to propagate it.

40

Request of the Israelites that Moses should receive for them the law from God

Deuteronomy 5

THE Israelites, terrified by the dreadful appearance at Sinai, requested Moses to approach to God in their place, and receive the law for them. In this they were no doubt influenced merely by their own feelings. But it was providentially effected in order to afford a type of the gospel. The true Israelites received God's law, and perfectly fulfil it, not personally by themselves, but in their Mediator Christ, with whom, by a divine constitution, they are one. The terrors of the Lord would destroy them, were they to approach in their own righteousness, or profess to keep the law as a ground of salvation. Not one of them all could look at God in this way. This great truth is taught us in a figure in this terrible display of the holy and righteous God promulgating his law. 'These words the Lord spake unto all your assembly in the mount out of the midst of the fire, of the cloud, and of the thick darkness, with a great voice: and he added no more. And he wrote them in two tables of stone, and delivered them unto me. And it came to pass, when ye heard the voice out of the midst of the darkness, (for the mountain did burn with fire,) that ye came near unto me, even all the heads of your tribes, and your elders; and ye said, Behold, the Lord our God hath showed us his glory and his greatness, and we have heard his voice out of the midst of the fire: we have seen this day that God doth talk with man, and he liveth. Now therefore why should we die? For this great fire will consume us: if we hear the voice of the Lord our God any more, then we shall die. For who is there of all flesh, that hath heard the voice of the living God speaking out of the midst of the fire (as we have) and lived? Go thou near and hear all that the Lord our God shall say: and speak thou unto us all that the Lord our God shall speak unto thee; and we will hear it, and do it. And the Lord heard the voice of your words, when ye spake unto me; and the Lord said unto me, I have heard the voice of the words of this people, which they have spoken unto thee: they have well said all that they have spoken.' What was Moses that he should undertake such an office? In himself he was utterly unfit for the office. Did he not exceedingly fear and tremble? Was he not sinful dust and ashes, as well as the rest of his brethren? God constituted him a type of the great Mediator, and in that light he was acceptable and sufficient, though his brethren had requested him to approach for them, yet their own observation on the occasion implied that none of all the earth could thus approach and live.

41
The hiding of the Israelitish spies by Rahab
Joshua 2

WHAT a lucky chance! What an instance of providential direction! What brought the spies to the house of Rahab? They came not by invitation. They came not by previous acquaintance, or information with respect to her faith and friendship towards Israel. Among all the houses of Jericho, why did they happen to lodge with Rahab? It has been uselessly, as well as foolishly, attempted to be proved that she had not been an harlot, but the keeper of a house of entertainment. There is no evidence that she kept a house of general entertainment at all. But were this even in evidence, why did the spies happen to lodge in this house, rather than in any other of the same kind? Rahab was the only believer in Jericho. Why was there one believer found in Jericho? The Lord in his Providence had need of Rahab's services. He took out of Jericho just what served his purpose. But could not Jehovah have performed his will without Rahab? Doubtless he could; but he chose to act by means, and by the means of his people, and in this case by a Gentle believer, as a figure of the calling of the Gentiles to the blessings of God's true Israel.

The king of Jericho is informed that Israelitish spies were in the country—in the city—in the very house of Rahab. Could not the watchful Providence of God have prevented this? Could not the overruling power of Jehovah have kept it secret from the king of Jericho that spies were in the country—in the city—in the house of Rahab? Did Providence in this instance fight against itself? If we see the hand of Providence for Israel in the faith of Rahab, may not our enemies claim a similar Providence in manifesting the fact to the king of Jericho? Such manifestation was God's purpose, and for God's glory, as well as the eventual success of the spies. It tried the faith of Rahab. It proved her faith and her ignorance of duty. It showed an important truth, that God's people often glorify him by their obedience, while in that very obedience there is sinful weakness. Rahab's faith and hiding of the spies are approved by God; her lying was the result of ignorance of duty or weakness of faith. There need not any singular defence be set up for Rahab. Every Christian needs a similar defence in many instances. Who is it who is perfect in the knowledge of the revealed will of God? Who is it, then, who commits not sins from ignorance of duty?

Rahab hides the spies, and denies that they are in the house. But the danger is not over. Why does this lie succeed? Why did the king's messengers take her word? They should have died for their negligence. They should have searched every corner of the house. Would the police of any city, on such information, take the word of the most respectable householder? The thing was of God, and the cautious are negligent, or forgetful, when it is God's purpose to keep them from succeeding. The messengers are deceived by Rahab, and go in pursuit where the prey is not to be found. The stalks of flax would have been no cover, had it been God's purpose to reveal. Who can hide when God would make manifest? Who can discover what God would conceal? Who is it that may not see the work of the Providence of the Lord in the history of this matter? 'And Joshua the son of Nun sent out of Shittim two men to spy secretly, saying, Go view the land, even Jericho. And they went, and came into an harlot's house, named Rahab, and lodged there. And it was told the king of Jericho, saying, Behold, there came men in hither tonight of the children of Israel to search out the country. And the King of Jericho sent unto Rahab, saying, Bring forth the men that are come to thee, which are entered into thine house: for they be come to search out all the country. And the woman took the two men, and hid them, and said thus, There came men unto me, but I wist not whence they were: And it came to pass about the time of shutting of the gate, when it was dark, that the men went out: whither the men went I wot not: pursue after them quickly; for ye shall overtake them. But she had brought them up to the roof of the house, and hid them with the stalks of flax, which she had laid in order upon the roof. And the men pursued after them the way to Jordan unto the fords: and as soon as they which pursued after them were gone out, they shut the gate.' — Joshua 2:1-7.

42

The punishment of Adoni-bezek

Judges 1:6

'BUT Adoni-bezek fled; and they pursued after him, and caught him, and cut off his thumbs and his great toes.' Cruel, cruel, cruel! It may be so; but it is of God. And in this point of view, it is right. The Ruler of the world in this affair executes an awful retribution. And he does it in the way of his Providence. There is no account of a command to punish in this way on this occasion. There is no evidence, that the Israelites knew that Adoni-bezek had punished in this manner the kings whom he had conquered. There is no evidence that they intended this punishment to be retributive. What, then, suggested the manner of punishment to them in this instance? Whatever it was, the Providence of the Lord secured its accomplishment. The tyrant himself confesses not only the justice of his punishment, but acknowledges that it was a retribution overruled by God. 'And Adoni-bezek said, Three score and ten kings, having their thumbs and their great toes cut off, gathered their meat under my table: as I have done, so God has requited me.' Hear this, ye foolish wise men. Hear the testimony of one of the kings of ancient Canaan. Here the heathen recognising the Providence of God in the manner of his punishment, while ye see no Providence but as the effect of general laws. Your ignorance is below heathen ignorance. It is brutish. It would blaspheme the light of heathenism to say that it was heathenish. Of all men living there are no such enemies of the Divine character, as those who profess to fathom the nature of God, and determine a bound to his conduct. All the wisdom of philosophers could not discover how God could do this, while, at the same time, it was the uncommanded act of the Israelites. And that for which they cannot account, they will, in the presumption of their ignorance, boldly deny. As they cannot see the way in which God can do such things, they will solve the matter by explaining it as if it were merely permitted or foreseen by God. But neither permission nor foreknowledge can warrant a thing to be ascribed to God; as his doing. I might permit or foreknow with the utmost certainty, what I could in no sense be said to do. Here, then, I may be asked, can God be said to do such things? Were I to attempt an answer to such questions, I would be as presumptuous as the inquirer. God tells me that he doth such things. He tells me also that men do these things. I believe both assertions, though I cannot make the smallest approach to reconcile them. Does not God tell me in his word, that 'his ways are past finding out'? If we could fathom all the ways of God, the Scriptures could not be his word.

43
The Kenites inhabit Canaan with Israel
Judges 1:16

' AND the children of the Kenite, Moses' father-in-law, went up out of the city of palm trees with the children of Judah into the wilderness of Judah, which lieth in the south of Arad; and they went and dwelt among the people.' As Canaan was typical of the heavenly inheritance, and the sojourning of the Israelites in it was typical of the spiritual inheritance, why are we not to see the residence of the Kenites with them as a typical representation of the union of Gentiles with the seed of Israel in the kingdom of glory? When God puts the key into our hands, why should we fear to use it? The New Testament shows us, in innumerable instances, that the Old Testament is a figure of the things of Christ. Is he a friend of either, who wishes as much as possible to keep the Christ of God from appearing in the history of Israel?

44

The Israelites commanded to extirpate the Canaanites, yet some of them providentially preserved to prove Israel

Judges 3

GOD commanded that the Canaanites should be expelled or destroyed without exception, yet he did not design that this should be accomplished universally. They were not eventually all expelled, yet Israel was guilty in not expelling them. Men may speculate on these points, and show their presumption in adjusting them, but they are a part of the ways of God which are past finding out. A child, in reading the history, may see this truth, but their adjustment is beyond the efforts of human intellect. 'And ye shall make no league with the inhabitants of this land; ye shall throw down their altars: but ye have not obeyed my voice; why have ye done this? Wherefore I also said, I will not drive them out from before you, but they shall be as thorns in your sides, and their gods shall be a snare unto you,' Judges 2:2,3. How awfully sovereign is this conduct! God keeps the Canaanites in the land, while in judgment he declares that they would be a snare unto his people! If he knew that they would be a snare to his people, why did he not, on that very account, drive them out? Would not, should not, every human father do so? God is a sovereign, of the measures of whose conduct we are not fit to judge; and we have no right to bring him to our law. In all things we are certain that he acts justly and wisely. But his justice and wisdom we are not able to comprehend. The idolatry of Israel might have been prevented or lessened by the total expulsion of the idolatrous nations, yet God does not expel them! Human rulers would not, should not, act after this example. The intention of this act of Divine sovereignty, God tells us, was to prove Israel. By this means it was manifested that the Israelites were by nature no better than the rest of mankind. Had they been preserved free from idolatry and great crimes, they would have gloried in their own righteousness; and all nations would have considered that Israel was chosen by God to their high destinies on account of their excellence. For a similar reason, Divine Providence left David, and others of his ancient people, to fall into grievous sins. In like manner, the gross immorality of the heathen world, and the sins even against nature, which were generally committed, were designed by God to prove the guilt and universal depravity of human nature.

There is another awful feature in the Providence that spared some of the Canaanites in the land. When God determined that any of them should remain, why did he give a universal command for extirpation? Why did he thus give occasion for the guilt of Israel in not executing his orders? Here is sovereignty in its awful and incomprehensible majesty. And will the pride and petulance of human wisdom never cease its attempts to fathom the counsels of the incomprehensible God? Divine Sovereignty designed also that some of the Canaanites should be spared, 'that the generations of the children of Israel might know to teach them war, at the least such as before knew nothing thereof.' Every spiritual Israelite is a soldier; and while he is in this world, he will never want enemies to exercise him in the spiritual warfare.

45
The Midianites providentially invade and waste Israel on account of their sins
Judges 6

WHEN Israel pleased the Lord, no nation dare invade them: all nations feared them. When they fell into idolatry and rebellion against God, they were constantly a prey to devourers. And we see that there was no need that God should expressly call foreign nations to invade them. He effected his purpose in a providential way, by the voluntary acts of their enemies. In one point of view, God excited and sent the enemies to destroy his people: in another, it was their own spontaneous action, without any known reference to the will of the God of Israel. Here is a sample of the incomprehensible ways of Jehovah. God sent the invaders, yet the guilt of the invasion is all the invaders' own. As the swallow knows her season, so the Midianites, as if by a divine instinct, conceived and executed the purpose of invading Israel, at the very moment that their conduct merited this punishment from the Lord. It was punishment from the Lord, yet the executioners of this punishment acted entirely from their own thoughts, resolves, and hopes. Wonderful are thy ways, O Lord God Almighty! They alone are wise who study thy character in thine own word and works, renouncing their own wisdom, and relying on the enlightening of thy Holy Spirit. The entrance of thy word gives light, and makes wise the simple.

46
The dream of the Midianitish soldier
Judges 7:13

THIS dream was providential, and shows us how God, in the ordinary course of his Providence, without any proper miracle, gives occasion to victory, or defeat, in armies. A dream, or an impression, or even a superstitious omen, may be the means which Providence employs to effect its purposes. It is amazing upon what trivial circumstances the most momentous events depend. God employs whatever means he pleases; and he can make his enemies predict the victory of his people. Here a Midianitish soldier was a prophet to Gideon, to encourage him to the battle of the Lord against the mighty. 'And when Gideon was come, behold, there was a man that told a dream unto his fellow, and said, Behold, I dreamed a dream, and lo, a cake of barley bread tumbled into the host of Midian, and came unto a tent, and smote it that it fell, and overturned it, that the tent lay along. And his fellow answered and said, This is nothing else save the sword of Gideon the son of Joash, a man of Israel: for into his hand hath God delivered Midian, and all the host.'—Judges 7:13,14.

47

Jephthah's vow

Judges 11:31

WHATEVER may be supposed to have been the nature of the vow of Jephthah, it was rash and sinful. It injured his daughter, and brought himself into trouble. From his own confession this is perfectly obvious. 'And it came to pass when he saw her, that he rent his clothes, and said, Alas, my daughter, thou hast brought me very low, and thou art one of them that trouble me: for I have opened my mouth unto the Lord, and I cannot go back.' Divine Providence might have delivered her from the consequences of his rashness. His daughter might have been out of the way on his return, and something else might have been the first to meet him. He that so seasonably provided a ram caught by the horns in a thicket for the occasions of Abraham, could be at no loss to direct events so as to relieve Jephthah. But Providence did not so. It brought him into the very snare that he had set for himself. His

THE HISTORY OF PROVIDENCE

daughter was the first to meet him. 'Behold, his daughter came forth to meet him with timbrels and with dances; and she was his only child: besides her he had neither son nor daughter.' Human wisdom would have acted differently. Had we the direction of Providence on such an occasion, events would have been different, and all would have ended *fortunately*. The joy of victory and glory would not have been alloyed with the greatest calamity that could befall the house of the conqueror.

48
Samson married to a Philistine
Judges 14

SAMSON goes down to Timnath. Accidental. He saw a woman in Timnath of the daughters of the Philistines. Accidental. He loved her. What is strange in this? But he desires his parents to get her for him in marriage. Samson, this is wrong. Hast thou forgotten the commandment of the Giver of all thy strength and glory? His parents remonstrate: Samson is obstinate. The Philistine wife he must have. 'Then his father and his mother said unto him, Is there never a woman among the daughters of thy brethren, or among all my people that thou goest to take a wife of the uncircumcised Philistines? And Samson said unto his father, Get her for me, for she pleaseth me well.' Nothing could divert him from his purpose. The problem is solved in the next verse. The whole was providential, though effected through the sin of Samson and his parents. 'But his father and his mother knew not that it was of the Lord that he sought an occasion against the Philistines.' God designed by the hand of Samson to punish the Philistines, and this is the way in which his Providence chose to bring it about. May we not also in this affair behold an emblem of the calling of the Gentiles?

Taking this fact for a key, we may open much of the Providence that we behold with our own eyes. How many events owe their origin to circumstances equally casual and trivial as the love of Samson for a Philistine woman! Things that are accidental and unimportant in our view, may be the wise arrangement of Providence to lead to the most important consequences.

49

Awful wickedness of the Benjamites

Judges 19

THE fact here recorded by the pen of inspiration is one of those by which Providence shows the guilt and depravity of human nature, even in his own people. Had the grossness of crime been found only in the most unenlightened of the heathens, some plausibility would have been given to the apologists of human nature. But here is an instance of the most awful wickedness, even in one of the favoured tribes of Israel. The seed of Israel are by this proved to be by nature nothing better than the seed of Cain. All are equally, by nature, the children of wrath. By what a chain of seemingly fortuitous events is the event here recorded brought about? Had any one of the links been taken away, the event would not have happened, and Benjamin's depravity would not have been manifested. The marriage of the Levite to this particular woman; the character of the woman herself, and her misconduct; the relative situation of the district where the Levite lived, with respect both to the habitation of the father of his wife, and the country of the Benjamites; the Levite's resolution to bring back his wife, and not to abandon her,—these, and other things, are all necessary links in the chain of Providence by which this event took place. The Levite on several days purposes to set out, yet is prevailed on to remain. At last, though he rose early to depart, he was prevailed on to stay till evening. Why did he not either go in the morning, or remain this day also? Her father is his benefactor, and presses him to stay that night also, and set out early next morning. But he is obstinate. Now he will go. No importunity can move him. If he was in haste to return, why did he not go sooner? If he was not in haste, why did he not patiently stay till morning? What folly was it to set out, even in the most civilized country, at an hour which obliged him to lodge by the way? Go, he will go. 'But the man would not tarry that night, but he rose up and departed.'

It was late when they came to Jebus, and his servant advised him to turn in and lodge there. No, he will not lodge in a city of strangers; he will go to Gibeah to his brother Benjamin. To Gibeah of Benjamin they did go, and there they found no hospitality except from one of another tribe. Instead of the children of Abraham, they found the children of Belial. Had it not been for the hospitality of an old Ephrathite, they must have lodged in the streets. In this way the sin of Sodom was brought home to the Benjamites, and the people of Gibeah committed a crime which certainly never was exceeded by the most profligate of the heathen nations.

50

The history of Ruth

THIS whole history is a chain of providential events. It is delightful, it is instructive to trace the connection of the links. One of the ancestors of the Messiah is to come out of Moab; and by the process related in the book of Ruth, the thing is effected.

The redemption of the inheritance is typical, and in Providence it happened that, by this redemption, Ruth must be adopted into Israel, and become the wife of Boaz. The Gentiles are here shown to be fellow-heirs with the children of Abraham. 'Then said Boaz, What day thou buyest the field of the hand of Naomi, thou must buy it also of Ruth the Moabitess, the wife of the dead, to raise up the name of the dead upon his inheritance.'—Ruth 4:5.

To bring this Gentile wife to Boaz, and place her among the ancestors of Christ, a famine sent Elimelech and his family to the land of Moab, his son was married to a Moabitess, this son dies, Naomi, Elimelech's wife, returns to her country, a most extraordinary attachment incites Ruth to follow her, and a chain of providential events makes her the wife of one of the ancestors of Jesus.

Ruth finds favour with Boaz. He is a near kinsman; but not the nearest kinsman. Another has the previous right of redemption. Why does he not redeem? He is willing to redeem. Why then does he not redeem? Providence so ordered it. He was not able to redeem without marring his own inheritance; and this his caution did not dispose him to risk. The right, then, is given over to Boaz. But why was Boaz able to redeem? Why was he willing to redeem? Why was he so long an unmarried man? Why was he disposed to marry this poor stranger? All things work together to fulfil the purposes of the Most High.

51
The people of Israel ask a king
1 Samuel 8:5

IT WAS a sin in Israel to seek a king: it was of the Lord that they sought a king. By asking a king they virtually rejected God as their

THE HISTORY OF PROVIDENCE

king: yet the king of Israel is eminently a type of the King Messiah.
God, then, can bring about his purposes by the free actions of sinful men. Saul, in the divine sovereignty, is to be made king of Israel;
and to bring this about, the sons of Samuel are not like their father.
They are corrupt in judging, and they take bribes of the people. In
consequence, Israel asks a king, and God commands Samuel to give
them a king. Had Samuel's sons been like himself, the people would
not have asked a king. Why, then, did not Providence prevent this
occasion of sin to his people? Why did his Providence lay this stum-
bling-block before them? If he designed to give them a king, why
did he not give them a king in a way that would have presented
them with no occasion of rejecting himself as king? God designed
to show what rebellion was in them, and his Providence manifests
this, even in the way of fulfilling his own purposes, which coincide
with theirs. Here is sovereignty.

52

Loss of the asses of Kish

1 Samuel 9:3

SAUL must be anointed by Samuel to be king of Israel. How is
this to be effected? The asses of Kish, the father of Saul, must go
astray; Saul must be sent by his father to seek them; they must not
be found by him; he is providentially led in a course that places him
in the neighbourhood of the city where Samuel was at the time; it
is suggested to Saul by his servant to inquire of the Prophet, when
he himself had resolved to return to his father's house; Saul and his
servant arrived at the city in which Samuel was, just at the time
that served the purpose, and every thing succeeded to bring about
the event which Providence designed. Thus is Saul anointed king

of Israel. Nothing is accidental. Things which to us are accidental, may be the beginning of a train that is to effect some of the most important events in Providence. What can apparently have less connection with the anointing of Saul to his office as king, than the straying of his father's asses? This, in itself, was a disagreeable accident, that gave great trouble to the family of Kish. But it was connected with the glory of his house, and was not only in wisdom, but in goodness. Let us use this key to open disagreeable occurrences in Providence that may be for us which appear against us.

53
Samuel's delay in coming to Saul at Gilgal
1 Samuel 13:8

WHY did not Samuel come within the appointed time? Was it accident, was it necessity, was it negligence, which was the cause of his delay? Whatever it was, it was providential. God designed it to be a touchstone to try the obedience of Saul. And it was a test peculiarly adapted to try the strength of the faith and obedience of the new king to the King and God of Israel. No arguments for disobeying a divine injunction could be more plausible than those pleaded by Saul on the occasion. The people were scattered, and the piety of the king will not engage in battle without sacrifice to the God of Israel. As Samuel had disappointed him, does not necessity oblige him to offer sacrifice himself? 'And he tarried seven days, according to the set time that Samuel had appointed; but Samuel came not to Gilgal; and the people were scattered from him. And Saul said, Bring hither a burnt-offering to me, and peace-offerings. And he offered the burnt-offering. And it came to pass, that as soon as he had made an end of offering the burnt-offering, behold, Samuel came; and Saul went out to meet him, that he might salute him. And Samuel said, What hast thou done? And Saul said, Because I saw that the people were scattered from me, and that thou camest not within the days appointed, and that the Philistines gathered themselves together at Michmash; therefore said I, The Philistines will come down now upon me to Gilgal, and I have not made supplication unto the Lord: I forced myself therefore, and offered a burnt-offering. And Samuel said to Saul, Thou has done foolishly; thou hast not kept the commandment of the Lord thy God, which he commanded thee: for now would the Lord have established thy kingdom upon Israel for ever. But now thy kingdom shall not continue: the Lord hath sought him a man after his own heart, and the Lord hath commanded him to be captain over his people, because thou hast not kept that which the Lord commanded thee.'—1 Sam. 13:8-14. When Providence puts it out of the power of his people to observe his ordinances according to his own appointment, they are not guilty in not observing them; and they are guilty when they observe them, under any pretence, contrary to the Divine appointment. God could have given victory to Saul without sacrifice, when sacrifice could not be legally observed. And when Saul observed it illegally, God was not only displeased with him, but on that very account rejected him as king of Israel. And had Saul waited a little longer, he would have had sacrifice in a legal way. Samuel made his appearance as soon as Saul had ceased to offer the burnt-offering. The Providence of God tries his people, even with their conviction of the utility of his ordinances.

54

David, as a type of Christ, brought by Providence into the field against Goliath

1 Samuel 17

DAVID, as a type of Christ, must engage and defeat the champion of the Philistines. Providence brings him to the spot at the precise moment of time, and by a train of circumstances brings him to the encounter. His father providentially resolves to send a supply of necessaries to his son in the camp of Israel. Why at this moment? Why not the day preceding, or the day following? Why not in the evening, after the hosts were on both sides retired into their tents; or in the morning, so early as to return before the engagement? Why was David sent? Had not his father other messengers? Why was David taken from the sheep? David made some inquiries which showed that he was conceiving the resolution to encounter Goliath, and his soul is fired with zeal for the glory of Israel and of Israel's God. He is discouraged by his brother Eliab, and insulted; yet he is not driven from his purpose. The thing providentially reaches the ears of Saul, and eventually David engages and defeats the enemy of Israel. Here is a chain of providential circumstances, undoubtedly planned, formed, and connected by the hand of God. David slings a pebble. What a lucky hit! The unerring hand of God led it to its destination. Goliath is killed by a pebble from a sling, at the first discharge. How many have escaped from the field of battle, amidst the discharge of the most powerful cannon! One man is killed by a fall from his feet on the open field; another falls ninety feet perpendicular, and is uninjured.

55
David's preservation from Saul

DAVID must be king in the room of Saul; therefore none of the plans of his enemy can take his life. Yet, in general, he was providentially preserved; in the very way in which God usually preserves his people. Saul cast a javelin at him: David escaped. Saul sent him on an errand, that he might perish among the Philistines: David executed the commission and returned in safety. That the thing was providential, Saul himself was convinced. 'And Saul saw and knew that the Lord was with David.' Among the means of safety which Divine Providence prepared for David against the snares of Saul were the love of Michal, and the unexampled love of Jonathan. By the means of his wife and of his friend in the house of Saul, David was generally aware of the dangers that awaited him. These things were merely providential. How could David escape the wrath of the king, when even Jonathan, the king's son, was in danger of his life from his father, for his love to David? In reading the history of David's dangers and escapes from Saul, we read the history of the ordinary Providence of God. By this key we ought to unlock all the escapes of ourselves and the people of God. He who providentially defended David can with equal care providentially deliver us. Nothing is more erroneous, or more pernicious to the comfort of God's people, than to consider the deliverances of his people recorded in Scripture as being extraordinary or miraculous works, without any bearing on after-times.

56

Doeg present when David came to Ahimelech

1 Samuel 21

FOR the sin of Eli with regard to his sons, God rejected his whole house from the priesthood. Providence fulfills his word. Doeg happened to be at Nob when David on his flight came to Ahimelech: he saw what David received from the priest, and gave information. With the exception of Abiathar, the whole house of Ahimelech was cut off. 'Now a certain man of the servants of Saul was there that day, detained before the Lord; and his name was Doeg, an Edomite, the chiefest of the herdsmen that belonged to Saul.'— 'Then answered Doeg the Edomite, (which was set over the servants of Saul,) and said, I saw the son of Jesse coming to Nob to Ahimelech, the son of Ahitub. And he inquired of the Lord for him, and gave him victuals, and gave him the sword of Goliath the Philistine.'—'And the king said to Doeg, Turn thee, and fall upon the priests. And Doeg the Edomite turned, and fell upon the priests, and slew on that day fourscore and five persons that did wear a linen ephod. And Nob, the city of the priests, smote he with the edge of the sword, both men and women, children and sucklings, and oxen, and asses, and sheep, with the edge of the sword.'

Abiathar, one of the sons of Ahimelech, escaped and fled to David. But he afterwards conspired with Adonijah, and was expelled from the office of the priesthood by Solomon. 'And unto Abiathar the priest said the king, Get thee to Anathoth, unto thine own fields, for thou art worthy of death: but I will not at this time put thee to death, because thou barest the ark of the Lord God before David my father, and because thou hast been afflicted in all wherein my father was afflicted. So Solomon thrust out Abiathar from being priest unto the Lord; that he might fulfill the word of the Lord which he spake concerning the house of Eli in Shiloh.' Thus did

Providence fulfill the word of the Lord against Eli for his negligence with respect to the restraint of his sons. The wisdom of this world would see nothing here but the hand of man: the pen of inspiration refers all things to the will of God.

57
David put in possession of the kingdom
2 Samuel 3:6

O N THE death of Saul, the men of Judah anointed David to be their king. But he must be king over all Israel; and Providence opens the way. Ishbosheth was made king by Abner. How can this obstacle be providentially removed? Abner is a man of might and of wisdom. If he has espoused the cause of David's rival, hopes of speedy success are not to be entertained. But Providence dissolves the union between the son of Saul and his protector. Though Abner had made himself strong for the house of Saul, Providence turned his power to assist in effecting what he was endeavouring to prevent. It happened that Abner had taken a concubine of Saul's and that Ishbosheth had imprudently reproved him. Abner is disgusted, rebels, and translates the kingdom to David.

But Ishbosheth still lives. He must be removed to make way for David. Two of his own captains, even of his own tribe, conspired against him, and slew him. By wicked instruments, and by a deed which was disapproved and punished by David, was the rival of David taken out of the way. None can work like the Almighty. He effects his purposes by the wicked as well as by the righteous; by means which he condemns as well as by means which he commands. This is a depth unfathomable to our intellect.

This, however, might have only exasperated the minds of the

friends of the house of Saul against David. Divine Providence turned it otherwise. All Israel were now unanimous in calling the man after God's own heart to the throne. 'Then came all the tribes of Israel to David unto Hebron, and spake, saying, Behold, we are thy bone and thy flesh.' Why did they forget this lesson? Was it at this moment that their relation to David commenced? It was now that God impressed them with this sentiment; for now David must be the acknowledged king of all the tribes of Israel. David, as the type of Christ, must have a willing people in the day of his power. 'Also in time past,' they continue to say, 'when Saul was king over us, thou wast he that leddest out and broughtest in Israel.' Why, then, was this so shamefully forgotten hitherto? Why does their gratitude now revive? 'And the Lord said to them,' say they, 'thou shalt feed my people, and thou shalt be captain over Israel.' Why, then, did they, till this moment, rebel against what they knew to be the appointment of the Lord? Why do they now yield with child-like submission to this authority?

58

Ill-treatment of the messengers of David by Hanun, king of the Ammonites

2 Samuel 10:2

THE message of David to Hanun, king of the Ammonites, in condolence on the death of his father, was a most effectual way to secure peace between the two nations. This God did not design: this his Providence prevented. When David's messengers arrived, the princes of Hanun excited him to suspect the sincerity of David, and grossly to insult him in the person of those commissioned by him. It may be politic in statesmen to guard against insincerity in the most friendly professions. But to betray these suspicions, and return insult for kindness, is both inhuman and grossly impolitic. Had there been just grounds to suspect the sincerity of David, it was the wisdom of Hanun's court to overlook this, and return the compliment that was so politely conferred. But when God determines to punish nations, he makes their rulers mad, even though they may be in other respects wise and cautious men. So was it on this occasion. 'Then said David, I will show kindness unto Hanun the son of Nahash, as his father showed kindness unto me. And David sent to comfort him by the hand of his servants for his father. And David's servants came into the land of the children of Ammon. And the princes of the children of Ammon said unto Hanun their lord, Thinkest thou that David doth honour thy father, that he hath sent comforters unto thee? hath not David rather sent his servants unto thee, to search the city, and to spy it out, and to overthrow it? Wherefore Hanun took David's servants, and shaved off the one half of their beards, and cut off their garments in the middle, even to their buttocks, and sent them away.' Thus vengeance came on Ammon. And thus it is in every age. When God designs to send the sword, his Providence often employs the rashness of mutual insults as the means of unsheathing it. A point of honour may deluge nations with blood.

59

David's scheme to hide his crime with respect to Bathsheba providentially defeated

2 Samuel 11

IN THE awful sovereignty of Divine Providence, David is presented with a temptation by which he falls, and by which is clearly seen that the best of men are by nature capable of the worst of crimes, and that they are preserved only by the power of God through faith. In the scheme of David to hide his sin, and in the manner in which all the expedients of his wisdom and power united were defeated, we have a striking instance of the acting of Providence. In this conduct David is seen as a most heinous transgressor. What a variety of ingredients are combined in his crime! He is guilty of the greatest injustice that man can commit against man. He uses that power which God gave him to protect his subjects as a means of inflicting injury. He is guilty of treachery, cruelty, and ingratitude, with respect to the most deserving of his servants. In the fall of David we see the guilt and depravity of human nature. But God puts him to shame. All the expedients of his artifice cannot conceal what God would reveal. A sort of romantic, extravagant, and chivalrous principle providentially guides the conduct of Uriah on this occasion. He will not go down to his house. David urges and invents expedients to break his resolution. All expedients are ineffectual. Uriah is as obstinate as Balaam's ass. Who is so blind as not to see the hand of a sovereign Providence here? Yet, by this sovereign Providence, occasion is presented to David to contrive the death of this deserving servant. How easily could Providence have prevented not only the issue of David's temptation, but the occasion of the temptation? How deep is that wisdom, how awful is that sovereignty, which afforded occasion to the commission of such crimes in a beloved servant—in a dear son! Without the slightest difficulty, Providence could have prevented that conduct in David, which, in every age since its commission, has been the means of opening the mouths of his enemies, and of hardening their hearts. Human wisdom cannot fathom the depth of the divine counsels: it cannot receive it. But can any thing be more self-evidently true, than that, if any earthly father would act so by his son, or even by his enemy, he would be justly the abhorrence of mankind? Who, then, can judge the Almighty? His ways are past finding out. The silly philosophist reasons, and distinguishes, and defines, and thinks he can explain the divine conduct satisfactorily in all things. He is wise only in words. He neither has a distinct meaning himself under his own words, nor can he give any satisfaction to another, who tries to comprehend his distinctions. True wisdom submits to the divine testimony, and on that ground believes with confidence what it finds utterly beyond its comprehension.

60

Punishment of David's crime with respect to Uriah providentially executed

2 Samuel 13

GOD denounced the most grievous afflictions against the house of David on account of his conduct towards Uriah. These afflictions were all executed in a way of Providence. Amnon trespasses against nature with respect to his sister. Absalom murders Amnon out of revenge. This might have been prevented, had Amnon married Tamar. But against this he was immovably resolved the moment after the commission of the crime. His aversion is equal to his love. From this followed his murder. Absalom is restored from banishment; he steals the hearts of the people; he rebels, and his rebellion succeeds. At last, contrary to the most cautious and strict commands of David, Absalom, being entangled in an oak, is slain by Joab. Every part of the divine sentence against David is executed by his Providence without a miracle. Who can work like God?

61

Ahithophel's prudent advice providentially rejected by Absalom

2 Samuel 17

NOTHING could be more prudent than the advice of Ahithophel. The advice of Hushai is sophistical declamation. Yet Absalom rejects the counsel that was wise, and follows that which was for his ruin. The thing has happened a thousand times, and no doubt for a similar reason. 'And Absalom and all the men of Israel said, The counsel of Hushai, the Archite, is better than the counsel of Ahithophel. For the Lord had appointed to defeat the good counsel of Ahithophel, to the intent that the Lord might bring evil upon Absalom.' The rejection of Ahithophel's counsel was the free action of Absalom and his friends; yet God appointed this free choice to effect his own purpose. Can human intellect conceive how God could appoint the choice of a voluntary agent? Millions of volumes of incomprehensible nonsense have been written to explain these mysterious ways of God. But it is an attempt to fathom the abyss of infinity. That the thing is so, we know, because God declares it. How it is so, we cannot know, because the manner of it is not declared. We may as well attempt to fathom the incomprehensible nature of God, as to fathom his equally incomprehensible ways.

In the fact here presented to our view, we have a key put into our hands by which we may open the events of the history of nations. Why does folly often prevail over wisdom in the counsels of princes, and in houses of legislators? God has appointed the rejection of good counsel in order to bring on nations that vengeance that their crimes call down from heaven. God rules the world by Providence, not by miracle. See that grave senator. He rises and pours forth wisdom. But if God has determined to punish the nation, some prating speculatist will impose his sophisms on the most sagacious assembly.

62

Solomon's decision with respect to the mother of the child

1 Kings 3:16

GOD determined to impress the people of Israel with a high opinion of the wisdom of Solomon in the beginning of his reign. But how was this to be effected? Providence provided the occasion. A dispute arose between two persons, of a very perplexing nature, as to which of them was the mother of a child which each of them claimed. There was no witness of the matter but themselves, and they were both equally confident in their assertion of their right. Solomon's plan for finding out the true mother is well known, and will ever be admired, as the highest specimen of the knowledge of human nature, promptness in inventing expedients, and sound judicial discrimination. But the Providence of the Lord in the matter, I think, has been generally overlooked or neglected. In this affair we are not only called to contemplate the gift of God in the wisdom of Solomon, but the direction of Providence on the occasion of displaying that wisdom. For the purpose of making a favourable impression on the people, what would it have signified that Solomon had actually possessed such wisdom, had not an opportunity of manifesting it occurred to him at the proper time? The dispute, then, between these two harlots was not a fortunate accident, but was a wisely directed Providence. This is another proof that things which to us are purely accidental, are essential parts of a Divine plan in the government of God. This is another instance in which Providence makes use even of the wickedness of men to fulfill his purposes. The falsehood and wicked purpose of this cruel woman were employed by Providence to display the wisdom of his servant Solomon. Deep and incomprehensible are thy counsels, O thou unsearchable Jehovah! Instead of scrutinizing thy ways as censors of thy conduct, let us admire, and submissively adore. Who shall successfully contend with the Almighty?

63
Rehoboam's rejection of the old men's counsel
1 Kings 12

HERE we have another Absalom. Here good counsel is rejected, and the most absurdly foolish advice is providentially followed, in order that the word of the Lord should be fulfilled. Could any thing be more obvious to any man of ordinary understanding, than that Rehoboam should, on the application of his people, without a moment's delay, have given them satisfaction? A very child could hardly need advice on this emergency. But Rehoboam rejects the obvious dictates of common sense urged on him by his aged friends, and listens to the silly counsel of his young advisers. The thing was of the Lord. God had declared that, on account of Solomon's sins, he would take a part of the kingdom from his son. And here his Providence executes his threatening. 'Wherefore the king hearkened not unto the people; for the cause was from the Lord, that he might perform his saying, which the Lord spoke by Ahijah the Shilonite unto Jeroboam the son of Nebat.' Can any thing be more clearly asserted than it is here, that the reason why Rehoboam rejected the claims of the people, and the counsel of the old men, is, that the Lord might effect what he had declared? Here God fulfills his purposes by the free actions of men. How God does this, while the actions remain the actions of men, human intellect cannot comprehend. It is easy to refine, and to talk nonsense learnedly and metaphysically. But a satisfactory account of the manner of the harmony of these two things, man will never succeed in giving. How foolish is that wisdom which grapples with such a subject!

64

The land of the Shunammite providentially restored

2 Kings 8

HOW wonderful is the Providence of the Lord, in accompa-
nying the steps of his people! All things are arranged with
reference to their interests; and when they are in difficulties which
may appear insurmountable, a train of circumstances is in progress for their deliverance. The Shunammite woman, warned by
the prophet of an approaching famine, left the land of Israel, and
resided seven years amongst the Philistines. She returned, but her
land was occupied by others. How shall she now prove her title?
It may be impossible at the time to prove her title. At all events, it
may be very troublesome and expensive to produce evidence. The
Providence of her God makes the matter easy. Proof is in court, the
witness is in conversation with the judge, at the very moment of
application. Nay, what is still more wonderful, at that very time the
king *happened* to be talking with Gehazi, the servant of the prophet
Elisha, about this very matter. How did it happen that Gehazi was
brought into a situation to have intercourse with the king? How
many chances were against this? How did it happen that Gehazi was
with the king at that particular time? He might have been nearest in
attendance on the king, yet have been absent at that time. How did
it happen that it came into the king's mind, at that particular time,
to ask Gehazi about the great things that Elisha had done? How
many chances were against this? How did it happen that at the very
moment in which he was telling the king about the restoration of
the Shunammite's son to life, she came into the presence of the king,
crying for her house and for her land? What power connected these
events? The man who will not recognize Providence here may deny
that there is light in the sun. 'Then spake Elisha unto the woman

whose son he had restored to life, saying, Arise, and go thou and thine household, and sojourn wheresoever thou canst sojourn: for the Lord hath called for a famine: and it shall also come upon the land seven years. And the woman arose, and did after the saying of the man of God: and she went with her household, and sojourned in the land of the Philistines seven years. And it came to pass at the seven years' end, that the woman returned out of the land of the Philistines: and she went forth to cry unto the king for her house and for her land. And the king talked with Gehazi the servant of the man of God, saying, Tell me, I pray thee, all the great things that Elisha hath done. And it came to pass, as he was telling the king how he had restored a dead body to life, that, behold, the woman, whose son he had restored to life, cried to the king for her house and for her land. And Gehazi said, My lord, O King, this is the woman, and this is her son, whom Elisha restored to life. And when the king asked the woman, she told him. So the king appointed unto her a certain officer, saying, Restore all that was hers, and all the fruits of the field since she left the land, even until now.'—2 Kings 8:1-6. How many independent wheels are here moving in concert! It is easy to see how the wheels of a watch all move in concert. They are all mechanically connected, and move by the same spring. But here are wheels unconnected, all moving in harmony, with all the exactness of mechanical influence. Here is really the harmony of the Monads of Leibnitz; who accounted for the sensations of the mind in concert with impressions on the senses, by the hypothesis that the soul and body are like two independent clocks, keeping exact time, which are perfectly independent of each other, but always in harmony. This was arbitrary, and unphilosophical in the philosopher; for the doctrine is not philosophy but figment. But in the fact before us, we behold several human agents acting as independently of each other as the same number of clocks; and all these independent agents act in as much harmony as exists between the impressions made on the sense, and the sensations of the mind. Here is wisdom. Where are you, ye philosophers? Try your line in fathoming this depth. Your wisdom in these deep things of God is only folly: your boldness is the presumption of madness. You idly waste your time in attempts to fathom infinity; and bewilder your readers with incomprehensible refinements under the name of science.

65
Jezebel eaten by dogs
2 Kings 9

IN EXECUTING predicted punishment on the family of the king of Israel, Jehu did many things by express command. Here, contrary to his design, contrary to his orders, Jezebel is devoured by dogs. This was a providential fulfillment of prediction. By the command of Jehu, Jezebel is cast down from a window. But instead of designing to give full accomplishment to the Divine prediction with respect to this woman, Jehu said, 'Go, see now this cursed woman, and bury her; for she is a king's daughter.' But buried she cannot be. God's word has denounced her doom. She is to be eaten by dogs in the portion of Jezreel. 'And they went to bury her; but they found no more of her than the skull, and the feet, and the palms of her hands.' These fragments were a proof that she was devoured, and not removed for burial by some friend. Here is the hand of Providence. Though Jehu gave orders for the burying of Jezebel, yet, providentially, these orders are not given immediately after her death. A space intervened for the dogs to do their part of the work. And why were the dogs so voracious in the streets of Jezreel? Surely this is not usual. It is strange that Jehu knew the prediction about Jezebel, and did not fulfill it. He either neglected this part of the business, or it did not at first occur to him. But when he was told what had happened, he immediately recollected the word of the

Lord. 'Wherefore they came again, and told him. And he said, This is the word of the Lord, which he spake by his servant Elijah the Tishbite, saying, In the portion of Jezreel shall dogs eat the flesh of Jezebel: and the carcase of Jezebel shall be as dung upon the face of the field in the portion of Jezreel; so that they shall not say, This is Jezebel.' — 2 Kings 9:36,37.

66
Providential preservation of Jehoash
2 Kings 11

NOTWITHSTANDING the transgressions of the house of David, God remembered his covenant given to him; and his Providence took care that his seed should not fail him on his throne. On the death of Ahaziah, his mother destroyed the seed royal, yet Providence saved one of them to sit in the seat of David. 'And when Athaliah, the mother of Ahaziah, saw that her son was dead, she arose and destroyed all the seed royal. But Jehosheba, the daughter of king Joram, sister of Ahaziah, took Joash the son of Ahaziah, and stole him from among the king's sons which were slain; and they hid him, even him and his nurse, in the bed-chamber from Athaliah, so that he was not slain.' — 2 Kings 11:1,2. In due time the true heir to the kingdom was manifested and invested with royal authority. Conspiracies may take place in kingdoms, but their success or failure is of the Lord. It would be as easy to dethrone the sun in the firmament, as the greatest of the tyrants of the earth, unless the thing is of the Lord. 'The powers that be are ordained of God.' In any other kingdom under heaven, it would have been rebellion against God to resist Athaliah. God for the time had put her into power. But his express authority gave the throne to the house of

David, and made it duty to put Jehoash on the throne. Even in Israel a similar thing would have been rebellion against God, except when God had expressed his will. In Judah the throne was at all times exclusively confined to the heirs of David's house.

In the catastrophe of royal houses, how many providential escapes do we find similar to that of Jehoash! The deepest counsels, the most subtle substances of statesmen, are, often providentially defeated, or, when they succeed for a time, are ultimately frustrated.

67

Captivity of Israel effected providentially

2 Kings 17

HOSHEA did that which was evil in the sight of the Lord, and Shalmaneser, king of Assyria, subjected him. This was quite in the way of ordinary Providence. No command was given to the king of Assyria to attack the king of Israel. No miracle was wrought to effect subjugation. But mere subjugation was not enough. Israel had fallen almost universally into idolatry; and must be removed from their land. Hoshea rebels, and the captivity is effected. 'The Lord was very angry with Israel, and removed them out of his sight.'

In these events we have a specimen of what is continually going on in the world. The rise and the fall of nations are in every step the work of Providence.

68

The book of the law found in the temple in the time of Josiah

2 Kings 22

WHY did the book of the law so long lie hid from Judah, who had received the treasure from the Lord? Why was it now found? There was now a Josiah to make a good use of it, and to make known its contents to all his people. It was found, like the loadstone, when God designed to use it for his own glorious purposes. The finding of the law was accident; it was Providence. In like manner, the Scriptures, for many centuries, lay hid in an unknown language. But when God determined to make them known for salvation, they are beginning to be published in all languages.

69

Captivity of Judah

2 Kings 24

JEHOIAKIM was, for his sins and the sins of the kingdom, subjected providentially to the king of Babylon. But the sins of Judah called for greater vengeance. The king rebelled, and the nations are let loose on his people. 'And the Lord sent against him bands of the Chaldees, and bands of the Syrians, and bands of the Moabites, and bands of the children of Ammon, and sent them against Judah to destroy it, according to the word of the Lord, which he spake by his servants the prophets. Surely at the commandment of the Lord came this upon Judah, to remove them out of his sight, for the sins

of Manasseh, according to all that he did; and also for all the innocent blood that he shed: for he filled Jerusalem with innocent blood;
which the Lord would not pardon.' The assailing nations are all
urged on by ambition and selfish motives. Yet they are all going at
the bidding of the Lord, though he had given them no express command. Why are they now excited? Why are they all excited at once?
Why now more than formerly? Why were they now successful, when
they had so often failed? Jehoiakim succeeds to the throne, and sins
like his father: Nebuchadnezzar comes and carries him, with the
principal part of the people, to Babylon. Zedekiah succeeds, madly
rebels, and the captivity is completed. 'For through the anger of the
Lord it came to pass in Jerusalem and Judah, until he had cast them
out from his presence, that Zedekiah rebelled against the king of
Babylon.' All this is effected by the Lord in a way of Providence. He
works here as he is every day working in the kingdoms of the world.
Zedekiah's rebellion, and madly persevering obstinacy, was his own
work, yet it was 'through the anger of the Lord.'

70

Glory and wealth of the kingdom of Israel in the time of Solomon

THE house of God in Jerusalem was a type of the church of
God. An inspired apostle tells us, that the house of God is the
church of God. It was necessary, then, that the glory and magnifi-
cence of the one should in some measure correspond to those of the
other. God, in his Providence, provided Solomon with the means.
Let us learn from this, that in building his temple, Jesus, who sits on
the throne of his Father, will be at no loss in providing the means.
When he chooses he will bring down every temple of Dagon; and

the mountain of the Lord's house will be established on the top of the mountains, and all nations shall flow into it.

71
Disasters and miserable death of Jehoram
2 Chronicles 21

FOR his sins, 'The Lord stirred up against Jehoram the spirit of the Philistines, and of the Arabians, that were near the Ethiopians. And they came up into Judah, and brake into it, and carried away all the substance that was found in the king's house, and his sons also, and his wives; so that there was never a son left him, save Jehoahaz, the youngest of his sons. And after all this the Lord smote him in his bowels with an incurable disease. And it came to pass, that in process of time, after the end of two years, his bowels fell out by reason of his sickness; so he died of sore diseases.'

Can the wisdom of man show in what manner the Lord stirred up the Philistines and Arabians against Jehoram? It was their own work; it was the work of God. In like manner God, in his Providence, in every age stirs up nations to punish those whom his purposes doom to ruin. Yet one son is preserved to the transgressor. Why? God remembered his covenant with David, and an inscrutable Providence preserved Jehoahaz. Even when the dogs of war are let loose, destruction is guided by the finger of Providence. Here, also, in the Providence of God towards this persecutor and encourager of idolatry, we may learn to ascribe to Providence the singular diseases and deaths of tyrants and persecutors, which the pen of history records. An infidel philosophy, in its affected wisdom, refuses to see the hand of Providence in judgment. But the Christian ought not, from fear of ridicule, to hide his eyes, against the works of

Providence. If God smote Jehoram with an incurable and excruciating disease, why may he not, from time to time, manifest his Providence in punishing signal persecutors of his people? True science has no evidence on which it can lawfully deny or question this doctrine. Science, falsely so called, in its attempts to banish Providence from an immediate concern in the calamities of mankind, is influenced not by scientific evidence, but by enmity to God, and to his ways.

Nothing can be more consoling to the man of God, than the conviction that the Lord who made the world governs the world; and that every event, great and small, prosperous and adverse, is under the absolute disposal of him who doth all things well, and who regulates all things for the good of his people. The child had no fear of shipwreck when he knew that his father was at the helm. The Christian will be confident and courageous in duty, in proportion as he views God in his Providence as ruling in the midst of his enemies; and acting for the good of his people, as well as for his own glory, even in the persecution of the Gospel.

72
Wicked people — oppressive rulers

IT IS an inestimable advantage to a nation to have the right of succession to the throne settled by laws with definite and indisputable precision. This prevents all that mischief which arises from disputed succession; and shuts up every avenue from designing men to excite disturbances on the death of a sovereign. An objection apparently strong presents itself to this doctrine. Rulers ought to be the wisest and most just of men. In succession by birth, it cannot be known whether the monarch may be a wise man or a fool, a righteous man or an oppressor of the people. All very true.

But the people of the Lord have no reason to be disquieted on this account. Their God rules the world, and appoints the rulers in his Providence. It is an incalculable blessing to have wise and righteous rulers; but, if it is otherwise, God designs it for his own inscrutable purposes. He never sends a tyrant or an oppressor, when a righteous and merciful ruler would serve the end he has in view for him. When wickedness greatly abounds, it may be necessary that Providence should grind the people by oppressive rulers; and even in countries where tyranny cannot exist, he can baffle the wisdom of statesmen, and increase the burdens of the people, through the very means which policy has devised to lighten them, or effect prosperity. The whole history of the kings of Judah and Israel shows that God sent oppressive rulers to a wicked people. The history of all nations manifests the same Providence. Christians who waste their time in speculations or attempts to bless a wicked world by a perfect civil government are as foolish as the man who proposed to regulate the weather by machines constructed on the laws of electricity.

73

A way of return providentially opened to the Jews on the overthrow of the Babylonish empire by Cyrus

Ezra 1:1

THE Jews must return from Babylon at the end of seventy years. God has said it. Failure,—delay, is impossible. But how shall they be delivered? If they could not defend themselves with all their resources in their own country, how shall they deliver themselves from captivity in the midst of a mighty empire? God delivered them, it is true, from the bondage of Egypt; but it was by mighty signs and wonders. From Babylon he delivers them without a single miracle. His Providence, by a long train of events, effected his purpose as fully as if all had been done by a display of power as manifest as that on Sinai.

What a wonderful train of preparation was put into operation to effect this purpose! The birth, genius, talents, education, and character of Cyrus, were all providentially adapted for the office that God assigned him in this business. Follow him through his wars, and be astonished at his enterprise and success. Reflect on the office which the God of Providence assigned him, and let your wonder terminate in more exalted views of the power and government of God. Empire was given to Cyrus because he was the anointed of the Lord to deliver his people out of Babylon.

But when Cyrus is in Babylon, what secures the deliverance of the Jews? Had not the conqueror the same interest with the king of Babylon in keeping them in bondage? Was Cyrus a worshipper of the true God? No, he was a heathen. What, then, inclines his heart to deliver the people of Jehovah? Was he now made a convert? No, he continues a worshipper of his own gods. He dies a heathen. Why, then, does Cyrus, rather than the king of Babylon, deliver the people of God? Cyrus was the man appointed by the Lord, and the hour of fulfillment was now come. God has the hearts of all men in his hands, and he turns them as rivers of water. He makes his enemies, as easily as he does his friends, the instruments of effecting what he decrees. God put it into the heart of Cyrus to set the Jews free from captivity. This is clear from the book of Ezra; 'Now in the first year of Cyrus, king of Persia, that the word of the Lord by the mouth of Jeremiah might be fulfilled, the Lord stirred up the spirit of Cyrus, king of Persia, that he made a proclamation throughout all his kingdom, and put it also in writing, saying, Thus saith Cyrus, king of Persia, The Lord God of heaven hath given me all the kingdoms of the earth; and he hath charged me to build him an house in Jerusalem, which is in Judah. Who is there among you of all his people? His God be with him, and let him go up to Jerusalem, which is in Judah, and build the house of the Lord God of Israel, (he is the God,) which is in Jerusalem. And whosoever remaineth in any place where he sojourneth, let the men of his place help him with silver, and with gold, and with goods, and with beasts, besides the freewill offering for the house of God that is in Jerusalem.'—Ezra 1:1-4. Here we see that it was the Lord who stirred up the spirit of Cyrus to make this proclamation. The prophecy concerning himself, it is evident from this document, had been laid before him; and the providential effect was the proclamation of liberty. Had it been the will of God that Cyrus should be hardened, the prophecy would have been neglected or mocked. How did Pharaoh resist amidst all the mighty works of Jehovah! The effect, then, that the knowledge of the prophecy concerning himself had on Cyrus, is said to be a stirring up of his spirit by the Lord. Success depended on this, and not merely on the natural effect of the document submitted to the conqueror. God here effects through his Providence, by Cyrus, as mighty a deliverance to his people, as he had done by all the display of his power against Pharaoh in their deliverance from Egypt. God's people, then, have, in every age, a right to look to him with confidence for deliverance from the greatest dangers, and the most inextricable difficulties. Surely, the life of no sovereign, in the midst of his most faithful and attached guards, is so safe as the man who has his trust in the God of Israel. From this fact we may see, that God can easily effect all that remains in his predictions and promises with respect to his ancient people. Without the supposition of a single miracle, he can remove every obstacle in the way of his purpose, and effect the greatest work of power. The prospects of the Jews ought to be determined by a fair exposition of the word of God, by the laws of language, consistently with all that any where in Scripture bears on the subject. But no objection can be allowed from difficulty of accomplishment, or opposition of the rulers of the world. God rules on earth as absolutely as he does in heaven. No being can resist his will. Every thing must fulfill it. The stars do not know their course more certainly than every event that takes place on earth fulfills the designs of Providence.

As God stirred up the spirit of Cyrus to deliver his people, so he stirred up some of the people to return. At first view, we may be ready to think that all the Jews would have with avidity seized the opportunity to return to their native land, in which they had so high prospects. But it was not so. And, as a matter of fact, all did not return. Very many, induced by connections which they had formed in the land of their captivity, chose to remain. But God stirred up the spirit of a number to return on the proclamation of Cyrus. 'Then rose up the chief of the fathers of Judah and Benjamin, and the priests and the Levites, with all them whose spirit God had raised, to go up to build the house of the Lord which is in Jerusalem. And all they that were about them strengthened their hands with vessels of silver, with gold, with goods, and with beasts, and with precious things, beside all that was willingly offered.'—Ezra 1:5,6. Some were providentially excited to return, others to assist in persuading those who were inclined to remain.

74

Obstacles in the way of the Jews, in building the temple, on their return to Jerusalem, providentially thrown in their way and removed

Ezra 4

THE house of God cannot be rebuilt without opposition,—opposition that will sometimes prosper, but at last will be completely overcome. For a long time the building of the temple was opposed by the enemies of the Jews, and for a long time it was hindered. 'Then the people of the land weakened the hands of the people of Judah, and troubled them in building, and hired counsellors against them, to frustrate their purpose, all the days of Cyrus king of Persia, even until the reign of Darius king of Persia.'—Ezra 4:4,5. Plausible objections were made to excite the fear of the kings of Persia, and at first had the designed effect. The building of the temple is forbidden. Examine every step of the process in the history, and see how naturally every thing is effected, both in the temporary interruption of the building, and in the final permission to build. When Providence designs that the work of building should for a time be interrupted, the enemies are led to a procedure that is most effectual to secure this event. They advert to the records of the former state of Jerusalem, and this confirms their allegations, and excites the suspicions of the king. When Providence designed to frustrate the opposition of the enemies of his house, they are led to refer the king to a decree of Cyrus, which effectually inclines him to encourage the work. The design of the enemies of God's people is not only frustrated, but the very thing by which they thought to succeed is employed to excite the king to great zeal and ardor in accomplishing the building of the temple of God. So shall it be with the house of God, which is the Church of God.

75
Book of Esther

THE book of Esther is peculiarly the book of Providence. In it we see the people of God providentially brought to the very brink of ruin, and delivered without a single miracle. The means employed by their enemies to effect their destruction are by Providence employed as the means of their exaltation and glory. The hand of God in his ordinary Providence has linked together a course of events as simple and as natural as the mind can conceive, yet as surprising as the boldest fictions of romance. This subject I have handled in a separate work, and shall take no farther notice of it in this place.

76
Book of Job

IN THE book of Job we behold the Providence of God bringing affliction on one of his most favourite servants, for the trial of his faith, the exercise of his patience, the humbling of his self-righteous pride, the growth of his godliness, and the manifestation of the Divine power in upholding him from falling. Here we learn that afflictions are sent by God on his people for wise and good ends, that he will not leave them under their afflictions, and that he will crush Satan under their feet. The people of God ought to take every affliction as coming from the hand of God. It may come by the instrumentality of Satan, or of wicked men, but it is also from God. Prosperity is also here seen to be from God. His Providence enriched Job in a most signal degree, and after he was stripped of all, he was increased in his latter end far above his former state. All this was in the way of Providence. Job himself recognised the hand of God both in blessings and in afflictions. 'Shall we receive good,' says he, 'at the hand of God, and shall we not receive evil?' Satan himself recognises the same truth, when speaking to God with respect to Job. 'Doth Job fear God for nought? Hath God then made a hedge about him, and about his house, and about all that he hath, and on every side? Thou hast blessed the work of his hands, and his substance is increased in the land. But put forth thine hand now and touch all that he hath, and he will curse thee to thy face.' The security of the Lord's people in this world of sin and misery is, that God makes a hedge about them, and Satan can injure neither themselves nor their property without the Divine permission. Had Satan his own will, he would continually harass the people of God. But his malice is controlled, and he can manifest none of it beyond what God permits for his own glory and the good of his people.

Job's afflictions were, in one sense, brought on him by Satan, but, in another, by God. Satan could act only subordinately. It is God who must put forth his hand and touch Job with affliction. Yet, in doing this, he used Satan as the instrument of bringing this affliction. 'And the Lord said unto Satan, Behold, all that he hath is in thy power, only upon himself put not forth thy hand.' – 'Put forth thine hand now,' says Satan to the Lord, 'and touch his bone and his flesh, and he will curse thee to thy face.' The Lord complies, but executes the afflictions through Satan. 'And the Lord said unto Satan, Behold, he is in thine hand; but save his life.' Here God acts, and Satan acts in doing the same thing. The Sovereignty of God in doing this is holy and good; in doing the same thing Satan is unholy and malicious in a most astonishing degree. Satan stript the house of Job of his goods and of his children: Job takes all from the hand of the Lord. 'The Lord gave,' says he, 'and the Lord hath taken away; blessed be the name of the Lord.' Let the children of God, then, view good and evil as coming from the hand of their heavenly Father. In the smallest things, as well as in the greatest, let them see his hand. Malice cannot vex, power cannot oppress, covetousness cannot strip, without a warrant under the seal of the Lord and Father of Christians.

When, in the Providence of God, any of his people are called to peculiar and signal trials, let them not suppose that this must arise from a peculiar aggravation of their sins. All afflictions suppose sin, but Job, who here suffers in a manner grievous and excessive, is testified, by God himself, as an eminently righteous man. It is good for them to see their sins in all their aggravations; but it is not according to truth to measure the guilt of the sufferer by the degree of his suffering. God is a Sovereign, and though he never afflicts without necessity, yet he may afflict the most righteous of his servants in a degree exceeding the affliction of those who are in their lives most defective. He may have wise reasons for calling the most righteous of his people to suffer the most grievous afflictions.

77

Sennacherib sent by God against his people, yet punished for going

Isaiah 10

THE wisdom of this world can never understand this part of the ways of the Most High. If the Assyrian was without any command from God, or any constraint on his mind, how can he be said to be sent by God? If in any sense he was sent by God, how can he be guilty in going? How can he be justly punished for doing the very thing which God appointed him to do? Here is the very essence of the question that has for ever agitated the wisdom of this world, the consistency of the decrees of God with the voluntary actions of men. Here the truth is practically exhibited. God appoints what his enemies act, yet the whole sin is theirs. How can this be? Foolish men, why ask the question? Are you able to measure the conduct of the infinite and incomprehensible Jehovah? That the thing is true, every impartial mind must here see. How it is true, is not revealed, therefore, can never be found out—should never be inquired after. What God reveals, let us know: what he conceals, let us not attempt to discover.

One thing we may here see plainly. Though Sennacherib was sent by God to punish his people for their sins; yet the instrument of wrath did not know that he was God's messenger; and did not act from obedience to God. He acted from selfish and wicked motives; and, therefore, was guilty in doing the very thing, which God had appointed to be done by him. 'O Assyrian, the rod of mine anger, and the staff in their hand is mine indignation. I will send him against an hypocritical nation, and against the people of my wrath will I give him a charge, to take the spoil, and to take the prey, and to tread them down like the mire of the streets. Howbeit he meaneth not so, neither doth his heart think so, but it is in his heart to destroy and cut off nations not a few.'—Isaiah 10:5-7. In a sovereign way utterly inscrutable to human wisdom, God sends the Assyrian to do his work, while he did his own work, and satisfied his own pride and passions. Instead of intending to execute the purposes of the Lord, the conqueror boasted of doing all by his own power, and turns all to his own glory. The Lord, therefore, denounces. 'Wherefore it shall come to pass, that, when the Lord hath performed his whole work upon Mount Zion, and on Jerusalem, I will punish the pride of the stout heart of the king of Assyria, and the glory of his high looks.'

Here we have an infallible commentary on the Providence of God with respect to the desolators of the earth in every age. God sends them as his scourge, yet they go to gratify themselves; and are, therefore, justly guilty of all the evils which they cause to mankind. Whether they are ultimately successful or unsuccessful, God will call them to account for all the blood which they have shed, and all the miseries which they have brought upon the earth. Cyrus and Alexander, Julius Caesar and Napoleon, all executed the purposes appointed by the Lord for them to perform; yet they are all guilty of every aggression on the happiness of mankind. They served God, but they did not intend to serve him. And what are all the wars that still spread desolation and misery among the nations? Their authors are commissioned by the Ruler of the world to the work of violence, but for every drop of the oceans of blood that have been shed since the murder of Abel men must give account. Princes and statesmen may think that the interests or aggrandisement of their nations is a just apology for their wars. But justice is the same thing among nations as among individuals. If the pirate is to be blamed by Alexander for disturbing the seas, Alexander is equally to be blamed by the pirate for disturbing the world.

78
Destruction of Babylon
Isaiah 13

BABYLON was employed by Providence for the chastisement of his people, and commissioned to carry the Jews into captivity. Babylon was guilty in executing the will of the Lord, and was providentially destroyed by him with an unexampled destruction. The Medes and Persians are sent by God to execute his vengeance on Babylon. He calls out their hosts and gives them victory, yet the Medes and Persians were excited by their own passions. 'Besides,' says God, 'I will bring up the Medes against them, which shall not regard silver; and as for gold, they shall not delight in it. Their bows, also, shall dash the young men to pieces; and they shall have no pity on the fruit of the womb; their eye shall not spare children.' How awful does Providence appear here! Even when savage idolaters violate every dictate of humanity, they are the executors of the judgments of the Almighty. While their conduct is most horridly guilty, in the Divine sovereignty it fulfills God's will. Who can fathom this depth? In Spain acts of barbarity that disgrace humanity are constantly occurring, yet men in general see nothing of the hand of the Lord in this. The just and holy God is pouring out his vengeance, and in the reciprocal cruelties of these children of blood, God is avenging the cause of his martyrs. In God's dealings with Assyria and Babylon we ought to find a key to his Providence in his dealings with the western nations of Europe. Does not Jehovah govern the world? Is there evil in a city, and the Lord hath not done it? Statesmen and philosophers in their blindness may overlook the hand of God when it is outstretched over their heads, but his own children may see it as clearly as David did the sword of the destroying angel over Jerusalem.

79

Destruction of Tyre

Isaiah 23:11

IN THE destruction of the cities and nations denounced by prophecy, we are not merely to view the fulfillment of prediction, but we are to consider that the thing predicted is to be effected by the Lord, so that the destruction is the Lord's work. 'He stretched out his hand over the sea, he shook the kingdoms: The Lord hath given a commandment against the merchant city, to destroy the strongholds thereof.' God does the thing: man does it. In doing the work of the Lord, man acts freely; and is justly accountable for doing what is directly appointed for him to do. Philosophy cannot plumb this ocean by its line; philosophy, therefore, denies what it cannot comprehend. But does she show wisdom in this? No; she manifests her folly. The amount of her unbelief is this—'There is nothing in the ways of the Almighty but what I am able to comprehend.' Can there be a purer specimen of Atheism and madness?

In the accomplishment of the threatenings against the nations, we are also to consider that God usually works in the way of Providence. He works effectually, but in such a manner that his hand is not generally seen. The wisdom of this world sees nothing but the agency of man. Here is the great wisdom of God; he manifests himself in his works of Providence; yet, as in the works of creation, he is not seen.

80

Famine in Judah

Jeremiah 14

FOR the existence of plenty as of famine, the wisdom of this world looks no higher than to what are called second causes. God, it is considered, is no farther concerned in these matters than as the author of certain general laws. He has set the machine a-going, and it continues to work by its own construction, without any regulation of a superintending hand. Climate, soil, cultivation, need, it is confessed, favourable seasons, but any divine direction of weather is supposed to be unnecessary. Timely rain—or the want of it, is a matter below the attention of the Ruler of the world. The blight and the mildew, the wet and the caterpillar, are enemies with which the farmer is to struggle; but they are never considered as armies of devastation sent into the fields by a righteous Providence. The history of the Old Testament gives us a key to Providence in the production of famine or of plenty. God regulates the supplies of the children of men as exactly as if each individual of the human race had his rations assigned him by the angels of heaven every rising sun. 'The word of the Lord that came to Jeremiah concerning the dearth. Judah mourneth, and the gates thereof languish; they are black unto the ground; and the cry of Jerusalem is gone up. And their nobles have sent their little ones to the waters: they came to the pits, and found no water; they returned with their vessels empty: they were ashamed and confounded, and covered their heads. Because the ground is chapt, for there was no rain in the earth, the ploughmen were ashamed, they covered their heads. Yea, the hind also calved in the field, and forsook it, because there was no grass. And the wild asses did stand in the high places, they snuffed up the wind like dragons; their eyes did fail, because there was no grass. O Lord, though our iniquities testify against us, do thou it for thy name's sake: for our backslidings are many; we have sinned against thee.'—Jer. 14:1-7. As in creation and in Providence, so in redemption, God hides himself in the midst of a blaze of light. In all his works he reveals himself, yet the enmity of the human heart will not allow men to see him. And what is most strange, the savage sees a divine hand in the works of Providence; it is unseen and denied by philosophical wisdom. The illiterate peasant hears God in his voice of thunder and storms, and acknowledges divine wrath in pestilence, sword, and famine. But the philosopher perceives nothing in all these but the course of nature. The wisdom of man makes itself ignorant of what the very beasts seem to feel.

81

Field of Hanameel providentially offered for sale

Jeremiah 32:7

THE captivity and expatriation of Judah were at hand. But their return is as necessary as their expulsion. God, then, designs to confirm this truth; and his Providence provides the means. A field purchased by the prophet will be both a figure and an evidence of this. At this moment his cousin Hanameel comes to the prophet and offers his field for sale. What made it necessary for this man at this time to sell his inheritance? Why does he come at the very time that the occasion demanded? God sent him. But how did he send him? By his Providence, and not by express command. Every thing occurred with the exactness of the movement of a watch; yet Hanameel was doing his own business according to his own volitions and sentiments.

82

Life of Jeremiah providentially saved by Ebed-Melech

Jeremiah 38

JEREMIAH must soon have perished in the mire of the pit. God could have delivered him by the hands of hosts of angels, or he could have delivered him without man. Even in his situation, he could have preserved him for years, without injury or pain. But God usually works by means; and his Providence always provides the means that are necessary. When Jeremiah was cast into the pit, Providence directed that Ebed-melech applied to the king, and succeeded in the deliverance of the servant of God. How did it happen that in so profligate a time such a man as Ebed-melech was about the person of the king? How did it happen that so good a man had such interest with such an enemy of God? Consider, also, how seasonably the fact comes to the ears of Ebed-melech. It might not have reached him till the man of God had died. Providence! Providence! Verily there is a God who ruleth in the earth.

83

Capture and fate of Zedekiah

Jeremiah 39:7

HOW wonderfully is Divine Providence displayed in the capture and fate of king Zedekiah? He was to be taken, and with his eyes to see the eyes of the king of Babylon. He was to go to Babylon, but his eyes were not to see it. He escaped from Jerusalem and fled; but neither death nor flight could deliver him from what God had awarded him. The king of Babylon, in every thing which he did, acted spontaneously, without any reference to the fulfillment of prophecy. Yet Providence directed that his free actions performed the thing decreed by the Almighty.

84

Preservation of Jeremiah and of Ebed-Melech in the capture of Jerusalem

Jeremiah 39:11

THE same Providence which secured the punishment of Zedekiah, preserved Jeremiah from injury. The king of Babylon issues orders for his protection, and he is guarded in safety and in honour. The preservation of Ebed-melech was still more strange: for, as being about the person of the king, he was not likely to escape. But Providence can preserve in the midst of danger. Verily, in the end it will be seen that the service of the Lord is wisdom. The wise men of this world, mighty and mean, are fools. Let the Christian ponder on the Providence that preserved Jeremiah and Ebed-melech in all the confusions of a stormed city. Can any thing be more consoling in the present times? The wisdom of this world is seeking for safety from compliances with spreading corruptions and errors. The standard of divine truth is lowered by many of his own professed people. Men of God raise high the banners of the cross: and, if desolation comes, look to the God of Jeremiah and Ebed-melech.

85

The forgetting of his dream by Nebuchadnezzar providential

Daniel 2:5

THE king of Babylon forgets his dream. Why? Because this was the means of calling forth Daniel, and of giving the true interpretation of the dream that was from God. Had the king remembered his dream, and told it to his wise men, they might have made a shift to deceive him, and plausibly have interpreted it according to their art. But neither they nor their master, the devil, could tell what passed in the mind of Nebuchadnezzar in his sleep. The thing, then, must come to Daniel, and from him we have God's interpretation of a dream, much of which is still to be fulfilled. But why does the king act so tyrannically with respect to the wise men? Was not the thing he required unreasonable? Is not their justification perfectly sufficient? Their art did not profess what he sought. But he is tyrannical, arbitrary, and obstinate. They must die. Was ever conduct or caprice of tyrant more absolute? All the wise men of Babylon must die, because they cannot declare what is known only to Omniscience! But all this is necessary to bring Daniel forward. This explains the mystery of Providence. How wonderful is this! Jehovah, the Ruler of the world, serves his purposes by the caprices and cruelty of tyrants, as well as by the exertions of saints. The passions and caprices of a Henry VIII have a place in the work of Providence, as well as the peaceful labours of the followers of the Lamb of God.

86

The lot fell upon Jonah

Jonah 1

'THE lot is cast into the lap,' says Solomon, 'but the whole disposing thereof is of the Lord.' This is true, and in every instance true; true as to the smallest matters, as well as to matters of the utmost importance, — as true in gambling, as in the choice of an apostle. But this does not import that God always answers to the appeal by lot, or in this way distinguishes the righteous from the unrighteous cause. Here, then, there are two opposite errors: one excludes Providence, and sees nothing but atheistic chance, — the other by lot appeals to Providence, and expects the event to be the oracle of the Divine judgment. Both errors are dishonourable to God, and dangerous in their practical influence. To deny the agency of God in the casting of the die, even in folly and in sin, is to deny the existence of Providence, and to lead away the mind from seeing God in the government of the world. To pledge God to the appro-bation of the decision by lot, is to mistake the true nature of the doctrine of Providence, and to make the Just and Holy One the abettor of sin. Though the lot is always disposed by God, yet it may spoil the righteous man, and enrich the unjust. God determines the fall of the lot, but he does not determine the justness of the cause by that fall. Providence even rules the lot, when it is unwarrantably employed, to accomplish its own purposes. But it gives the issue no sanction.

I speak this with regard to the lot, in cases where it is employed without the Divine command. For God has on different occasions commanded decision by lot; and in these not only is the fall of the lot by the disposal of the Lord, but the decision has his approba-tion. In such cases God speaks as really as he did on Mount Sinai. In casting the lots with respect to the scape-goat, the Lord chose the animal that was to die, as truly as if he had declared his choice by a voice from heaven. So also with respect to the inheritance of the children of Israel in Canaan. In their battles, also, the children of Israel, when it was not necessary for the whole host to attack, went out by lot against the enemy. In like manner, the Lord pointed out Achan by lot, in this way declaring him the guilty person, as truly as if he had named him. Even in the case of Jonathan, when the conduct of his father was rash and sinful, the appeal was solemnly made to God, and God answered it. Jonathan was pointed out as the offender, though in ignorance. In many other things the Israelites determined by lot, when the decision was the Lord's decision.

In the New Testament also, after the fall of Judas, an apostle was chosen by lot. Two reasons induce some interpreters to reject the authority of this choice. On the supposition they cannot have the exact number of twelve apostles. But is it so necessary always to keep up this number of apostles, that men should on that account venture to bring such a charge against the apostles, and against the inspiration of the Scriptures? The number twelve might be necessary for the apostles on their setting out, without the necessity of keeping up that number. In fact, that number was not always kept up. The breach made by Judas was filled up, because he was a false apostle, and not a true foundation stone. But the vacancy by the death of James was not filled, nor any other vacancy to the death of John. Besides, what will be done with Barnabas on this supposition? Paul, then, may have been, and was an apostle as truly as Peter, though he was supernumerary, or as one born out of due time. The mystical number was at first necessary, to correspond with what is written in the Scriptures. But there was no need to keep always exactly to that mystical number. I think the same observation will apply to the ten horns of the beast, if the necessity of facts demands its aid.

Another reason induces some to reject the authority of this decision, on the apprehension that the allowance of its Divine inspiration will sanction all appeals to the decision of God by lot. But let consequences be what they may, we must not reject Scripture truth on the authority of theory. Hence, I do not look on the objection as valid. This lot was in the choice of an apostle, and nothing like it can ever occur. God only could choose an apostle, and an appeal to him in a way of his own might be necessary on that occasion, without giving a sanction to appeals of that nature on any other occasion. When we have to choose an apostle, let us choose him by lot, for we have no rule or guide for our choice. That Matthias was a divinely appointed apostle appears quite evident. The proposal of choosing an apostle in the room of Judas was made by Peter, and coincided in by all the rest of the apostles. That they had the authority to act as they did should not be doubted. Had they not already received their commission? And from the moment of receiving that commission, were they not fit to discharge all the duties of the office as far as they were necessary? Even after his nomination, did not Jesus again renew their commission, giving them power to fulfill it? 'As my Father,' says he, 'sent me, even so send I you. And when he had said this, he breathed on them, and said unto them, Receive ye the Holy Ghost, Whosesoever sins ye remit, they are remitted unto them; and whosesoever sins ye retain, they are retained.' Are they not, then, from this moment, invested with all authority to act for Christ? Was Christ's breathing on them a mere ceremony? Had they not now the Holy Spirit to guide them in a matter as important as the choice of an apostle, even in declaring the way of salvation? They had not yet, indeed, received the gifts of the Spirit on the day of Pentecost, but that was a distinct thing from the inspiration by which they had preached the gospel. If there is truth in the words of Jesus, the apostles are now empowered and fitted to act for Christ in every thing necessary for the time. Farther gifts might be necessary or useful for the evidence and confirmation of their office, and the truths which they promulgated. But now they want no apostolic authority. The day of Pentecost gave them no additional commission.

Let us now take a glance at Peter on this occasion. 'And in those days Peter stood up in the midst of the disciples, and said, (the number of the names together were about an hundred and twenty,) Men and brethren, this scripture must needs have been fulfilled, which the Holy Ghost by the mouth of David spake before concerning Judas, which was guide to them that took Jesus. For he was numbered with us, and had obtained part of this ministry. Now this man purchased a field with the reward of iniquity; and falling headlong, he burst asunder in the midst, and all his bowels gushed out. And it was known unto all the dwellers at Jerusalem; insomuch as that field is called in their proper tongue, Aceldama, that is to say, The field of blood. For it is written in the book of Psalms, Let his habitation be desolate, and let no man dwell therein: and his bishoprick let another take. Wherefore of these men which have companied with us all the time that the Lord Jesus went in and out among us, beginning from the baptism of John, unto that same day that he was taken up from us, must one be ordained to be a witness with us of his resurrection. And they appointed two, Joseph called Barsabas, who was surnamed Justus, and Matthias. And they prayed, and said, Thou, Lord, which knowest the hearts of all men, show whether of these two thou hast chosen, that he may take part of this ministry and apostleship, from which Judas by transgression fell, that he might go to his own place. And they gave forth their lots; and the lot fell upon Matthias; and he was numbered with the eleven apostles.' — Acts 1:15-26.

Is not Peter here the inspired Peter? How unlike he is to himself! He had from the first strong and clear faith in Jesus as the Messiah. But verily, till after his commission, he would have made a bad expounder of Scripture. Had Peter, before his inspiration, made such a progress in knowledge as to interpret the Scriptures in this authoritative manner? Did he know that David, in the passage referred to, spake of Judas? This of itself would decide the matter with me. Peter's exposition of the Psalms referred to is the work of the Holy Spirit. God has spoken by Peter, as much as he spoke by David in the Psalm interpreted. Why does Peter confine the choice to those who had associated with them from the beginning? What did uninspired Peter know of this matter? Why does he say '*must* one be ordained?' What does uninspired Peter know of this necessity? Did not the assembly, which acted on this occasion, act as for the Lord? If they had no authority, they must have been the greatest fanatics, or the most presumptuous antichrists. Every line of the document contributes to impress me with the conviction that the choice of Matthias was the Lord's choice.

Let not the Lord's people be rash in adopting the crude interpretations of God's word by men who are guided by their presumptuous theories; and for the sake of avoiding difficulties in their system, will not scruple to advance principles that degrade the word of God, and tend to bring doubt and suspicion upon every page of Holy Writ. The same boldness that rejects the inspiration of this choice, may at pleasure make havoc of every part of the divine word, which stands in the way of their theories. It is no light matter to charge the apostles of Christ with acting beyond their commission, after they received that commission. To me the crime is not less than blasphemy against the word of the living God.

The decision by lot, or the voice of an overruling power, is found among heathen nations. No doubt, like other things, it is a tradition founded on God's appointment to his people. A striking instance of this we have in the proposal of the sailors on the occasion of the storm, related in the account of Jonah. More wise than many philosophers, they saw a Providence in the tempest; and though every tempest is not to discover a Jonah, yet every tempest is from the Lord, and has in view some purpose. God's people should not shut their eyes against that which was visible to ignorant heathens. They thought that the violence of the tempest indicated that there was on board some notorious transgressor who must be cast out. In this they were in ignorance. They were right in viewing the tempest as sent by a superior power. They believed beyond evidence, when they judged that this was an indication, that vengeance demanded some one to be cast into the sea. But God made use of their ignorance to effect his purpose. It would be wrong in a storm at sea to imitate the conduct of the sailors with Jonah. But God employed their view of the lot to find out Jonah. On this occasion it was God's lot. On all occasions God decides the lot; but if men would attempt to find out a murderer, or any other violator of justice, by lot, they would often destroy the innocent. God, when he pleases, may make the lot to fall on the guilty, but he may make it fall on the innocent when it serves his purpose. It would be as sinful and unwarrantable to decide on criminals by lot, as it would be to judge them by the laws of phrenology. Let it never be forgotten, that though God decides the falling of the lot, he does not decide the cause at issue. The lot is guided by the Lord, yet it may condemn the righteous, and save the guilty, in all cases in which it is not appointed by the Lord.

But in the case of Jonah, an unerring hand guided the lot, even when used not according to divine appointment. God here directs the expedients of superstition to effect his purpose. How wonderful is the wisdom of God in the government of the world! He makes ignorance and knowledge, tyranny and good government, cruelty and compassion, crime and virtue, fulfill his will. 'And they said everyone to his fellow, Come and let us cast lots, that we may know for whose cause this evil is upon us. So they cast lots, and the lot fell upon Jonah.'

We have a similar instance of divine interference in regulating the lot cast by Haman for the destruction of the Jews. Pur was the devil's oracle, but, like the persons possessed by demons, it was obliged to speak for God. Balaam intends to curse, but he is obliged to bless.

One great use of the lot, according to Solomon, it might still serve, even although it should not be considered as in its decision involving an appeal to God. 'The lot causeth contentions to cease, and parteth between the mighty.' In dividing an estate between heirs, the most perfect skill and impartiality may not be able to make both sides equally eligible. Who, then, is to have his choice? There is no ground of preference, and neither has a right to yield to the other. Let the lot decide. This will cut away all ground for complaint. Yet this decision is not to be looked on as involving God's approbation of the division. In other words, it is not God's lot, as in the division of Canaan. It is a human expedient useful to prevent disputes. God casts the lot, but does not pledge himself for the righteousness of the result. And may not the lot often effectually part between the mighty? In the dispute with regard to the boundary between Great Britain and America, some part of territory it might be impossible with certainty to adjudge to either party. Who is to yield? Let the lot decide. Yet who will say that the decision implies that God pledges himself that justice is on the side of the successful lot? In reality, the just title might be on the other side, while the lot has been disposed by the Lord. But the Lord has given the territory by his Providence. And would not such a settlement be better than strife? Many persons would fear to make such a decision, because they consider the lot as a religious ordinance. But as a religious ordinance, it is not, as appears to me, in use. And in such instance, it does not pretend to be the oracle of God in declaring right. It decides the matter only as the will of Providence, not as the divine declaration of right.

Right views of this subject are of great practical importance; and error with respect to it has led to absurdities and evils. Some have appealed to God by lot, in order to determine between truth and error. There can be no more effectual engine of Satan than this. God has given us his word to direct us in all our conduct and faith; and his Spirit instructs us in the truths and duties of Scripture only by enabling us to understand them. We are sanctified by the Spirit, through the truth, only as far as it is understood. Even should we confess the truth without understanding it, we are neither justified nor sanctified. To know the will of God, it is his appointment that we search the Scriptures, and receive all truth and duty as we perceive them to stand on the divine testimony. We ascertain the mind of God, not by a lazy appeal to lot, but by a diligent search of his word, relying on the guidance of the Spirit of truth. It is obvious, then, that if God has not appointed the lot, to determine between truth and error, whoever uses this mode of decision lays himself open to deception and delusions.

Some make the Bible itself a sort of lottery book, by opening it at random, and taking as God's answer to their object of inquiry whatever passage first strikes their eye. This is absurd, fanatical, dangerous. God has not appointed this mode of consulting him, and he who employs it may be left to fall into the most serious delusions. He may be falsely comforted, or falsely discouraged. God answers his people through his word, not by a random appeal to it by lot; but by its true import, interpreted according to the laws of language. It is as unlawful to use the Scriptures in this manner, as to attempt to cure diseases by making an amulet of a portion of John's gospel.

Dr. Haweis, in his *Continuation of Milner's Church History,* observes, that the 'frequent appeal to the lot seems the peculiar characteristic of the Moravian Church.' Their missionaries have their stations assigned by lot, and the lot must sanction their marriages. The historian observes, that, notwithstanding this, 'no where fewer unhappy marriages are found than among the brethren.' Nothing, however, can warrant a restraint that God has not imposed, and that amiable body, to whose zeal all the friends of the gospel are so much indebted, would prosper not the less to rid itself of this unscriptural bondage. God does, indeed, direct his people in marriage; but he does not answer the appeal by lot. If their marriages are generally happy, it is not owing to this peculiarity. It is easy to misinterpret Providence. When Rachel had a son by her handmaid, whom she had given as a wife to her husband, she said, 'God hath judged me, and hath also heard my voice.' God might answer her prayer of faith, though he did not sanction what she had done. She misinterpreted his Providence, and claimed what was given to her faith as a sanction to that which was her sin. It is, indeed, a most comfortable truth, which may be drawn from this passage, that God blesses what he approves in his people, even though what is approved is mixed with much that is evil.

Leah also is under a similar mistake. 'God,' said she, 'has given me my hire, because I have given my maiden to my husband.' She was not justified in giving her maiden to her husband, yet we, are expressly told, that 'the Lord hearkened unto Leah.' If our prayers were never heard until our faith and conduct are without mixture, we need never pray at all.

'I confess,' says Dr. Haweis, 'I can see no Scripture order or warrant to countenance such appeal, nor any such practice adopted in the apostles' days, or in the primitive church. The single instance, Acts 1:26, where the sacred college was to be filled up by one of the two persons chosen by the church for the office of apostle, is no precedent, nor sanctions any similar appeal to the lot.'

Luther himself, in a most important concern, acted on a similar misinterpretation of Providence. After he had denied the divine right of the pope, for a time he consented to acknowledge his superiority over all bishops, among other reasons, on the ground that, 'unless it had been the will of God, the popes could never have attained so great and durable a dominion.' This does not distinguish between what is the will of God to exist, and what is sanctioned by God. On the same ground, he might have defended subjection to Satan. It was God's appointment that the Man of Sin should exist, but it was not his command to submit to him. The prosperity of a cause is no proof of a divine sanction.

In like manner, divine judgments are sometimes looked on as marking their objects as sinners beyond the rest of mankind. Divine judgments are always on account of sins. But the victims in them are not always the worst of mankind. Many very wicked people may escape; sometimes the righteous may fall. Were it otherwise, we would walk by sight, not by faith. But in all instances of divine judgment, by pestilence, by famine, by the sword, the people of God have a right to trust in him, with the assurance that he will glorify himself, and bless them in what happens to them. If it is not for his glory and their good, a hair of their head will not fall. And, in general, the Lord remarkably preserves his people. When it is otherwise, the wisdom and kindness of the dispensation of sovereignty should not be questioned.

Our Lord corrects this general mistake in interpreting this work of Providence. 'There were present at that season some that told him of the Galileans, whose blood Pilate had mingled with their sacrifices. And Jesus answering said unto them, Suppose ye that these Galileans were sinners above all the Galileans, because they suffered such things? I tell you, Nay: but, except ye repent, ye shall all likewise perish. Or those eighteen, upon whom the tower in Siloam fell, and slew them, think ye that they were sinners above all men that dwell in Jerusalem? I tell you, Nay: but, except ye repent, ye shall all likewise perish.'—Luke 13:1-5. The instances to which our Lord refers were the visitations of Providence. They were not accidental, but by divine appointment. They were in judgment. Our Lord does not question this. He denies only that those judgments marked out the sufferers as the greatest of sinners. Many greater sinners meet with no visible displays of judgment. Jesus does not affirm that the sufferers did not suffer in judgment, but that the judgment did not import that they were peculiarly sinners. He declares that without repentance all will also perish. This does not acquit the sufferers, but with them condemns all the rest of mankind who did not repent.

We often hear expressions of admiration that the earth does not open and swallow great transgressors, or that the thunders of the Almighty do not strike them dead. But though God occasionally does give witness to his own existence and government by the display of his immediate judgment, yet in general, he waits his appointed time of vengeance. It is the will of God to give scope for the manifestation of the guilt and depravity of human nature, and the manner of his Providence is adapted to this purpose. If God would on the spot strike down every blasphemer, every perverter of his word, and, in general, every open transgressor, we would have a world of decent hypocrites, but we would not have a world less at enmity with God. It is the Divine wisdom, then, to allow opportunity for man to show what he is. Were it not for this, man would be thought to be less wicked in his nature than the word of God asserts him to be. It is, then, in every view, of great importance to understand the ways of God in his Providence, as well as in his grace.

The absurd and murderous custom of duelling was originally founded on an appeal to Providence. It was thought that God would defend the right. At no remote period the judicial combat was known to the law, as well as trial by jury is known now to us. Various other appeals are made to Providence on the principles of the lot, in attempting to discover guilt, or manifest innocence. As might be expected, this misinterpretation of Providence was the cause of much misery to society; and Satan reigned under an appearance of giving honour to God. Even Sir John Oldcastle, Lord Cobham, a man of God in the fifteenth century, proposed such an appeal to Providence. When accused of heresy, he begged to be permitted to vindicate his innocence by the law of arms. He said he was ready, 'on the ground of his faith,' to fight for life or death with any man living—the king and the lords of his council being excepted. Lord Cobham was a brave soldier. But his proposal was evidently not confidence in his own prowess and skill in arms. It was a reliance on Divine interposition. In no other view could he have challenged to fight any man living. This, then, is to be viewed, not as a modern challenge but as a relic of ignorance that in many things may be found in God's people. Modern duellists, who have no such opinion of appeal to Providence, have not the excuse of the good Lord Cobham.

A misinterpretation of Providence of a similar nature is the opinion, that what Providence puts in our power, God warrants us in doing. When a man finds his enemy under his hand, he too often interprets it as the language of Providence, that punishment should be inflicted. So judged not David. When Saul was repeatedly in his power, and though his own life was constantly in imminent danger, he always refused to kill him. How opposite to the conduct of David was that of Archbishop Laud! When Dr. Leighton, one of the Puritans, was, by the Archbishop's instigation, condemned in the Star Chamber, and sentence was pronounced in Court, Laud, pulling off his cap, and lifting up his eyes to Heaven, gave thanks to God who had enabled him to behold this vengeance on his enemies.

Dr. Leighton as recorded by the archbishop himself, was punished in the following manner: 1. He was severely whipt before he was set in the pillory. 2. Being set in the pillory, he had one of his ears cut off. 3. One side of his nose was slit up. 4. He was branded on the cheek with a red hot iron, with the letters S. S. On that day se'ennight,[1] his sores on his back, ear, nose, and face, being not yet cured, he was whipped again at the pillory in Cheapside, cutting off the other ear, slitting the other side of his nose, and branding the other cheek—See Haweis, C. Hist. And this is the thing that the infamous Laud ascribes to Providence! Providence, indeed, did appoint the thing for his own glory, and trial of the faith of his suffering servant. But Providence did not approve the actors: a righteous God will find the whole guilt in the inhuman perpetrators. God calls his people to suffering for his sake; but not to them who are the authors and abettors of their suffering. Good for them that they had never been born. Deep and mysterious are thy ways, Lord Jehovah! Thou reignest as an absolute Sovereign over all the earth: yet sin and misery now abound; and with many will abound forever. Let us bow with submission. We know the Lord God will always do righteously.

87

Jesus in a storm

Matthew 8:24

WHAT! Is the ship which carried Jesus overtaken by a storm? If there is a Providence, might we not expect that, when the Son of God was sailing, the sea should be quiet? Shall the rude winds heave the waves on high, or assail the ship which carries

---

[1] that is, 'seven nights', a week.—P.

the Creator? Would not human wisdom forbid every rude blast, and command gentle breezes to fill the sails? Not so in the wisdom of Divine Providence. Jesus goes aboard, and the howling tempest is let loose: the ship reels, and the yawning abyss threatens to overwhelm all in ruin. 'And when he was entered into a ship, his disciples followed him. And, behold, there arose a great tempest in the sea, insomuch that the ship was covered with the waves: but he was asleep. And his disciples came to him, and awoke him, saying, Lord, save us: we perish. And he saith unto them, Why are ye fearful, O ye of little faith? Then he arose, and rebuked the winds and the sea; and there was a great calm. But the men marvelled, saying, What manner of man is this, that even the winds and the sea obey him!'—Matt. 8:23-27. And this was a wise Providence. It glorified the Son of God, by giving him an opportunity of manifesting himself as the Lord of the seas and of the winds. 'Peace, be still,' said the Lord, and the sea was as smooth as a pail of milk. This was the same power that spake the world into existence. This Providence was also for the good of the disciples. It increased their faith in the Son of God.

When the Lord's people sail, they should not fanatically suppose that Providence will certainly give them fine weather. If the Son of God experienced a storm, his people cannot plead exemption. But they have ground to pray for a prosperous voyage, and reason to expect that Providence will give it, if Divine wisdom has no purpose to serve by a tempest. The Lord does not put his people to trial without necessity: if he presents dangers before their eyes, it is to excite them to call on him, and trust in his power and love. Jesus rebukes the fears of the disciples. Where was their faith? Was not Jesus at hand? And is not Jesus always at hand with his people? Let them, then, with confidence call on him, Lord save us.

88

The two Gergesene Demoniacs meet Jesus

Matthew 8:28

'AND when he was come to the other side into the country of the Gergesenes, there met him two possessed with devils, coming out of the tombs, exceeding fierce, so that no man might pass by that way. And, behold, they cried out, What have we to do with thee, Jesus, thou Son of God? Art thou come hither to torment us before the time?' How opportune is this meeting! Is this a lucky chance? Is it a wisely ordered Providence? What brought the demoniacs to meet Jesus? Was it intention in the men? They were mad; and though they had been as wise as Solomon, they knew nothing of the coming of Jesus. Was it the act of the demons with whom they were possessed? What power constrained them to meet their great enemy? Wicked men, in ignorance, do what the Lord appoints, and act freely. The demons, with their knowledge, do what they dislike. They obey and recognise Jesus. They seem to act freely, yet they do what must be against their desires and their interests. Who can understand the grounds of God's government of the angels that fell? They do his work, while they are his greatest enemies.

Many a child of God will here recognise his own picture. How many of the slaves of Satan, maddened with rage against the Son of God, by meeting him in his word are brought to soundness of understanding! By chance they hear the gospel, and, though they may have gone to mock, their eyes are opened, and they are found sitting at the feet of Jesus, clothed with his righteousness, and in their right mind. Happy meeting!

89

The barren fig-tree blasted

Matthew 21:17-20

HERE is a concurrence of circumstances, which, in connexion with the conduct of Jesus on the occasion, no well-instructed Christian will call accidental. Was it in wrath, or in peevishness, that Jesus cursed the tree? Whatever was the cause of the barrenness of the fig-tree, was not the ultimate cause to be found in God himself? In man, all the guilt of sin is to be found in himself; but in the productions of the earth, the barrenness, as well as the fertility, is to be ascribed ultimately to God. In cursing the fig-tree, then, Jesus had a reference to spiritual barrenness, which is a just object of the divine displeasure, and which will be punished as it deserves. If, then, Jesus had this design in his rebuke of the barren fig-tree, the circumstances that led to the cursing of the tree must all be providential. 'And he left them, and went out of the city into Bethany; and he lodged there. Now in the morning as he returned into the city, he hungered. And when he saw a fig-tree in the way, he came to it, and found nothing thereon, but leaves only, and said unto it, Let no fruit grow on thee henceforward for ever. And presently the fig-tree withered away. And when the disciples saw it, they marvelled, saying, How soon is the fig-tree withered away!'—Matt. 21:17-20. The hungering of Jesus at that time was a providential circumstance. Why was he attacked with hunger, just at the spot where stood the barren fig-tree? Was it not to give him an occasion to seek fruit from the tree? Why was that fig-tree barren on that occasion? Was it not to afford an occasion for what Christ did at that time? Why was it the season that figs should be found on the trees? The time of gathering the figs had not yet arrived, and fruit should have been on the tree, had it been good. Does not every circumstance, even in this trifling matter, that afforded illustration to the things taught by Jesus, appear providentially arranged for the purpose?

90

The death of Christ providentially accomplished

Matthew 26:14

THE death of Jesus was foreordained, and the instruments in sovereignty appointed. Yet they did the deed with wicked hands and a guilty mind. 'Him,' says Peter, 'being delivered by the determinate counsel and foreknowledge of God, ye have taken, and by wicked hands have crucified and slain.' These two things must be in harmony. But who can reconcile them? Presumption objects, and presumption in vain attempts a reply. Speculations on such a subject are fit only for Milton's devils. Men of God ought to abhor discussions of this kind as they do the gates of hell. What God has said, let us confidently receive: beyond what he has said, let us not dare to inquire. Christ must die by the appointed instruments: these instruments acted wickedly in what they were appointed to do. This much is said. How these things can be so is not said, and it is vain to attempt the solution. An attempt to solve is not only vain but impious. It invades the prerogative of God, and presumes to comprehend what is incomprehensible. But the objector rages and blasphemes; and shall we do nothing to stop his mouth? Yes, stop his mouth with proving the truth by Scripture, according to the force of language. Grind him to powder if he perverts. But if he will not submit to receive what God testifies on his own authority, leave him to his blasphemy. If he blasphemes the character which God has given of himself, there is a day appointed for his judgment, when vengeance will be executed on all 'the hard speeches which ungodly sinners have spoken against him.'

As Jesus was to die by guilty hands, his death must be accomplished providentially. Had God commanded the Jews to kill Jesus, they would not have been guilty for executing the command. But it was to be effected by wicked counsel and by wicked hands. The chief priests, then, were given over to such folly and hardness of heart as to seek to kill him; and Judas was given over to covetousness, that he might sell him. 'Then one of the twelve, called Judas Iscariot, went unto the chief priests, and said unto them, What will ye give me, and I will deliver him unto you? And they covenanted with him for thirty pieces of silver. And from that time he sought opportunity to betray him.'—Matt. 26:14-16. See the blindness and the hardness of heart that man is capable of when given up to himself. How senseless was it in the chief priests to suppose that they could succeed in this manner! They saw that the power of God was with Jesus, and how could they expect to succeed? And Judas—how suited to the work assigned him!—his covetousness fitted him for the betraying of his Master. There are millions of the most wicked men who would not have done what Judas did. Yet among the twelve there was a man so covetous as to sell his Master for a mere trifle. And how do all circumstances now combine to give effect to the design! The life of Jesus was often attempted, but his enemies could never succeed. Now is the appointed time, and all things concur to give effect to the design. Judas conceives the design of selling Jesus, and the chief priests bribe him. At the appointed moment he dies on Calvary.

91
Purchase of the Potter's Field
Matthew 27:7

IT WAS predicted by Jeremiah, the prophet, that the price of Jesus should go to the purchase of the Potter's Field, and the prophecy was providentially fulfilled in a very singular manner. Judas was so covetous that, for the reward of thirty pieces of silver he basely sold his Master. He was so hardened, that when he heard that Master declaring, that one of his disciples should betray him, and even pointing out himself as the traitor, he repented not. Yet when God's word demands its fulfillment, he regrets what he had done, and brought back the money. The chief priests would not take back the money, and he cast it down in the temple. These men who did not scruple to give money for the blood of an innocent man, were so scrupulous in their consciences, that they could not put the price of blood into the treasury. They consulted what should be done with the money, and the result of their free deliberation was, that they bought the Potter's Field for the burying of strangers; and thus was fulfilled the word of God. How many were the chances that this should not be the destination of the price of Christ? Why was it that this particular field was to be sold at this particular time? Do we not here see that the Providence of Jehovah directs all things even the most minute? The deliberations of the enemies of Jesus, whether statesmen or priests, are always overruled to fulfill the purposes of the Most High. Who can understand, who can explain this mystery? Man acts and resolves with perfect freedom, yet he acts and resolves only in fulfillment of the will of the Ruler of the universe!

92

Not this man, but Barabbas

Matthew 27:15, John 18:40

IN THE situation of Barabbas as an object of mercy in preference to Jesus, Providence afforded the Jews an opportunity of manifesting the utmost depravity of heart. Barabbas was a murderer, and was guilty of insurrection. Yet this man they chose to deliver from justice, not from concern for him, but from hatred to the Son of

God. What a singular coincidence, then, was it that brought Barabbas and Jesus into competition, as candidates for the benefit of this Jewish privilege! What a stain on human nature, that Barabbas was the favourite of the electors! Christian reader, need you think it strange, then, that the enemies of your Lord should treat you in the same manner? Under no forms of government, monarchical, aristocratic, or popular, will the man of God, of a decided fearless character, be a favourite. There is no greater mistake than to think, that Christianity would be better treated under a pure democracy than under a pure despotism. Neither monarch nor mob will love the people of Christ, but as they are individually themselves the partakers of the knowledge of God. Better to stand before a single despot, than to encounter the bigotry of the multitude. Paul stood before Caesar, and was delivered out of the mouth of the lion; Pilate desired to save Jesus, but the multitude condemned him. Do we not every day see the same thing, as far as circumstances allow it to be manifested? God's people are far from being perfect, but with all their imperfections, they are better to be trusted in places of trust than the most apparently virtuous of their enemies. But are they, either as to the prerogative of the powerful, or to the privilege of the bulk of the people, the objects of selection in choosing to places of honour or emolument? Barabbas would have a better chance than Nicodemus or Nathaniel.

93
Dream of Pilate's wife
Matthew 27:19

WHATEVER may be the philosophy of dreaming, this dream was evidently providential. Yet, why providential? What did it effect? What was it designed to effect? It did not prevent Pilate from giving up Jesus to his enemies, that they might put him to death: nor was it intended for such a purpose. Jesus must die. Why, then, a waste of means to prevent it? Was not this dream a thing dissuasive to Pilate from condemning Christ? Yet God intended that Jesus should now die by the hands of his enemies. If, then, it did not serve to save Christ from death, and was not intended to be successful for that purpose, what other purpose could it serve? One purpose it served. It showed that the counsel of God must stand, notwithstanding the strongest efforts that can be made to prevent it. Pilate was fully convinced of the innocence of Jesus; he was apprehensive when he heard of his pretensions of being the Son of God; and he was now warned by this dream of his wife, to keep himself free from the blood of Jesus. Yet, after all, he gave him up.

It shows us also, that Divine Providence affords to the wicked an occasion of aggravating their guilt. Pilate knew that Jesus had done nothing worthy of death; yet for unwarrantable reasons he was giving him into the hands of his enemies. At this moment he is warned by a wonderfully providential dream, against what he was about to do, yet he did it notwithstanding. His guilt, then, is providentially aggravated.

94

Jesus given up by Pilate

Matthew 27, John 19

PILATE was fully convinced of the innocence of Jesus; he was alarmed by the pretensions of Jesus to be the Son of God; he was urged by his wife, from a dream, to have nothing to do in condemning him. But he was overborne by the importunity of the people. To satisfy his scruples of conscience, he marks his sense of the innocence of Jesus by a most impressive ceremony. 'When Pilate saw that he could prevail nothing, but rather a tumult was made, he took water, and washed his hands before the multitude, saying, I am innocent of the blood of this just person: see ye to it.' No, no; Pilate. This will not do. All the water in the ocean will not wash you from the blood of the Son of God. You condemn the guiltless, knowing him to be guiltless. Had you been a private man, this impressive way of showing that you did not participate with the murderers of Jesus would have been very proper. But it is not valid for your excuse as a magistrate. You should have done your duty.

But if this did not excuse Pilate, it added greatly to the guilt of the Jews. Hence the solemn testimony of a heathen—of a governor, that Jesus was innocent. This circumstance, then, affords the occasion of an aggravation of the guilt of the murderers of Jesus.

All men condemn Pilate, but there are but few who would not have acted just as Pilate acted. Pilate tried every means which he could think of in order to save Jesus. The Jews at last employed an argument that he could not overcome. 'And from thenceforth Pilate sought to release him; but the Jews cried out, saying, If thou let this man go, thou art not Caesar's friend; whosoever maketh himself a king, speaketh against Caesar.' Jesus had fully declared that his kingdom was not of this world, and, consequently, that his claims could not interfere with the power and right of Caesar. Pilate understood this; but he was overawed by the consideration that the complaint might ruin him with his master. What might be the consequence if Pilate had refused to give up the man whom the whole nation of the Jews accused as a competitor for a throne that now belonged to Caesar? Here was the trial of the integrity of Pilate, and he fell by the temptation. Who, without the faith of Abraham, would have stood?

We all know what Pilate should have done, but few would have done otherwise. Even absolute sovereigns are sometimes overawed by the importunity of a powerful faction, and, desiring to do justice, are compelled to listen to the voice of the mob. Even in free governments, rulers will sometimes bend to the clamour of a powerful religious faction, when they are far from wishing it to prosper. Our own country is blessed with the freest government on earth, yet there are seasons in which I would expect full justice neither from Whig nor Tory. All rulers occasionally sacrifice justice and impartiality to expediency and popular clamour. Lynch law is not with us legitimate, yet 'wild justice' comes to the same amount; and the freaks of wild justice may be overlooked in our own country, as Lynch law is tolerated in another. Are there no instances in Ireland in which violence may be committed against the opposers of the popular religion, where justice becomes lame in the pursuit of the transgressors of law? 'And so Pilate, willing to content the people, released Barabbas unto them, and delivered Jesus, when he had scourged him, to be crucified.' Are there no countries in modern times, in which jails are emptied of their most noxious inmates, in order *to content the people*? Are there no countries in which the protection ordained by law may not in some instances be withheld from the righteous, *in order to content the people*? What Pilate did is often repeated. Expediency, not pure justice, is in many things the foundation of the procedure of power.

95
Adversity no evidence of providential disapprobation
Matthew 27:42

SUCCESS is usually interpreted as the divine approbation of any cause. The bulk of mankind are affected with this kind of evidence more than with any other. It is obvious, then, that there must be some point of view in which the argument is good. The argument is to be approved, as being honourable to God, and an acknowledgment of his particular Providence, as well as that he is the author of truth. These are two grand fundamental points which deserve entire approbation. But when it is inferred, that because God directs all things, and is the author of truth, therefore success must always be the test of truth, the conclusion is not warranted. It is possible that, in the sovereign wisdom of God, it may be for his glory to give a temporary triumph to error; success, therefore, is not a test of truth. And that God actually in his Providence proceeds on this principle, the Scriptures leave us no room to doubt. But in certain circumstances the argument is good. Though success of itself cannot prove any cause to be of God, yet success in certain circumstances may prove this as convincingly as demonstration. The success of the gospel is proof of the truth of the gospel, not from the evidence of simple success, but from that success in connection with the nature of the gospel, and with the opposition which it is calculated every where to provoke, and which, as a matter of fact, every where it met. In this light, we contend that the success of the gospel is proof of the gospel; while we deny that the success of Mahomet is proof of his doctrine, or the success of antichristian apostasy is evidence that it is of God.

As men are prone to interpret simple success as proof of divine approbation, so they are equally prone to consider failure as indicative of the disapprobation of Providence. But as God, in his sovereign wisdom, may give a temporary triumph to error, so may he give temporary failure to truth. The advocate of error may be hailed by the cheering voices, of the people, while the advocate of truth may be put to death, or afflicted. The Jews now triumphed when they had Christ on the cross; but it was on the cross that he defeated the powers of darkness, and all the enemies of his people. They thought that if God was on his side, he could not suffer him to be crucified. In their opinion, God had determined the controversy between them and Jesus in their favour. Men are still proceeding in error on the same principle; and truth and error are estimated by the census. Every party is prone to rely on its success as evidence of the divine approbation; whereas success can be evidence of truth, only when the nature of the thing is considered in relation to the people with whom it is successful, and the means employed in its support. Christianity may be true, though at some times, and in some places, it may fail of success. Socialism may be false, though it should spread for a time over the world. A French Atheist thought, as by a demonstration, to settle the question with respect to the existence of God, by appealing to his own life. He considered it proof that there is no God, because he did not destroy him who denied him. Some atheistic Socialists, we are told, have made the same appeal, and have challenged God, if he exists, to destroy them. And if God were such a one as themselves, he would be provoked to destroy them at the moment. But he is wise, and is not in haste. His enemies cannot fly and escape from him; and he has eternity before them for their punishment. They will find it will reach them time enough. It would not suit the purposes of God to cut off by visible judgment all his enemies. In that case they would be deterred from manifesting the wickedness that is in their hearts, while they would continue equally his enemies. By giving them a stage and free scope to exhibit themselves, the guilt of human nature is practically proved.

Let not the Christian doubt, that God will look to his own cause. But let him ground his belief of all revealed truth on the word of God. The cause of God, no doubt, will in all things ultimately triumph; but God may give Satan a temporary victory, and suffer him to trample on his cause and on his people. Success, when men use nothing but means appointed by God, without any mixture of their own wisdom, is evidence of the cause of God. But the friends of truth, like their Master, may suffer shame, and loss, and death.

96

Appointment of a watch at the tomb of Jesus

Matthew 27:62

WHAT a providential thing was it that his enemies took so much precaution with respect to Jesus in the tomb! By this means they confirm the evidence of his resurrection in the strongest manner. Had no sentinels of the enemy watched at his grave while he lay in the earth, it would have been with more plausibility alleged that he might have been carried off by the disciples. Was it not, then, of Providence that 'the chief priests and Pharisees came together unto Pilate, saying, Sir, we remember that that deceiver said, while he was yet alive, After three days I will rise again. Command therefore that the sepulchre be made sure until the third day, lest his disciples come by night, and steal him away, and say unto the people, He is risen from the dead: so the last error shall be worse than the first.' Here it is providential that the chief priests and Pharisees knew the prediction of Jesus with respect to his resurrection. Had they not known this, they would not have used this precaution. But Jesus might have communicated this prediction to his disciples, while his enemies might have been unacquainted with it. It was providential, then, that they had known it. It was providential that it occurred to them to make this precautionary use of their knowledge of this prediction. It was, indeed, obvious enough; but still, in the moment of victory, they might not have looked farther when their enemy was dead at their feet. It is providential that they themselves drew the right conclusion from the fact of his resurrection. They virtually admit that his resurrection would be proof of the truth of his mission from God. Here they condemn themselves. For though, after all their precautions, he rose from the dead, they did not then believe in him. This shows that it was not from want of evidence that they did not believe in Jesus. It shows that they estimated the evidence of resurrection in the case of Jesus as proof of his pretensions. They confess that evidence of a resurrection in the case of Jesus would be a worse thing for their cause than any thing that had yet happened. The resurrection, then, in their estimation, must be accounted evidence of his Messiahship. Yet, when the resurrection was offered to them in evidence, they were as far from believing it as they were before it happened. The chief priests and Pharisees have here set to their seal, that the resurrection of Jesus would, in their estimation, be proof of his mission, and virtually recorded their own condemnation.

'Pilate said unto them, Ye have a watch; go your way, make it as sure as ye can. So they went, and made the sepulchre sure, sealing the stone, and setting a watch.' It was providential that Pilate went beyond their request. Instead of commanding the thing to be done by the soldiers, without any reference to the enemies of Christ, he gave orders to them also to manage the affair, and so no negligence nor collusion can be suspected. The watch was at their disposal, and the tomb was carefully sealed.

Thus it is that the very efforts of the enemies of the truth are overruled to the elucidation and establishment of truth. This caution in watching against imposture is divinely appointed to exhibit evidence in its full force. Truth shines the more brightly by being continually under friction. Let the opposers of every part of the Divine will use all their efforts to keep it from using false evidence. In this they do it a favour. It stands safely only when it stands on its own basis.

97
Report of the soldiers that the disciples stole the body of Jesus

Matthew 28:13

DIVINE Providence not only defeats the most crafty designs of the enemies of the gospel, but makes them subservient to his own purposes, and sometimes employs them to effect the very purpose which they were intended to prevent. So was it in this matter. In the proposal of the chief priests, and the execution of it by the soldiers, we have a manifestation of the inconceivable depravity of the human heart, and a proof that no evidence can enlighten the darkened mind of man, without the leading of the Holy Spirit. The proposal of the chief priests and elders in council implied that they knew that Jesus was risen from the dead, while their hatred to the truth impelled them to discredit it by so wicked a stratagem. They were not only so hardened as not to believe in Jesus on the evidence of his resurrection, which they could not but believe; but they were so unprincipled as to avail themselves of the basest means to hide the evidence from others, which they had before their own eyes. Who can estimate the guilt of this unbelief? They knew that Jesus was risen; they felt that this was proof of his pretensions; yet, to hinder the effect, they bribed the watch to say that, while they slept, the body was stolen by the disciples. Is it, then, for want of sufficient evidence that men reject the gospel? No, it is hatred to the gospel, that is the ground of rejecting it. Men love darkness rather than light, because their deeds are evil.

And what shall we say of the watch? They beheld all the wonders at the tomb from which Jesus rose. 'And behold, there was a great earthquake: for the angel of the Lord descended from heaven, and came and rolled back the stone from the door, and sat upon it. His countenance was like lightning, and his raiment white as snow; and for fear of him the keepers did shake, and became as dead men.' Do they now believe? Are they converted to God? Are their hearts changed? No such thing. They are as dead as they were before—as dead as they who lie in the grave. Instead of becoming the disciples of Jesus from the ocular evidence of his resurrection, and the awful display of the divine glory which took place on that occasion, when a bribe was offered, 'they took the money, and did as they were taught.' Such is the blindness and hardness of heart in man, that nothing can open his eyes, and change his heart, but the power of the Spirit of the Almighty. The gospel is the only means of conversion, and the Spirit of God is the only agent. The word is mighty, but it is mighty as the sword of the Spirit. A sword as sharp as a razor is as harmless as a rush in the hands of an infant. In the hands of a vigorous and skilful soldier it does dreadful execution.

In this occurrence, then, we have, in the wisdom of Providence, a display of the natural blindness and guilt of man, and proof that no evidence is sufficient, without the Holy Spirit, to raise men to spiritual life. But the cunning project of the enemies of Jesus was providentially calculated to contribute to the establishment of the truth, which it was designed to destroy. The story was, in itself, utterly incredible. The guards could not be supposed to have been all asleep at such a risk to their lives; and they could not depose to a fact which, they alleged, took place while they slept. Besides, had they really slept, it never would have been confessed, unless they had been actually detected. Now, they were not found asleep. What made them their own accusers? Nothing but the bribe, and security of impunity. The story is worth nothing for the purpose for which it was invented. It served to deceive only those who loved to be deceived.

But the story is of great importance in proof of the resurrection. It is the confession of the enemies of Jesus on the spot at the time, that the body was really out of the tomb. As the account given by the bribed witnesses is self-evidently false, there is increased evidence that he was really raised from the dead. 'This saying,' we are told by Matthew, 'was commonly reported among the Jews,' to the time of his writing. There can, therefore, be no manner of doubt that, in one way or other, the body of Jesus left the tomb. As the story of the watch is utterly incredible, the only rational conclusion is, that he was raised as the Scriptures report. Thus, the wrath of man is made to praise God.

98
Christ crucified between two malefactors
Mark 15:27

AND is not the cross itself sufficiently disgraceful? Must Christ on the cross be a companion of malefactors? Yes, so is the will of God. And that it was designed for wise purposes is evident from the fact, that the thing was predicted by the Spirit of prophecy. It was, then, no accidental thing. It is a matter adjusted by Divine wisdom. When he died between two malefactors, 'The Scripture was fulfilled, which saith, And he was numbered with the transgressors.' And great wisdom appears in the fact. It not only served to increase the humiliation of Jesus, but afforded him, in the very depth of that humiliation, an occasion of manifesting his almighty power, and his sovereign grace. One of the malefactors he saved through the blood which was then shed; the other, in his sovereignty, he overlooked, and suffered to perish in ignorance and sin. By the occasion now providentially offered, he manifested himself in some of the most awful characters[1] of God. Even while suffering on the cross, he exercised almighty power, and displayed sovereign grace. Here he gives hope to the guiltiest of mankind who believe on him. Here he gives hope to the guilty even under the very grasp of death. If they now believe, like the Israelites stung with the fiery serpents, they are

[1] that is, awesome characteristics, or attributes. —P.

saved from the most deadly sins. When they look on this Saviour, their wounds are instantly healed.

99
Combination of the Pharisees and Herodians to ensnare Jesus
Mark 12:13

WHAT a vile conspiracy of seditious zealots, and courtly sycophants of power, to ensnare Jesus! Whigs and Tories are opposed in everything. But they unite in opposing the gospel. Radicals and loyalists, monarchists and democrats, all, all combine to oppose the Saviour of the guilty.

On one point the Pharisees had a very tender conscience. It was not, they thought, lawful to pay tribute to Caesar. The Herodians, from their name, doubtless, were base sycophants, who, so far from considering it sinful to pay the taxes, approved the sacrilegious and idolatrous innovations introduced by Herod. The one would not give Caesar his own; the other would give him what belonged to God. Both were wrong, and Jesus gave an answer to the ensnaring questions, which equally condemned both.

What a providential thing was it for us that this thing took place! It gave occasion to Jesus to give us a lesson which, in a few words, teaches us our duty to civil rulers in all circumstances in which we can possibly be placed. Let us give all our substance rather than resist the arm of that power which Divine Providence has put over us. But in the things of God, we owe them no allegiance. Should they presume to dictate to us in religion, or to regulate or modify any of the doctrines of Christ, let us die rather than comply. This is the patriotism of a Christian.

100

Jesus brought before Herod

Luke 23:5

JESUS must stand before the rulers of the earth, both Jewish and Gentile. Herod, then, must hear him, that in the day of judgment he may give account to the Judge of the world for his conduct with regard to the Son of God. Herod was providentially at that time in Jerusalem. We are not told the occasion, but it was a *chance* divinely ordained. But though Herod was at Jerusalem, Jesus might have been put to death before Herod would have had an opportunity of seeing him. Providence, then, brought the thing about by another *chance*. The high priest, in urging Pilate to put Jesus to death, happened to speak of Galilee, and the mention of Galilee happened to remind Pilate that Herod was in the city; and the thought *happened* to occur to Pilate to send Jesus to Herod. We are told by the inspired historian that Herod and Pilate had quarrelled, and on that occasion were made friends. It appears, then, that Pilate designed it as a compliment to Herod when he sent Jesus before him; and Herod felt it as a compliment, so that a mutual good understanding was restored. Now, all these *happenings* were links in the chain which drew Jesus before the tribunal of Herod. Besides, as Jesus was declared innocent by Pilate, so is he justified by the verdict of Herod. Base man, then, why did you condemn him? The thing was ordained of God, yet the guilt is yours. You must answer for it. Every man is responsible for every thought, word, and action. How this thing can be ordained of God, without affecting the responsibility of the agents, is a thing beyond the grasp of human understanding. He is a fool who will either deny it or attempt to grapple with it. 'Then said Pilate to the chief priests and to the people, I find no fault in this man. And they were the more fierce, saying, He stirreth up the people, teaching throughout all Jewry, beginning from Galilee to this place. When Pilate heard of Galilee, he asked whether the man were a Galilean. And as soon as he heard that he belonged to Herod's jurisdiction, he sent him to Herod, who himself also was at Jerusalem at that time. And when Herod saw Jesus, he was exceeding glad; for he was desirous to see him of a long season, because he had heard many things of him; and he hoped to have seen some miracle done by him. Then he questioned with him in many words; but he answered him nothing. And Herod with his men of war set him at nought, and mocked him, and arrayed him in a gorgeous robe, and sent him again to Pilate. And the same day Pilate and Herod were made friends together; for before they were at enmity between themselves. And Pilate, when he had called together the chief priests and the rulers and the people, said unto them, Ye have brought this man unto me, as one that perverteth the people: and, behold, I, having examined him before you, have found no fault in this man touching those things whereof ye accuse him: no, nor yet Herod: for I sent you to him; and, lo, nothing worthy of death is done unto him.'—Luke 23:4-15.

IOI

Cross of Christ borne by Simon

Luke 23:26

'AND as they led him away, they laid hold upon one Simon, a Cyrenian, coming out of the country, and on him they laid the cross, that he might bear it after Jesus.' What can be more purely accidental? What Providence can you discern here? Stop a moment, and consider the matter a little more attentively. Jesus himself said, 'He that taketh not his cross, and followeth after me, is not worthy of me.' The same declaration is repeatedly made by our Lord, and urged on those about him. Everyone knows that this peculiar phraseology is grounded on the manner of execution by the cross, and is an allusion to the circumstance of Christ's carrying his own cross, and of Simon's substitution on the occasion here referred to. By taking of the cross and following after Jesus, there is an allusion to the taking up of Christ's cross by Simon, who thus followed his Master to the place of execution. In this way of speaking, Christ includes all the labours, difficulties, reproaches, trials, and persecutions, which his people are to bear after him for his sake. He bore sufferings and shame himself first for them, going before them. They must in turn bear such things for him, going after him; and thus they take up their cross and follow him. So far none will dispute. But what has this to do with Providence? A great deal. Let it be observed that the declaration of Jesus, repeatedly made in this phraseology, was *prospective* in its allusion. The thing to which it refers, and on which the phraseology is grounded, had not happened at the time when Jesus used it. It was still future till the time of his death. Christ, then, used the phraseology from his foreknowledge of what was to take place at his death, with respect to the circumstance of his carrying his own cross, and of Simon's being met on the way to the place of execution, and his being compelled to carry the cross for the remainder of the way. Here, then, is the Providence. At the particular time in which this phraseology could have its reference accomplished, Simon *chanced* to be coming out of the country, and *happened* to meet the party who led Jesus to the place of crucifixion. Had he not come, or had he come a few minutes sooner, or a few minutes later, the reference of the language of Christ would have wanted the ground on which it was to rest. Besides, when they met Simon, what excited the thought to make him carry the cross? Was not this providential? Here we see that the most casual things are under providential direction; and that the most trifling things recorded in Scripture are calculated to give edification to the man of God. Simon's taking up the cross and carrying it after Jesus, when led to the place of crucifixion, like Christ's washing of the feet of the disciples, is a symbolical action, including all the trials of the Christian for Christ's sake. The cross itself many may never be called to bear. Perhaps, as a matter of fact, none of them may be called to carry their own cross to the place of crucifixion. They may not be called at all to suffer death. But taking up the cross refers to all trials for Christ's sake; and every Christian must take up his cross and follow Jesus. None of the people of Christ, who live any time in the world after they are called to the knowledge of him, are without their trials in proportion to their strength. This shows the great importance of right views of the inspiration of the Scriptures. Many tell us that inspiration cannot be necessary in historical facts known to the narrator. But, had the historian been left to himself, he might have omitted the fact about Simon, and in that case we would have wanted the very foundation on which one of the most commonly repeated sayings of Jesus was grounded. They who have loose notions of inspiration are not in the tract in which they can make discoveries in the word of God. They read it as a common book. It should be read as being, every line of it, God's book. The savage wonders at the process of the man of science in examining the bowels of the earth to make discoveries. Such a savage in the things of God is the man who does not examine the Scriptures in the way in which the philosopher examines the earth.

102

Christ's death by crucifixion

John 18:31

CHRIST was to die on a cross. This was predicted, and this was accounted by the Jews an accursed death. 'Cursed is everyone that hangeth on a tree.' Christ, then, who was made a curse for his people, must die on a cross. But how is this to be brought about? It was properly the Jews who put him to death; and had they performed the business without the intervention of the Roman government, he would not have been so executed. He was condemned by the Jews for blasphemy, and the blasphemer was stoned to death by the law of Moses. Pilate acquits Jesus, and how can he crucify him? He saw that the thing was inconsistent, and, therefore, when he yielded to the importunity of the Jews, he gave him up into their hands to do with him as they pleased. 'Then said Pilate unto them, Take ye him, and judge him according to your law. The Jews, therefore, said unto him, It is not lawful for us to put any man to death.' Here is the hand of Divine Providence. The power of life and death was now taken from the Jews, otherwise Christ would not have been put to death by crucifixion. He would have died in the way in which the Jews put blasphemers to death. But there is another providential interposition in this matter. Pilate, unwilling to put Jesus to death himself, offered to give him into the hands of the Jews to put him to death in their own manner. Yet they would not accept the offer. How scrupulous they have become! The men who a thousand times endeavoured to kill Jesus without even the colour of trial, now refuse to execute him when he is given up into their hands! What did they fear? Could they really fear the Roman government, when the Roman governor gave up the prisoner to them, and desired them to judge him according to their law? Were the Jews, on other occasions, so very conscientious in yielding obedience to the Roman authority? Whatever might be their reasons, it was evidently of God that they refused to execute Jesus according to their own customs. They refused, and Pilate complied. Why did he comply? Had he not here a good pretext for saving Jesus as he wished? Might he not have said, 'I have judged him innocent. As you have judged him guilty according to your law, you must put him to death, or let him live.' Why did he not reason thus? Why did he yield? The reason is, 'That the saying of Jesus might be fulfilled which he spake, signifying what death he should die.' How wonderfully does God work in his Providence! He does his pleasure as well by his enemies as by his friends. Pilate and the Jews, on this occasion, were the ministers of Providence, and fulfilled his purpose, while they broke his law!

103
The title on the cross of Christ
John 19:19-22

HEROD and his men of war arrayed Jesus in mock majesty, and insultingly treated him as an impostor pretending to the throne of David. The title on the cross of Christ, composed by Pilate, was not given on this principle. Pilate, unhappy man, though overcome by faction and the fear of false accusation, gave up Christ to his enemies, yet he never insulted him. He feared him even while he condemned him to death. And now he is providentially led to compose a title for the cross of Christ, that proclaims him in his true character. The Jews felt the thing as an acknowledgment of the pretensions of Jesus, and requested him to change it. But he sternly and steadily refused. It must stand written in Hebrew, Greek, and Latin. Even on the cross Jesus is exhibited by his very crucifiers in his true character. The cross of Christ calls to men of all nations in their own language, that Jesus is the true King of Israel, who sits on the throne of his father David. The very devils were obliged to confess the Son of God; and his opposers in every age are obliged to serve the interests of his kingdom, even in the persecution of his people. 'And Pilate wrote a title, and put it on the cross. And the writing was, Jesus of Nazareth, the King of the Jews. This title then read many of the Jews: for the place where Jesus was crucified was nigh to the city: and it was written in Hebrew, and Greek, and Latin. Then said the chief priests of the Jews to Pilate, Write not, the King of the Jews; but that he said, I am King of the Jews. Pilate answered, What I have written I have written.' Here the wrath of man praises God with a loud voice.

104
Lots cast for the coat of Jesus
John 19:23

'THEN the soldiers, when they had crucified Jesus, took his garments, and made four parts, to every soldier a part; and also his coat: now the coat was without seam woven from the top throughout. They said, therefore, among themselves, Let us not rend it, but cast lots for it, whose it shall be; that the Scriptures might be fulfilled, which saith, They parted my garments among them, and for my vesture they did cast lots. These things, therefore, the soldiers did.' Here we are expressly assured, that the thing done was done, that prophecy might be fulfilled. But we see that the fulfillment was altogether providential. The casting of the lot for this part of the raiment of the Messiah was the work of the soldiers themselves, the thought of which occurred to their own minds. Never did men act more spontaneously; Stoical or Mahometan fate could not more exactly have accomplished the thing predicted. In an inconceivable manner God performs his purposes by the voluntary thoughts and actions of all men, even by his enemies. Philosophy may attempt to explain and to reconcile by forced modification on one side or the other. Some, in order to have action voluntary, will deny that God ordains voluntary action, because they cannot comprehend the consistency. Some, in order to maintain the universal ordination of God, deny that action is voluntary, because, in their little wisdom, they cannot philosophize on the subject. Some force a harmony by obliging both parties to soften their expressions, and submit to modification; because they are not hardy enough to take either alternative, yet still wish to be esteemed wise. The attempt to fathom this subject is as vain as to attempt to ascertain the boundary of space or time. That God doth all things by the counsel of his own will, yet that man is voluntary and responsible, are truths exhibited in Scripture, written as with a sun-beam. Our business is to believe both, without any attempt to comprehend the incomprehensible ways of Jehovah.

105
The legs of Jesus not broken
John 19:31-37

How watchful is Providence in the fulfillment of the Scriptures! A bone of the Messiah is not to be broken; yet a general order was given to the soldiers on the occasion to break the legs of those who were hanging on the cross. How is Jesus to escape? Providentially he was already dead; and as the breaking of the legs was for the purpose of hastening death, by an equal Providence the soldiers took the liberty not to observe the letter of their instructions. Soldiers generally are machines, and it is seldom they fail in literally executing their orders. Surely none but God could so execute his purposes. Had not Jesus been dead, his legs must have been broken. How critical was the juncture! How seasonable was the order!

The same thing was overruled to occasion the piercing of the side of Jesus, for the fulfillment of the Scripture, and the exhibition of a miraculous symbol of salvation. A soldier wantonly, without orders, pierced the side of Jesus with a spear. That the bones of Jesus might not be broken, the soldiers did not fully execute their orders: That the side of Jesus might be pierced, a soldier pierced him without orders, moved by some capricious but divinely appointed suggestion. What a complication of the wonders of Providence! Philosophy endeavours to lessen our astonishment, by telling us of the structure of the body. The pericardium, they tell us, was pierced, and this accounts for the issuing of the blood and water, without the help of any miracle. Down, driveller! Did not the blood and water come in two distinct streams? Is this to be accounted for by the structure of the heart?

106
The disciples pluck the ears of corn on the Sabbath-day
Luke 6

THE occasions of many of the miracles of our Lord were providential. While their great object was to prove Jesus to be the Christ, they were often performed in such circumstances as to instruct his disciples in other truths. The occasion of several of them seems evidently to have been to show the true nature of the Sabbath. In the fact here recorded, we have an occasion afforded to our Lord to condemn the Pharisaical notions of the Sabbath; and show those works that are not inconsistent with its most sacred observance. Jesus and his company happened on the Sabbath to go through the corn-fields: it happened, also, that his disciples were hungry, and that, in consequence, they plucked the ears of corn, and ate. This gave occasion to the Pharisees to complain, and to Jesus to expound to them the true nature of the Sabbath. Whoever reads the account of the works of our Lord will see much of these providential leadings in his life. A similar Providence presented before him the man with the withered hand on a Sabbath; and afforded an opportunity for that answer so confounding to his adversaries.

In like manner, in every age, the Providence of Jesus often brings his people into situations that afford them an opportunity of manifesting the difference between religion and superstition, between enlightened obedience to the authority of God, and a bigoted attachment to human additions to the Divine law. The Lord's day is a most precious appointment for the disciples of Christ, but they do not honour it aright who speak of it in a way that would condemn the conduct of the Lord of the Sabbath.

107

Certain disciples minister to the Lord Jesus of their substance

Luke 8:3

JESUS, who could supply others by miracle, lived himself by Providence. The Lord of the universe, who at first created the world, and who still by his Providence makes the earth fruitful for the supply of man and beast, instead of supplying his wants by immediate creation, drew his supplies from his people. Wonderful humiliation! The Lord of heaven and earth condescends to live on the bounty of those who are supplied by his own Providence! Thus he gave not only the most amazing instance of humility, but afforded an opportunity to his disciples to manifest their faith in him, and their love of him. In this way he still acts. He makes some of his people poor, that others of them may have an opportunity of ministering to Jesus by ministering to the saints. What is done to his children is done to himself. His gospel is not preached, as it might be, by angels; but is to be sent over the world by his redeemed people. Here they have an opportunity of ministering to Jesus, by contributing to extend his kingdom. The service of the Lord Jesus requires the substance of his people; and they who rest on his power to uphold his kingdom, without connecting it with the means of his appointment, separate what God has joined together. When Jesus had to ride in triumph into Jerusalem, he sent a messenger to the owner of the ass, saying, 'The Lord hath need of him.' Is it not enough for a disciple, when the cause of God says to him, 'The Lord hath need of thy substance, or thy services'?

108
The calling of Zacchaeus
Luke 19

ZACCHAEUS is to be brought to the knowledge of Christ: mark how the Providence of God puts him in the way of being effectually called. Jesus is in the place where this chief of the publicans resided; but so were thousands whom Jesus overlooked. Providentially, however, Zacchaeus was singled out from the rest in a remarkable manner. He had an uncommon curiosity to see Jesus, and to have a satisfying view of him. But he was low of stature. Had he been a tall man, he might have gratified his curiosity without notice. Jesus, indeed, could have called him in any way he chose. But he generally did things in a way of Providence. The man was little; and in order to get a full view of Jesus, he climbed up into a tree on the road side. This was the occasion of presenting him to the notice of the Lord Jesus; and in his sovereignty he called him down, in the same style of language in which he called the world into existence. 'Zacchaeus, make haste and come down; for today I must abide at thy house.'

And thousands are led by curiosity, or a worse motive, to hear the gospel, when it becomes to them the means of eternal life. Many preachers upbraid their hearers with the carnal motives which bring them to hear the gospel. This is wrong. It is a proclamation to keep them from coming again. Jesus did not so with Zacchaeus. No matter to us what brings sinners to hear the gospel, let the preacher do his part, which is to commend the truth to every man's conscience in the sight of God.

109
The enemies of Jesus restrained from injuring him by fear of the people
Luke 19:48

JESUS sometimes delivered himself miraculously from his enemies. But he oftener did this in a way of Providence. One very usual means was the fear of the people. The mass of the people were not so hardened as their leaders; and they were uncommonly taken with his teaching and miracles. Except when their dearest prejudices were touched, they heard the Lord with much attention. Accordingly, on many occasions, when the Scribes and Pharisees would have destroyed Jesus, they were prevented by the fear of the people. So was it on the present occasion. 'The chief priests and the scribes, and the chief of the people, sought to destroy him; and could not find what they might do: for all the people were very attentive to hear him.'

But when the hour was come for the Lord to depart from this world, this providential restraint was removed; and the people themselves were excited by their rulers to call out, 'Crucify him, crucify him!'

In how many instances may we find this Providence exemplified in the history of God's people! Divine Providence often raises up ungodly men, and puts them in such situations as enable them to be a screen to his people. As long as the cause of the Lord needs this, he will continue it. When it ceases to serve him, he will remove it. And sometimes the protector will be removed, or prevented from giving aid: sometimes he will be himself turned into a persecutor.

IIO

Providential preservation of Peter when he smote the servant of the high priest

Luke 22:50

HOW often does the Lord preserve his people from the conse-quence of their ignorance in their service of him! It would, indeed, be bad for us were it otherwise. There is much evil in the best of our services. Our very zeal has in it what would condemn us. Is it not perfectly surprising that Peter escaped after striking the servant of the high priest? Why was he not cut down on the spot? Why was he not made prisoner, and tried with Jesus? And justly he would have been condemned; for he resisted the power that God had placed over him. His Master suffered unjustly; he would have suffered righteously. But he acted in ignorance of his duty; he acted out of love to his Lord. This the Lord approved, and preserved him from the consequences of his rashness and ignorance. Here we have an instance of sovereign providential restraint on the hearts of wicked men. Peter opposed the authorities, and openly drew his sword; yet there is not a hand to cut him down, while a band of soldiers are before him; nor was there a voice to bring him to judg-ment, though he was by several persons recognized. Jesus rules the hearts of ungodly men, as well as he guides the wheels of nature.

From this we ought to learn, that preservation in any exploit is no evidence that God approves it. Peter was preserved, while he did what his Lord reproved.

III

Providential circumstances leading Peter into the situation in which he denied his Master

Compare Matt. 26:51; Mark 14:47; Luke 22:50; John 18:10

PETER was to deny his Master, and the circumstances that led to this event were providentially ordered. Peter begins to fear, but he loses not all courage at once. He followed Jesus, though at a distance. In this way he saw no danger. He still loves the Lord, and wishes to hear how the matter would go in the high priest's hall. But how shall he gain admittance? There is a person that keeps the door, and he has no interest. Here a link is furnished for the chain in John. He knows the keeper of the door, and gains an entrance for Peter. Had it not been for this circumstance, Peter would not have been put to the trial, and Peter would not have fallen. What a sovereignty is in this Providence! By keeping Peter out, Jesus might have kept Peter from denying him, and preserved his own cause from the reproach. Yet it was the sovereign will of his Providence that they should take place. Peter, then, is introduced into the place where he falls. Peter is so cautious as not to stand by the side of Jesus; yet he is not so cautious as to hide in a corner. He mingles with the officers and servants round the fire. Here he is again and again recognized. Yet not a word about the recognition of John, or of any other! Peter is the only man that is so often identified. He who sees not Providence in this affair is as blind as Bartimaeus. He who will not recognize Sovereignty in this Providence may deny design in the works of creation.

112

Providential meeting of Jesus and the woman of Samaria

John 4

THE woman of Samaria, and many others of the city of Sychar, were to be called to the knowledge of Jesus. But how was this to be brought about? In passing near the city, Jesus apparently was about to proceed without entering it. His disciples went into the town to buy victuals, while he rested at Jacob's Well. How many chances, then, were there, that neither this woman, nor any of the other persons, should hear of him! Had the disciples brought provisions with them, or been previously provided on the way, there would have been no need for delay; and the Lord would have passed before the woman came to the well. Now, when he is sitting at the well, why is it that at this moment the woman came? Why was she not a little sooner or a little later? Why was she a woman of such a particular character? Were not all these circumstances arranged by Providence to lead to the calling of the woman of Samaria, and to Christ's entrance into the city, where he had others to call? In this we have a specimen of the ways in which God opens an entrance for the Gospel into different places. How often is this by accidents, which are all appointed by Providence to fulfill his purposes!

113

The man born blind

John 9

SICKNESS and afflictions of every kind are all wisely ordered by the Lord. In every case they have an end. But they are not always in judgment. Men, however, are prone to ascribe them to judgment, and to decide rashly on particular cases. Judgment is one end of afflictive providential dispensations; but there are other ends to the Lord's people, which ought always to be distinguished. Taking it for granted that blindness was always the effect of some particular heinous sin, the disciples, on passing a blind man, asked Jesus whether the sin had been committed by himself, that he was visited with blindness; or his parents had sinned, that he was born blind. Jesus, without denying that the thing might happen on either of the accounts referred to, ascribed the affliction to another reason. The man was born blind, yet it was not for any particular sin of his parents; but 'that the works of God should be made manifest in him.' He was born blind that Jesus might have an opportunity of giving him sight. Here we see the Providence of God in the blindness of an infant, whom God designed that Jesus should cure in manhood. All this previous affliction must be endured by this individual, because that at a particular time God was to be glorified by his cure. And is not this great consolation to any of the Lord's people who have been born blind, or who may have lost their sight? They must not, indeed, expect a miracle to give them sight; but they may be assured that their affliction is for the glory of God; and, consequently, must ultimately be for their own good. God has some purpose to serve by their blindness, and in that state there is some way in which they may glorify God, more than they would have done with sight. There are many ways in which this may be true; each individual may undoubtedly discern something in his own case, in which he can realize its truth.

The same thing is true with respect to deafness, and many other calamities with which God's children are afflicted. This affliction is in one way or other for the glory of God. And a conviction of this, firmly and abidingly impressed upon the mind, would enable them to support their affliction with patience.

Sometimes Christians are inclined to suspect God's love towards them, when they are greatly afflicted. Nothing can be more without foundation in the word of God. In the school of Christ, this discipline is as necessary as teaching. Christians ought to take affliction as medicine from the hand of a loving parent. In the question of the disciples, we may see the opinion of the Jews with respect to Providence. It proceeds upon the principle that God governs the world by a particular Providence, and that afflictions are always from his hand. How unlike to this is the philosophical doctrine now held by many who call themselves Christians, in which God is in a manner excluded from working, and acts merely by general laws. The clock was made by him, and wound up at the beginning, and it can go on without him till it has run down. This Atheism ought to be the horror of Christians. It was not the doctrine of the Jews. The disciples were aware of a particular Providence: they erred with respect to the grounds on which it proceeds. Their views were too limited on this subject. Afflictions may arise from particular sins, or be the fruit of the sins of parents; but they may also be without a view to either, and be sent for the glory of God, as well as the good of the sufferer.

114

The sickness of Lazarus

John 11:4

HERE we have an instance of providential sickness. Lazarus was visited with grievous sickness, so that he died, for the very purpose of being brought to life by Jesus for the glory of God. This is the interpretation which is given by Wisdom itself, the Lord Jesus Christ. 'This sickness is not unto death, but for the glory of God, that the Son of God might be glorified thereby.' Now, who was Lazarus? He was a true disciple of Jesus. Was he the least in the kingdom of God? He was one who was the peculiar object of the love of his Master. His sisters sent to Jesus, saying, 'Lord, behold, he whom thou lovest is sick:' and the Jews exclaimed, 'Behold how he loved him!' Yet this peculiar favourite of Jesus was visited with sickness unto death, that God in him might be glorified. Let not God's people, then, think that they are not the objects of his favour, or that they are comparatively little in his favour, because he has visited them with sickness, or any other grievous affliction. Let the case of Lazarus answer, and silence all the murmurings of unbelief. Their affliction is for the glory of God, and for their own good. And if it was not to answer these purposes, it would not have been sent. For, though God afflicts his people, he never afflicts them willingly. He never afflicts out of caprice. Sometimes parents may injudiciously and capriciously put to pain with a good intention. God never acts in this manner. He never sends a single instance of affliction in which he is not one way or other to be glorified; and which will not turn out for the good of his people. This ought at once to give them confidence against the power of affliction when they are without it; and patience and resignation when they are in it. 'The bud may have a bitter taste, but sweet will be the flower.' God will not wound his people wantonly. He will keep them from all evil in the midst of all the evils of the world, except when his glory and their good require affliction. Lazarus, the beloved friend of Jesus, was called to suffer much pain in sickness. His sisters, whom Jesus loved, were called to the most painful affliction in the death of a brother whom they loved beyond measure. The beloved Lazarus must suffer the pains of death, that Jesus might prove himself to be the Son of God, by raising him from the dead. But what is still more remarkable, Jesus glorifies himself by the suffering of his dearest friends, when he could have proved his Sonship by the death and restoration of his enemies. Christians, take notice. It is not the revilers and blasphemers of the Son of God who are put to suffering and visited with death, in order to prove his dignity. It is his friends who are called to this high honour. The best soldiers are called to mount the breach. God's children are honoured and blessed by being selected to suffer for his glory. If afflictions were not for the good of his children, Christ would have exercised his sovereign power in the sickness and cure of his enemies. His friends he could cover from every evil, and from every danger. When he selects them for suffering, it must be for their own good as well as for his glory.

Let us mark the conduct of Jesus in this affair. Though he loved Lazarus exceedingly, yet he intentionally delayed setting out to visit him for two whole days. This was evidently that Lazarus might be dead before he would arrive. He tells his disciples expressly:—'I am glad for your sakes that I was not there, to the intent that ye may believe.' The design of all was, that Lazarus might be dead, and for a considerable time in the grave, in order to confirm the faith of the disciples, as well as afford evidence of his pretensions to his enemies. For this reason the feelings of the family of Lazarus must be long distressed, and the sorrow of death must affect them for several days. This was a trial of their faith.

And the Lord's people are often kept in affliction long for a similar reason. The person whom God designs to raise up from the bed on which he lies is kept long under sickness, and brought to the very gates of death, that God may at last be glorified in his recovery. And when any dies, as he lived not to himself, so he dies not to himself, but by his death glorifies God.

In this case we see that it is no evidence that the Lord does not hear the prayers of his people, that he does not answer them immediately. The sisters of Lazarus pressed Jesus to come, that their brother might not die. For a long time he came not. He intentionally delayed after the message. But yet he came in time to deliver. In like manner, the Lord may hear the prayers of his people to spare the life of their beloved relation, though he afflicts long after they call. They should ask, and faint not, till the event shall show the mind of the Lord. When this is the case, they should submit in patience, and be satisfied that God has done all things well. Even then their prayers are not lost. If God has not given them what they asked, he can give them what is better. He can perfect strength in their weakness, and make his grace sufficient for them.

115

Thomas not at the meeting of the disciples when Jesus appeared after his resurrection

John 20

IT IS remarkable that one of the disciples should have been absent from the assembly on such an interesting occasion. What was the cause of his absence it would be worse than useless to conjecture. But the intention of Providence in it is obvious. It was to display the natural unbelief, as to the things of God, that is in the heart of man; and to teach us the kind of evidence that God accounts sufficient for his saving truth.

Why was one of the disciples absent? Why was this disciple Thomas? The narrative itself affords an answer to both questions.

Divine Providence intended to give us a specimen of unbelief even in his own people. Thomas was peculiarly incredulous; therefore he was the person fitted to act the part designed for him on this occasion. If Thomas was afterwards convinced, there is no room left for captiousness to allege that the fact of Christ's resurrection was received by the disciples on slight grounds, without sufficient evidence and caution.

The unbelief of Thomas was unreasonable and sinful in a degree beyond expression. Why did he not believe the united testimony of the other apostles? He should have received the testimony of any one of them. Unbelief justly exposed him to eternal condemnation. Has Thomas a licence for unbelief, more than any other of the human race? Must he not be liable to condemnation on the same ground with the rest of mankind? Must he be satisfied in his own whims with respect to the evidence of this fact? Can he say with innocence, 'Except I shall see in his hands the print of the nails, and put my finger into the print of the nails, and thrust my hand into his side, I will not believe?' Did ever any infidel express a more unreasonable demand for the evidence of Christ's resurrection, and the truth of the Christian religion? The demands of sceptics are moderate and sober, compared to this intemperance of unbelief. The most unreasonable of them demand only that a particular revelation of the gospel should be made to every man. This falls far short of the extravagance and unreasonableness of the unbelief of Thomas.

But there is wisdom in this madness. If Thomas is unreasonable, God uses his unreasonableness to effect a great purpose. By this means, in the satisfaction given to Thomas, we have the fact of the resurrection established on evidence beyond all suspicion. The possibility of delusion is removed; and the reality that it was Jesus whom the apostles saw, rests not merely on the testimony of their eyes, but of the hands of the most unreasonable unbeliever that ever was in the world. Of all the infidels that ever existed, Thomas was the most extravagant. Voltaire and Hume are men of moderation, compared to this prince of infidels. Nothing will satisfy this philosopher but the handling of the prints of the nails in his Master. Was it not possible that the risen body of Jesus should have had no scars? Was not this the most likely thing to be expected? That Almighty power which could raise him, could raise him without a mark of his crucifixion. But Thomas was in all respects unreasonable; that through this, Jesus might exhibit himself with evidence of his resurrection, that the most extravagant incredulity could presume to demand.

By this providential fact the Lord teaches us that his own disciples believe in him, not because they are naturally more teachable, or less incredulous than others. It is God only who overcomes their unbelief. They are not only by nature the children of wrath even as others; but after they are brought to faith and life, the only security of their perseverance is the favour and love of God in Christ. They are kept by faith, and that faith is not of themselves, but is the gift of God. The strongest of all the disciples of Christ would not abide in the faith for a single day, if, like Peter or like Thomas, they were to be given up to their own natural unbelief. But if the strongest would not stand in their strength, the feeblest will not be plucked from the hand of the heavenly Father. After the fearful example of Peter and of Thomas, let no disciple of Christ trust in his own steadfastness. We are strong only when, seeing our own weakness, we have our strength in the Rock of our salvation. The world in general, and philosophers in particular, look upon Christians as a weak-minded people, who are prone to believe without sufficient evidence. The man of science, even when he can find no fault with the man of God, still thinks himself justifiable in considering him as utterly below himself in mental powers. He thinks there must be a soft place in his head somewhere. The best thing that he can find to say is, that he is 'an amiable enthusiast.' The truth, however, is far otherwise. Whether the believer is a man of strength of intellect, or feeble in mind, he would be equally an unbeliever with the most talented of his enemies, were he left to himself. Yea, the weakest would likely be the most presumptuous, and rash, and blasphemous in the extravagance of their complaints against the gospel. Thomas would not be behind Paine in the rashness of his demands and assertions. The Christian is made a little child by the word and Spirit of God, but by nature he receiveth not the things of the Spirit, for they are to him, as well as to others, foolishness, until his eyes are opened to discover them.

It is a matter of fact, worthy of particular attention, that the simplest of the men of God make a more correct and a more scientific estimate of the philosopher, than the philosopher can make of him. The philosopher, with all his knowledge, knows not God by his philosophy. He knows not, then, the correct and enlightened views of the man of God on the highest of all sciences. The philosopher, not appreciating the value of the soul, nor the amount of the unspeakable glory of the heavenly inheritance, as well as of the danger of overlooking condemnation, sees not the wisdom of the conduct of the man of God. He has no way to judge of him but by himself; and, therefore, as he himself is wise, the other must be a fool. The pleasure of knowledge, and the glory of fame are, with the philosopher, the very essence of the happiness of the third heavens. In all this, the man of God, even the weakest of them, can enter into the feelings and sentiments of the men of science: for, by nature, he is such a one himself. And he still finds, in his very best moments, that if he would lose sight of heaven, and be left of God, he would make his paradise with the philosophers, or, at least, according to his taste, with some group of those who are, in different ways, in pursuit of earthly joys. The Christian is not amazed that men seek the praise of men more than that of God; and that they pursue the things of this world rather than the things of God. He is rather amazed that God has turned himself out of this course, and enables him to resist the temptations which he daily meets in the world. To him there is no mystery in the character and choice of the philosopher, of the sensualist, of the men of the world. In them he sees himself as he is by nature. It is with new eyes that he sees spiritual things in a correct manner. 'The natural man receiveth not the things of the Spirit of God: for they are foolishness unto him: neither can he know them, because they are spiritually discerned. But he that is spiritual judgeth all things, yet he himself is judged of no man.' The Christian is the true philosopher. He not only has knowledge of the most sublime of all the sciences, of which the wise men of this world are as destitute as the wild ass of the wilderness, but he has that discernment of human views and character which human wisdom never has attained. The Christian knows the philosopher better than the philosopher knows himself. Of all the sciences, the science of mind is the most sublime; and Christians have a knowledge of the mind of man which no mere philosopher can obtain by his art. The philosopher gives an account of himself and of others, and of his own notions and views, which every Christian can detect as delusive and unreal.

In this providential fact, we see the forbearance and condescension of Christ to his people, even when they are unreasonable. He graciously removes the doubts of Thomas, though he might justly have left him to perish in his presumptuous unbelief. From this we may be assured, that, in one way or other, the Lord will remove the doubts of his people with respect to the evidence of the gospel. If he will not give them that evidence which extravagance may rashly demand, he will keep them from such extravagance, or remove their doubts by opening their eyes to understand the proper evidence. This will be the same thing with presenting to their view and to their touch his hands and his side. He will assuredly overcome the unbelief and hardness of heart of the most obstinate of his chosen ones. If he was not provoked to give up Thomas, his patience cannot meet with a more extravagant case of incredulity. He could call a Saul of Tarsus in the midst of his furious enmity to him, and he did overcome the unbelief of the incredulous and obstinate Thomas. What a consolation is this to the believer! What thoughts of unbelief arise in the heart! And how Satan could perplex the mind of the highest saint on earth, none but the believer can have any conception. If we were for a few minutes, from a state of the most assured faith, to be given into the hands of Satan to sift us as wheat, how would our faith fail us! Who knows what effect the fiery darts of the wicked one would have upon our minds, if they were not quenched? And quenched they cannot be but on the shield of faith; and in the case supposed God permits that faith to fail. What, then, will support us? How shall we without dismay look into an eternal world? But though God may for a moment suffer us to be tried by the tempter, he will not suffer us to be tempted above what we are able, but will with the temptation make a way of escape, that we may be able to bear it. Our constant prayer to God ought to be, that he would not give us into the hands of Satan, or that he will continue to give us the shield of faith. In matters of so great moment, the mind, particularly at death, naturally looks for and wishes every evidence of the truth, and sometimes demands unreasonable evidence. Nothing but the blood of Jesus should be before our eyes; and we should always remember that we glorify God, not by doubting, but by believing his word. Were not Jesus present with his people in the time of their trial, and especially at the time of their death, nothing could deliver them from horror. That they are not only saved from fear, but enabled to rejoice and triumph in death, is the surest evidence that the gospel is true. It is not surprising that persons ignorant of the character of God, of their own character, and of the consequences of sin, should be stupidly unconcerned at death. But the Christian knows too much to be kept from the very agonies of hell, if he has not the light of heaven when he passes through the dark valley and shadow of death. In the removal of the doubts of reason, let us gain confidence that the Lord will not forsake us in the time of our need. To a Christian, who is deeply acquainted with his own weakness, hell itself is not a greater object of horror, than to be given up without assistance from God; to wrestle and combat with the prince of this world at the hour of death.

It is remarkable that the Lord, though he complied with the unreasonable demand for evidence in the case of Thomas, yet he would not listen to the request of the rich man in hell, for the conviction of his relations on earth. 'Then he said, I pray thee, therefore, father, that thou wouldest send him to my father's house: for I have five brethren; that he may testify unto them, lest they also come into this place of torment.' Did Abraham yield to the proposal, and admire the plan? No. 'Abraham saith unto him, They have Moses and the prophets; let them hear them. And he said, Nay, father Abraham: but if one went unto them from the dead, they will repent. And he said unto him, If they hear not Moses and the prophets, neither will they be persuaded though one rose from the dead.' Our sceptics are still calling for more or better evidence. If the gospel is true, they allege it should have evidence against which no man could find objection. Let them alone. Press on them the evidence that God has given of the truth of his gospel. If they believe not this, it will be found, in the day of judgment, that they have not rejected it from its insufficiency, but from their own enmity to the truth. Testimony is a sufficient ground of evidence; and if they reject the testimony of God by his apostles, they will justly perish.

And the same thing will hold true with respect to the denial of the testimony of God with regard to any particular doctrine, and any particular part. The enemies of the doctrine, or fact recorded, will allege a want of proof; and, on the authority of philosophical doctrines, will take on them to modify the testimony of God. They make the dogmas of human science an authority paramount to the testimony of God in the Scriptures. This is the boldness, the blasphemy of infidelity. If God has given his testimony on any part, it is evidence paramount in authority to every other. To prove the truth alleged on such authority, nothing is necessary but to show that it is the result of the fair exposition of the laws of language. Let God be true, and let all men be liars. Against the testimony of God the philosopher is not to be heard more than a convicted perjurer. Our Lord, even though, for his own wise purposes, he indulged Thomas, yet did not approve of his unbelief, nor of his demand. He did not ascribe his incredulity to greater talents, or greater caution, or greater concern about the truth, than were discovered by his brethren. On the contrary, he shows that they rather are blessed who will believe without such evidence as Thomas demanded. There are two extremes, equally to be avoided, into which men are prone to fall. Some believe without evidence, believe against all evidence, believe what all evidence, capable of being submitted to the mind of man, shows to be absurd and impossible. On the other hand, there are some who unreasonably refuse evidence that is sufficient, evidence which God has pronounced sufficient, and look on themselves as manifesting greater intellect, or greater wisdom, in demanding evidence of another kind, which God has not appointed. 'Thomas, because thou hast seen me, thou hast believed: blessed are they that have not seen, and yet have believed.'

116

The manner of the death of Christians adapted to glorify God

John 21:19

CHRISTIANS are often exposed to death or the denial of their Lord. They are always liable to innumerable dangers, and accidents, and diseases, that may take away their lives. Had they no security in the Divine protection, they could never be at peace. How gloomy would be the thought that chance would be the disposer of their lot; and that Divine Providence is not concerned in the manner and time of their death! What comfort is derived from the truth here presented to our view! *The manner of the death of Christ is adapted to glorify God.* When the inspired historian relates what Jesus said with respect to the manner of Peter's death, he adds, 'This spake he, signifying by what death he should glorify God.' It was a cruel death that was appointed to Peter. But was it not consolation, nay triumph, for him to hear that God was to be glorified by this cruel death of his servant? It is very natural for a Christian to turn his thoughts to the end of life, and to be concerned about the manner in which he may leave this world. It is not pleasant to think of the last struggles of life, and the agonies of death. We know not whether our exit shall be comparatively without pain, or whether it shall please God that we should writhe under the pangs of some terrible disease; and breathe out our souls amidst the torments of our bodies. We know not whether our death shall be sudden, or our tabernacle shall be taken down gradually by the process of a slow disease. We know not whether we shall meet death with the full possession of our faculties, and expire while we address our beloved relatives, or die in the delirium of fever, and know nothing of our death till we awake in the life of the eternal world. We know not whether we shall die in peace under the protection of law, or perish under the hand of the persecutor. We know not whether, in the last scene of life, we shall have a full view of heavenly glory, or whether Satan may be permitted to pursue us to the very banks of Jordan, and attempt to frighten us with the waters that are ready to overwhelm us. But this we know, and let it be enough for us to know this, that our death shall be for the glory of God; and that the time, and the manner, and all the circumstances of it, will be arranged by wisdom and love, as well as by Sovereign power. When we pass through the valley and shadow of death let us fear no evil. Jesus, the Shepherd of his flock, will be with us, and his rod and staff will comfort us. If Satan is permitted to annoy, we shall be enabled to quench his fiery darts with the shield of faith.

117

Population regulated by Providence

Acts 7:17

IT IS remarkable that the beginning of the history of Abraham's family by Isaac was distinguished by providential delays and hindrances to the increase of their numbers, while the other descendants were exceedingly multiplied and prosperous. The fathers of the promised numerous seed for a long time had no issue; and, at last, like the house of Ulysses, were confined to a single heir. Abraham was an old man before he was the father of Isaac, Isaac was a man of forty when he thought of a wife, and Jacob, though at last he was teased with the perplexities of a numerous polygamy, was upwards of seventy before he married. All this appears very strange to the carnal eye, looking at the fact in the same view with the former. But it is quite consistent with the ways of Providence, and manifests more clearly that the thing promised, when effected, has been effected by God. Till the term appointed for the seed of Abraham to enter into the possession of Canaan, there was no need of a very numerous progeny. Providence, therefore, did not increase the population. But when the time of putting them in possession of the promised land drew nigh, God altered his procedure, and Israel increased with great rapidity. 'But when the time of the promise drew nigh, which God had sworn to Abraham, the people grew and multiplied in Egypt.'

Malthus and the political economists may attempt to regulate population. So did Pharaoh. But they may as well attempt to regulate the winds. It is God who increases or diminishes the number of the inhabitants of the earth. It is impious in any government, by legislative enactments, to interfere with that which solely belongs to the prerogative of the Creator. Are rulers to deal with the human race as with cattle; and raise no more than the number for which they can find a market? Let men turn to God through the knowledge of his Son, and there will be no longer a complaint of dearth, scarcity, or famine. 'Then shall the earth yield her increase, and God, even our God, shall bless us.'

118

Dispersion of the church at Jerusalem, by the persecution on the death of Stephen

Acts 8

IF JESUS has all power in heaven and in earth; if his enemies cannot speak, nor move, nor breathe, without him, it may appear strange that his people should be persecuted, and his cause at any time trampled on. He must have great and wise purposes to be served by the event, when he suffers his people to be afflicted by wicked men for his sake. The Scriptures leave us not to conjecture these purposes. They bring them before us most explicitly. Persecution glorifies God, benefits the Christian as a trial of his faith, and purges the Church from the dross of hypocrisy. 'Beloved,' says Peter, 'think it not strange concerning the fiery trial which is to try you, as though some strange thing happened unto you: but rejoice inasmuch as ye are partakers of Christ's sufferings; that, when his glory shall be revealed, ye may be glad also with exceeding joy. If ye be reproached for the name of Christ, happy are ye; for the Spirit of glory and of God resteth upon you: on their part he is evil spoken of, but on your part he is glorified. But let none of you suffer as a murderer, or as a thief, or as an evildoer, or as a busybody in other men's matters. Yet if any man suffer as a Christian, let him not be ashamed; but let him glorify God on this behalf.'—1 Pet. 4:12-16. Here we see that persecution is both for the glory of Christ and

the eternal honour of his people. The same apostle tells us that the
'manifold temptations' endured by his people are for the end 'that
the trial of their faith being much more precious than of gold that
perisheth, though it be tried with fire, might be found unto praise,
and honour, and glory, at the appearing of Jesus Christ.' The Lord
Jesus makes use of persecution as a means of purging out the dross
of hypocrisy. In the furnace of persecution the real Christian is distinguished from the merely nominal. This is a great advantage to
the churches; and the purpose may be served as well by the ordinary
reproaches, insults, and injuries that believers are called to suffer, as
by the times when their enemies have the power of inflicting torture
and death.

Another reason why God exposes his people to persecution is, as
a chastisement for their unfaithfulness. God uses this as a whole-
some discipline, when his people corrupt his truths or his ordinances. Notwithstanding all the excellencies that we may find or
fancy in the early Christians, it is certain that they began very early
to corrupt the gospel, and mix their own wisdom with the appointments of God. The mystery of iniquity, we are expressly assured,
was at work even in the days of the apostles, and the persecutions
predicted by Peter are ascribed to '*judgment*.' 'For the time is come
that judgment must begin at the house of God; and if it first begin at
us, what shall the end be of them that obey not the gospel of God?'

If this is the case, what a call to all Christians to examine their
ways, and wait for the coming of Christ, with their lamps trimmed
and their lights burning! If God is about to pour out judgments on
our guilty land, let him have no controversy with his people. Let
them be found awake, and at their posts; and let everyone of them
be now employed as they 'would wish to be found employed at his
coming. If they would all act under this impression, glorious things
might be expected with respect to the city of our God. There is,
thanks be to God, a glorious number of true followers of the Lamb
in the present day. They are, it is true, much divided. But this is no
reason for inactivity in any. It is not necessary for any one of us to

call to the rest, saying, You can do no service to my Lord, unless in all things you receive my views, and follow me. We can act in concert against the common enemy, even when we cannot, from circumstances, fight regimental order. Let every soldier stand on the ground he occupies, and conquer there; and the field is ours. Caesar in one of his battles had no time to arrange his troops. But they knew their duty, and he knew his. Every man fought where he happened to stand, when he could not find his own proper place; and Caesar himself grasped a sword from him who stood next him, and fought as a common soldier. They carried the field after hard fighting. Soldiers of Christ, imitate these brave Romans. Fight, and you will conquer. If God's people are faithful, and alive to duty, he can cover their heads when he points his artillery against those around them. And if they are to be called to suffering, let it be for the Lord's sake, and not from judgment.

But the end of persecution which we are called to contemplate in this passage is its tendency to spread the gospel. When Christians are by persecution driven from their country, it is the means of carrying the gospel to other countries. This was on this occasion evidently the providential intention of the persecution which arose on the death of Stephen. 'And Saul was consenting unto his death. And at that time there was a great persecution against the church which was at Jerusalem; and they were all scattered abroad throughout the regions of Judea and Samaria, except the apostles. And devout men carried Stephen to his burial, and made great lamentation over him. As for Saul, he made havoc of the church, entering into every house, and haling men and women committed them to prison. Therefore they that were scattered abroad went every where preaching the word. Then Philip went down to the city of Samaria, and preached Christ unto them. And the people with one accord gave heed unto those things which Philip spake, hearing and seeing the miracles which he did.'—Acts 8:1-6. Here is a persecution cruel and bloody. But it is not a waste of blood and treasure on the part of the army of the Lord Jesus. The dominions of Immanuel their prince are greatly enlarged by it. By this means the city of Samaria received the gospel. And far and wide was the dispersion. 'Now they which were scattered abroad upon the persecution that arose about Stephen travelled as far as Phenice, and Cyprus, and Antioch, preaching the word to none but unto the Jews only. And some of them were men of Cyprus and Cyrene, which, when they were come to Antioch, spake unto the Grecians, preaching the Lord Jesus. And the hand of the Lord was with them: and a great number believed, and turned unto the Lord.'—Acts 11:19-21. Here are fruits of victory worth the blood and treasure expended in the procurement of it. Here is the wisdom of God making foolish the wisdom of the wise. The enemies of the gospel hunted the disciples as wild beasts. But in the Providence of the Lord, this carried them to many distant countries, and with them they carried the gospel. In like manner Providence works in every age. In our own country persecution hunted out those men of God who, by their flight, were ordained to plant the gospel in America. Similar facts may be pointed out without number. Even when civil constitutions give the protection of law, there are innumerable ways in which persecution may be excited, and Providence may disquiet the people of God in one place, that they may remove and carry the gospel to another. We should trace the hand of God in all his works; and the more we give ourselves to the study of Providence, the more clearly will we be convinced that Jehovah reigns on earth as well as in heaven.

119

Tranquillity and prosperity of the churches on the conversion of Saul

Acts 9:31

IT IS true that many useful purposes in the Divine Providence are served by persecution of the faith of Christ. It is equally true that persecution is always an evil in itself, and is only indirectly made subservient to the divine glory. The good that God effects by it is good brought out of evil. In its own nature it is calculated to injure, and would not only injure, but destroy the cause of God, were it not that his Almighty power and his wisdom can make the wrath of man to praise him. Instead, then, of being sought and longed for as a blessing, it ought to be deprecated and avoided as far as possible. Our Lord, therefore, charges us to pray that we enter not into temptation, because it is a grievous thing in itself; and unless we were upheld by the Almighty power of God, we should assuredly be overcome and fall. In this many of the earliest saints known to church history were to blame, and nothing shows more clearly a commencement, even at that time, of a defection from the faith, than the fanatical ambition that they had for the honour of martyrdom. They courted the stake and the teeth of the lions; and were displeased with those who endeavoured to save them, as if they had done them an injury. Christ does not command this. When they persecute you in this city, says he, flee you to another. We are to give our lives only when we must either yield them, or deny Christ. If we, out of ignorance, go beyond this, and throw away life without being called to it, the Lord, no doubt, will pardon our ignorance, but we will have no reward for ignorance. Ignatius was much to blame in this respect. His letters are rather a sort of pious raving about the glories of martyrdom, than an example of the strongest self-denial in parting with the thing of all things on earth most valuable—the life. He is like the warrior who is prodigal of life from the love of fame, and his own advantage from victory, rather than from a single eye to the authority and glory of his sovereign. Would that general deserve approbation who would grieve that a part of the dominions of his sovereign should be saved by the voluntary submission of the enemy, and that victory was not gained by the effusion of an ocean of blood?

Even in modern times, when, alas! there are no symptoms of the zeal of Ignatius, the common maxim, which in one sense is true, is generally quoted in a very false sense — 'The blood of the martyrs is the seed of the church.' Many quote this maxim, as if they longed for persecution, and as if they considered times of trial as the halcyon days of the church. Neither Scripture nor experience warrants this doctrine. God may always bring good out of evil, and always make persecution tend to spread the gospel somewhere. But persecution, while it may send the gospel to distant places, may almost extinguish it in the place where it exists. It may, indeed, afterwards arise from the ashes into new life. But it may also be in a manner extinguished for ages. Witness France, Bohemia, and many of the best reformed countries at the Reformation. They are still in the ashes of the conflagration. And, at all events, whatever is to be the result, the immediate consequence to many is a fall to rise no more. In every time of persecution, multitudes deny Christ. This ought to make everyone dread it even more than death; because no man could stand, unless God should uphold him. Instead, then, of fanatically congratulating one another that times of glorious persecution are shortly ready to arise, we ought to pray earnestly and constantly that God may not, in his Providence, lead us into temptation. And let us not only, being aware of our own weakness, and well informed of our duty in this respect, pray against times of suffering; but let us labour incessantly, and with every talent, to do the will of God, that so, when he comes, we may be found, like good servants, doing his will, and waiting for his coming. Whatever our hand finds to do, let us do it with all our might. This, we are sure, is right, whether times of prosperity or times of adversity are at the door. This is the course in which we shall have peace and confidence now; and this is the course which Jesus will approve when he comes to judgment. 'Well done, good and faithful servant, enter thou into the joy of thy Lord.' Let us not be ashamed of any truth, or of any duty. They who laugh at us now will shortly weep and mourn. Let every soldier of Christ attack the enemy with whatever weapons God has put into his hands. The metaphysician affects to prove not only the uselessness, but the absurdity of Christianity. Physical science insults the records of Holy Scripture by pretended discoveries, deduced from facts in the most philosophical manner; and a multitude of the undecided, who still wear the livery of the Lord Jesus, hover between the camp of Israel and the camp of the uncircumcised, under the pretence of mediating between the contending armies, and effecting a reconciliation in a way that will do full justice to the claims of both. A new philosophy has been invented by the prince of darkness for the vulgar; and the profane and ignorant rabble are made to talk with an appearance of the wisdom of Socrates. Heresy and fanaticism appear in all their forms, and almost in every party. If it were possible, surely, among them, they would deceive the very elect. Soldiers of Christ, arise; put on your armour! Onward, onward, brave companions of Christ. Fear not the multitude nor the talents of your adversaries. The Lord sits in the heavens, and shall laugh them to scorn. He entered into Jerusalem into the midst of his enemies, surrounded only by the body guards of little children singing hosannas. It is glorious to be called to fight the battles of the Lord: it is peculiarly glorious to be called to the encounter of the enemy at a time when they are so powerful and so determined. Dread not the number nor the fierceness of their hosts. Think of the resolution of Jonathan and his armour-bearer. 'Come and let us go over unto the garrison of these uncircumcised: it may be that the Lord will work for us: for there is no restraint to the Lord to save by many or by few.'

If it is wrong to wish for persecution, it is equally wrong to provoke it. As in the early ages of Christianity, some persons offered
themselves unnecessarily to danger and death, so at present some
seem desirous of provoking hostility and of exciting persecution.
They seem to think that they are never strictly faithful, except they
are giving studied offence. This is wrong: this serves not the gospel,
but effectually injures its progress. We are to give no offence to Jew
or Gentile, or to the church of God. Paul was faithful, and by that
made many enemies; but Paul, instead of wishing to give offence,
laboured to become all things to all men, that he might gain some.
There is offence enough in the cross, without adding any thing to
it. Let us profess, all the truth, and practise all the duties which
we have learned from the Scripture: let us defend that truth and
practice against all their enemies. But let us not suffer for our own
whims. Let it be God's truth only for which we can contend. Then
we will be enabled to despise ridicule and reproach; and with exul-
tation anticipate the promise to faithfulness, when the Lord comes
to judgment. We ought not to preach the gospel as a cruel magistrate would read the riot act, merely as a form to enable us lawfully to fire on the crowd. We ought to wish earnestly, and to pray
fervently, and to strive with all the zeal of love, to bring the opposer
and the persecutor to the knowledge of Christ.

In the fact before us in this passage, we see how easily the Providence of God turns the storm into a calm. By the conversion of Saul
of Tarsus, he gave rest to the churches. 'Then had the churches rest
throughout all Judaea, and Galilee, and Samaria, and were edified;
and walking in the fear of the Lord, and in the comfort of the Holy
Ghost, were multiplied.'

Here we see that, if persecution is always overruled by Providence for the good of the truth, the direct means of edifying and
multiplying believers is by giving rest to the churches. Many new
churches were planted through the means of the late persecution
which arose on the death of Stephen; but these churches were all
edified and multiplied in the time of rest from persecution. Let us

not, then, wish for persecution, but let us use that rest which we enjoy in energy of efforts for the prosperity of Zion.

Here we see also that Providence can give peace and rest to the churches as easily in countries which are arbitrary and tyrannical in their government as in the freest states. There is no external blessing more valuable to the Christian than a free government. When he enjoys liberty of conscience, he ought to be grateful to God, and grateful to the civil constitution which confers on him so valuable a privilege. Nothing is more unbecoming in a Christian than to encourage petulance, discontent, or a spirit of insubordination in the country in which he lives. But Christians who enjoy not this invaluable privilege ought not to be discouraged. They should remember that the supreme government of any country is in the hands of their Lord; and that he can protect them under a despot, as well as under a government limited by law. Here the churches have rest even in the countries in which they had been persecuted, without any change of rulers, or of the constitution of government.

Who is so blind as not to see Providence here? In Russia, the Christian ought not to meddle with those who should conspire to restrain despotism. His God can give him peace even from an absolute sovereign, even when that absolute sovereign might be himself an enemy of God. When God desires to change a wicked and tyrannical government, his Providence will employ the hands of the wicked to effect his purpose. His children, in all cases, should obey the existing powers, in all things not contrary to the laws of God. Another observation equally true, and equally important, and almost equally obvious, is, that as God can give rest to his churches under the most despotic governments, so persecution may take place in one form or other, in the most free countries under heaven. In every country, as a matter of fact, there is persecution under various forms. But even where there is protection by law, there may be annoyance and danger of life in the service of God. Who is ignorant that, under the British government, in some parts of the empire, a disciple of Christ could not oppose the superstitions of the people but at the hazard of life? Even where we live, then, in the countries that are blessed with liberty, we must, in the service of Christ, look to his Providence for protection. We may have liberty as an act of legislation, but the violence of irreligion may render it useless. What, then, I would wish to impress on all Christians is this: In free countries, let them not trust to their civil privileges for protection. Let their strength be the Rock of Israel. In despotic countries let them not be discouraged. If they have correct views of the duty of Christians to civil government, there will be no just grounds of suspicion against them, even to the most tyrannical rulers. It is to be regretted, that though the nature of civil subjection is taught in Scripture, with a clearness, and precision, and fullness beyond almost any other subject, yet few, very few, Christians fully understand it. They are all perfectly willing to obey government as long as government patronises themselves and their religion; but there are comparatively few who will not murmur when they are called to conscientious submission even under tyranny, and oppression, and persecution. Right views of Providence are as essential on this subject as right views of civil subjection. If Christians see their Lord ruling with an invisible arm in every thing that takes place on the earth, they will have no apprehension from the unreserved civil obedience that he allows them to give to their rulers. But if they overlook this, or look on Providence as ruling only by general design and original arrangement, they will wince when they feel the lash. The well taught Christian can see the Lord presiding in the fires of his execution. All things work together for the good of them who love God.

120

Means of detecting Simon Magus

Acts 8:18

IN THE awful sovereignty of God ungodly men will, from time to time, creep into the best governed churches; and they serve a purpose in the Divine wisdom. It is an opportunity for them to discover the deep depravity of their nature, and to try the faithfulness of the true disciples, when they are manifested. In judgment occasion of offence is given to the world, and unsound professors are, by heresies and licentious doctrines speciously introduced by persons under a cover of godliness, drawn aside from the truth. 'Woe unto the world,' says Christ, 'because of offences! For it must needs be that offences come; but woe to that man by whom the offence cometh!'

The Providence of God, however, will usually in course of time discover such persons. Sometimes they will either broach heresies, or fall into the heresies of others. "But there were false prophets also among the people, even as there shall be false teachers among you, who privily shall bring in damnable heresies, even denying the Lord that bought them, and bring upon themselves swift destruction. And many shall follow their pernicious ways; by reason of whom the way of truth shall be evil spoken of. And through covetousness shall they with feigned words make merchandise of you: whose judgment now of a long time lingereth not, and their damnation slumbereth not.'—2 Pet. 2:1-3. Here we see that in Divine Providence the authors of heresies are admitted into the churches to manifest their opposition to the truth; and to discover all who are disaffected to it. Many are led into the pernicious ways. But none are led but those who are in heart unacquainted with the truth. 'For there must be also heresies among you, that they which are approved may be made manifest among you.' This is the use of heresies in a church of Christ. They separate the gold from the dross. They are a test to ascertain the genuine disciple.

While the unsoundness of the profession of some is manifested by their false doctrine, others are discovered by providential occasions given them to discover themselves by licentious conduct, and falling into gross sin. Others, like Judas, are discovered by providential occasions to excite their covetousness. Simon the sorcerer almost immediately discovered his ignorance of the gospel which he had professed, by making a proposal which implied that he thought that the gift of God might be purchased with money. This proved that he had not been enlightened by the Spirit of God, nor truly made a partaker of his grace. Accordingly, Peter instantly denounced him as a child of the devil. 'Thy money perish with thee, because thou hast thought that the gift of God may be purchased with money.' Simon was not, properly speaking, a hypocrite. This implies that the person is not sincere in his profession, and was the usual character of the Pharisees, who knew that they were not the religious characters which they affected to be considered. Simon, though still in the gall of bitterness and bond of iniquity, considered himself a disciple, and really believed in Christ, in his own view of his character. That he believed is expressly asserted. 'Then Simon himself believed also: and when he was baptized, he continued with Philip, and wondered, beholding the miracles and signs which were done.' There is not the least appearance of insincerity in his profession. Where, then, it may be asked, was his faith deficient? Where is the Divine declaration, proclaiming that 'he who believeth shall be saved'? If Simon is granted to have sincerely believed, is it not true, that a man may have the faith of Christ to-day, and lose it tomorrow for ever? There is not the smallest difficulty in the matter. Though Simon sincerely believed, according to his own view of Christ, yet his after-conduct proved that his view was false. The faith that is salvation is faith in Christ according to his proper character, implying the knowledge of God in Christ, which nothing but the teaching of the Holy Spirit can communicate. Of this Simon was destitute, though, in his false view of Christ's character, he sincerely believed that his pretensions were true. The great body of the world, under a profession of Christianity, believe in this sense. When it is denied that they believe in Christ, there is no need to assert that they are insincere in their profession of faith. In fact, this way of convincing them cannot succeed; for they are conscious of sincerity in believing what they confess about Christ and the way of salvation. The best way to convince them is, not to charge them as hypocrites, but to show them that as long as they remain under the dominion of sin, they must be ignorant of God and his Christ; and that their faith is not the faith of the gospel, to which eternal life is promised. It was on this ground solely that Peter proceeded with Simon the sorcerer.

By the miracles of Christ multitudes believed on Jesus, who had not the faith of the gospel. 'Now when he was in Jerusalem at the passover, in the feast day, many believed in his name, when they saw the miracles which he did. But Jesus did not commit himself unto them, because he knew all men, and needed not that any should testify of man: for he knew what was in man.'—John 2:23-25. These persons truly believed that Jesus was the promised Messiah, but the conduct of Jesus showed that he considered that they believed in him under imperfect views of his character. It is by the thing believed, and not by the definitions of faith, that such persons must be detected.

In like manner, the whole multitudes, after witnessing the miracle of the feeding of the people with a few loaves and fishes, would have taken Jesus and made him a king. But these very facts proved their unbelief. His kingdom was not of this world, and his salvation was not a deliverance which he was to effect for his people from the Roman government, but the redemption of the soul.

There are many such apparent contradictions in the Scriptures, and they who are 'unlearned' in the things of God wrest them to their own destruction. There is perfect harmony between the assertion that Simon himself believed, and that which declares, 'He that believeth shall be saved.' On this principle, also, must be explained the temporary faith of those who receive the seed on stony ground, and 'believe for a while.' They were sincere in their belief, but their turning away from a profession of the truth proves that they never understood it; and, consequently, that they possessed not that faith to which is annexed the promise of salvation.

Here is the sovereignty of God in a strong and striking light. Who would act in their own affairs as God here does in his? He not only suffers the seducer to enter into his camp, to spread disaffection in the ranks, but he, by his Providence, designedly effects this. When a shining professor of the gospel manifests that he never was in the truth, it opens the mouths of the enemies of God, and they take occasion to glory as if all Christians were hypocrites. Well, we cannot help this; and it grieves us that it is so. But God could have ordered it otherwise, yet he has ordered it so. He designedly gives blasphemers an opportunity of opening their mouths; and the advantage that they thus take against the truth is evidence of the deep depravity of human nature, and of enmity to God himself. All this will not cause the loss of one soul to Jesus. It will manifest the hostility of the world to him, and draw his people nearer to himself. It will diminish their confidence in themselves, and make them sit with Mary at the feet of their Master. All things work together for the good of his people, and the very reproaches brought on them by the fall of false brethren is not an exception. Every raving fanatic, every licentious professor of the gospel, will be reckoned as the legitimate children of that faith which justifies the ungodly. But the gospel disowns them, and the foundation of God standeth sure, having this seal, The Lord knoweth them that are his.

How admirable is the Providence of God in detecting Simon the sorcerer! The very thing that confirmed the faith of the true disciples was the means of manifesting that he was not in the truth. The miracles wrought by the hands of Peter were the occasion that Providence employed to manifest the true character of this man of Belial. Instead of rejoicing in the display of the power of Christ, as an evidence of his being sent of God, and as the means of convincing the world, this ambitious man wished the power of working miracles only as a means of gratifying his carnal purposes. Let us, in the fall of Simon, bless God, who watches over the churches, and who, though he designedly, for wise purposes, gives occasion for the admission of his enemies, yet will manifest them by his Providence, when they have served the end which he designed by their admission. And let him who thinketh he standeth take heed lest he fall. We stand only by faith. Remember Simon Magus.

121

Herod eaten by worms

Acts 12:23

THE death of Herod was a judgment from the Almighty, yet it was providentially executed. He was 'eaten of worms.' The medical faculty, had they been called on a coroner's inquest, might have found nothing but natural disease, induced by the previous state of the body. But Divine inspiration teaches us, that through the means of disease God inflicts his judgments. This fact is of importance, as it establishes the truth that God, as the Ruler of the world, executes judgment in his Providence; and affords us a key to his providential conduct. Let it be observed, that this is not a miracle in immediate connection with the gospel, performed through the apostles in confirmation of the truth. It was a judgment executed by God, without any instrumentality; and for the purpose of vindicating his own glory as God. It had no reference to the gospel. It is a thing as much to be expected at this day as it was in the age of miracles. Should any, then, suppose that this judgment was among the miracles of the age of the apostles, and that it is unwarrantable or superstitious to interpret any similar fact as a judgment in our time, or in any other age, they speak in ignorance. Such an interference of Almighty power is as much to be believed in Britain at this day, should a similar thing occur, as it was to be in Judaea in the days of the apostles. God smote Herod, not for opposition to the gospel, but for not giving God the glory, and thereby usurping the prerogatives of God.

It is quite easy to give this interpretation of such facts a ridiculous appearance, and to represent it in the class of superstitious conceits. A philosopher might have said on the occasion of the death of Herod, that it was true that death followed the conduct specified. But what reason, he might have asked, is there to believe that Herod's conduct was connected with his death? This is superstition. It infers a general law from a single fact. Herod's death followed his impiety, but it would have happened without his impiety. It was not the consequence of his usurpation of the honours of God, but was the effect of natural disease. In this way exactly philosophers now reason; and when a thing can be accounted for by natural causes, they refuse to recognize the hand of God.

That calamity ought sometimes to be viewed as judgment is here asserted by inspiration. Herod was smitten by the angel of the Lord, because he gave not God the glory. When conduct is notoriously derogatory to the honour of God, and when calamity immediately and remarkably follows it, we have the warrant of inspiration to consider it as judgment. Indeed, if there is not a kind of self-evidence in the thing, God's design would be frustrated. He designs to manifest his displeasure at the conduct, yet such displeasure, upon this supposition, cannot be assuredly known. The thing, then, must have its own evidence. And as a matter of fact, whatever may be the hardihood of philosophical infidelity, the bulk of men will ever recognize the hand of God in judgment. Heathens, as well as men under the light of Christianity, recognize this. We should not, then, from the dread of the scorn of infidel philosophy, refuse to recognize the hand of God in the punishment of audacious rebels even in this world. This is necessary occasionally for the purposes of moral government.

The occasion of the judgment on Herod intimates the kind of

wickedness most likely to be visited with immediate judgment. It is not the sensual and grossly vicious that are most likely to be the objects of it. Such persons have no defenders; and if any are to be given up to future misery, all persons will point out these to punishment. The sin of Herod was the usurpation of the honour of God. God is jealous of his own glory; and in the government of this world he marks his displeasure at every thing that robs him of this, more than he does at any other sins. Herod, who gave not God the glory, is punished with a painful and loathsome death, while the multitude of profligates are allowed to go to the grave without any mark of divine vengeance. And I may appeal to facts, in daily events, that judgments befall the profane scorner, the blasphemer of God, and the violator of the Lord's day, more than the vilest outcasts of society. Men think sin against God a trifle, and reckon the injury done to their fellows as almost the only crime. On the contrary, God reckons sin against himself the chief of sins; and even our sin against men derives its greatest guilt from its relation to God.

Undoubtedly some may err on the other side, and find judgments where they do not exist. But if the fact here recorded is part of the word of God, divine judgments are sometimes providentially executed upon notorious insulters of the divine character. To explain such facts where they occur, without any reference to divine interposition, is infidelity. God reigns, and though he generally hides himself, even in the manifestation of his power, he occasionally shows himself even to the world.

The death of Herod is proof of a particular Providence. Philosophers talk of Providence, and speak gratefully of a gracious and kind Providence. But many of them mean no more by Providence than the original establishment of the laws of nature, and the Providence of design and arrangement. God, according to them, has nothing to do immediately with the occurrences that take place in the world, more than the maker of a clock has to do with the motion of the machine after it is set a-going. The fact before us refutes this impious doctrine. Even though Herod was eaten of worms, yet it was by being smitten by the angel of the Lord that the worms did their duty. Jehovah is not like the gods of Epicurus. Attention to his works is no trouble to him. He wearies not in working. He is immediately present with all his works, and, by his power, the things that are made are upheld in existence.

122

Contention between Paul and Barnabas

Acts 15:36-39

'AND some days after Paul said unto Barnabas, Let us go again and visit our brethren in every city where we have preached the word of the Lord, and see how they do. And Barnabas determined to take with them John, whose surname was Mark. But Paul thought it not good to take him with them, who departed from them from Pamphylia, and went not with them to the work. And the contention was so sharp between them, that they departed asunder one from the other: and so Barnabas took Mark, and sailed unto Cyprus.'—Acts 15:36-39. What! A quarrel between two of the apostles of Christ? Shame! Shame! Tell it not in Gath, publish it not in Askelon. But it really happened, and has been told both in Gath and Askelon. Divine inspiration has blazed it over the world. Then it must be for our good, although it was their sin. The thing, then, happened in Providence for a useful lesson to Christians in all ages. It shows us what man is. The pretended ministers of Christ have been deified, and God, who foresaw this, has in his Providence shown that even his best servants are sinful and imperfect creatures. Were it of any consequence to judge between the brethren, and settle the amount of the fault of each, there appears sufficient ground to believe that Barnabas was most to blame. It is a suspicious thing that he took the part of his kinsman. In the kingdom of Christ there is no carnal kindred. No man is to be known after the flesh. No man is to be brought into a church, or kept in it, or put into office, on account of carnal relation. Paul, it appears from the document, acted not from private hostility, but from the conduct of Mark. There was good reason to be reluctant to employ the man who had already, in a manner, deserted his post. He might be still reckoned a Christian, yet be accounted unfit for any office or place of trust. Paul, however, on another occasion, shows that he acted towards Mark from no improper motive, as he fully recommended him to the reception of the brethren, as soon as he was convinced of his returning to his devotedness and duty. 'Marcus, sister's son to Barnabas, (touching whom ye received commandment; if he come unto you, receive him.)'

We are sometimes told that infallibility is not impeccability, and reminded of the contention between Paul and Barnabas. Very true, impeccability is not to be expected in man. But there is a mighty difference between impeccability and monstrosity of vice. The best of God's servants have their faults. But monsters of iniquity none of them can be. With all the evil and infirmities of the children of God, still they must ever be distinguished by their fruits. All who are imbued with the gospel must deny all ungodliness and worldly lusts, living soberly, righteously, and godly in this world.

123

Paul protected by Gallio's enlightened views of the duties of the magistrate's office

Acts 18:14

A S THE world, in general, are enemies to the gospel, it might be supposed that protection to the Christian might be impossible under despotic governments. Shall the lamb be safe under the paws of the lion? Yes, as safe as by the side of the dam in an inclosed fold. Divine Providence can devise means of protection when there is no protection but in the capricious resolves of an absolute tyrant. Paul was brought before the judgment-seat, but the philosophic and enlightened views of Gallio refused to hear their complaint. Yet Gallio, as a philosopher and man of learning, would have been as great an enemy to the gospel, had he taken the trouble to inquire into its nature and pretensions, as were the Jews themselves. Indeed, the men of science and pretended virtue are usually more virulent enemies of the gospel than are the vilest of the vulgar. They have something to lose, and the gospel strips them of all their glory. But Gallio seems to have been a man who did not trouble himself to inquire into the nature of the dispute between the Jews and the Christians, and this was the protection of Paul. Gallio justly considered that it did not belong to the office of the magistrate to judge between different systems of religion. He had nothing to do but with crime, considered with respect to society. In this he was much more enlightened than many Christians. Gallio, then, was the very man that fitted the situation according to the purpose of Divine Providence at this time. The character and views of this magistrate were among the wise appointments of an overruling Providence to deliver the herald of salvation on this occasion. From the character and views of Gallio, Paul had deliverance from his enemies. Gallio fitted God's purpose on this occasion as exactly as if he had been an angel of heaven. 'And when Gallio was the deputy of Achaia, the Jews made insurrection with one accord against Paul, and brought him to the judgment-seat, saying, This fellow persuadeth men to worship God contrary to the law. And when Paul was now about to open his mouth, Gallio said unto the Jews, If it were a matter of wrong or wicked lewdness, O ye Jews, reason would that I should bear with you: but if it be a question of words and names, and of your law, look ye to it; for I will be no judge of such matters. And he drave them from the judgment-seat.' — Acts 18:12-16. There is one remarkable providential circumstance in this fact, to which I would call particular attention. Paul was ready to speak, and to defend himself. Who is it that at first is not inclined to regret that he was not permitted? He would have doubtless, in his defence, declared the gospel, and testified before the governor and many others with respect to Christ. This privilege, on other occasions, he availed himself of to great purpose, and commended the truth to the consciences of many who would not otherwise have had an opportunity of hearing him. Yet, on this occasion, Gallio prevented this. He very justly considered it as unnecessary, because the very accusation alleged by his enemies contained no crime. The governor, then, was not called to hear the defence, as he was not called to examine the accusation. No doubt, had God had any good purpose to serve by Paul's speaking, an opportunity would have been given him to speak. But his silence on this occasion served the purpose of Providence more than his defence would have done. Gallio needed no arguments to acquit the prisoner; and if Paul had proceeded to exhibit the distinguishing features of the gospel, the cool, the impartial, the enlightened judge, might have been turned into the furious persecutor. Nothing will make a philosopher grind his teeth but the gospel. His icy soul will boil like a furnace when he speaks of the doctrine that humbles the pride of man. The man who will apologize for the extravagance of the most frantic fanatics will denounce the friends of Paul's gospel as the enemies of mankind. This, in fact, is exemplified in the two great Roman historians, Suetonius and Tacitus. These writers can find no words adequately to express their contempt and hatred of the followers of Christ. And in modern times, is there not more virulence used by philosophers in speaking about the friends of a pure gospel, than there is when mention is made of Joanna Southcote?[1]

Yet it is wonderful to find this enlightened governor, who so plainly pointed out the unreasonableness of calling men to account to the State for their religious opinions, unable to distinguish the true province of the magistrate in matters to which it really extends. 'Then all the Greeks took Sosthenes, the chief ruler of the synagogue, and beat him before the judgment-seat. And Gallio cared for none of these things.' Here, Gallio, you are wrong. Though it is not your duty to judge in matters of other men's religion, yet you should judge in matters of assault. Whether Sosthenes was a friend or an enemy of Paul, he should have been protected from violence, and his assaulters should have been severely punished. A magistrate has no right to judge in disputes about religion, but he has a right to judge in acts of violence committed about religion. Yet, with all the superior light of our times, instances might be found, in which civil authorities refuse to take cognizance of a matter of violence, because it has been committed about religion. Even in Parliament we will hear it more than insinuated that the religion of the great mass of the people should not be spoken against. Even those who are eternally canting about the freedom of religion may often be detected in speaking thus. Is there no part of the British dominions

[1] Joanna Southcote, or Southcott (1750–1814). The daughter of a Devon farmer, she claimed to possess supernatural gifts in about 1792. Setting herself up as a prophetess, she wrote and dictated prophecies in rhyme. She then announced herself as the woman spoken of in Revelation 12:1–6. At the age of sixty-four she affirmed that she was pregnant and would be delivered of the new Messiah, the Shiloh of Genesis 49:10. The date of 19 October 1814 was that fixed for the birth, but Shiloh failed to appear, and it was given out that she was in a trance. She died not long after. The official date of death is given as 27 December 1814; however, it is likely that she died the previous day, as her followers retained her body for some time, in the belief that she would be raised from the dead. They agreed to its burial only after it began to decay. — P.

in which violence would be unpunished, if committed against those who expose the dogmas of a powerful party?

Liberty of conscience is a matter of the utmost importance to the Christian. Yet it appears to me, that, even in this country, we enjoy it, not so much from a real discernment, on the part of statesmen, of the true boundary of civil government, as from a kind of political necessity. If any one body were so dominant that it could crush all others, I would not wish to owe my liberty to its forbearance, from an enlightened view of duty. Persecution is natural to man, and the children of this world will never bear the gospel if they could crush it. It is to Divine Providence that we owe this invaluable privilege; and whatever be the means which he employs to bestow it on us, we ought to give him the praise. We ought to be thankful for the blessings of a free government, but it is idolatry and ingratitude to God to ascribe to the wisdom and benevolence of rulers that which is due to the Ruler of the world. Shall that praise be given to infidel statesmen, which is due to that Providence that employs the policy of rulers to effect his purposes? We ought to obey the very worst government that God puts over us. But we ought not to give to the very best that praise that is due only to God.

124

Paul preserved by the Recorder of Ephesus

Acts 19

PAUL was never in more imminent danger than on the present occasion, and Divine inspiration gives us here a specimen of one of the ways in which Providence works in the preservation of Christians. The eye of the wise man of this world sees nothing here but the puppets; the hand behind the screen is entirely hid from him.

With all his wisdom he is but a mere child in the knowledge of the works of God. 'Rise, and stand upon thy feet,' says Jesus to Paul at his conversion, 'for I have appeared unto thee for this purpose, to make thee a minister and a witness, both of those things which thou hast seen, and of those things in the which I will appear unto thee; delivering thee from the people, and from the Gentiles, unto whom now I send thee.' And here he does wonderfully deliver him out of the very mouths of ravenous beasts. The whole city was in a tumult, excited by Demetrius and the craftsmen, who thought their craft in danger by the overturning of idolatry. The people in a body rushed into the theatre; and when Paul was about to enter, he was providentially prevented by the disciples, and other men of chief distinction, who were friendly to the apostle. Paul himself yielded to their entreaties, though, on other occasions, nothing could stop him. God, it is true, could have preserved him in the theatre; but he works by means, and not usually by miracles. On this occasion he chose to preserve his servant by providentially keeping him out of the place of danger.

But Paul, though not in the assembly, might be found for vengeance, and his friends were most likely objects of revenge. The people were become frantic with rage, and were ready to execute any work that Satan might point out to them. How admirable is the Providence of God in soothing the infuriated passions of this hellish mob! By the prudence, and coolness, and skill in managing the passions of the multitude, possessed by one man, Providence restored tranquillity. There is nothing in all this, it is true, but what is perfectly natural, and which takes place on many other occasions. How, stupid Infidel, must Providence act against the nature of which he is the author, in order to prove that it is Providence that works? God, in his Providence, works by natural means, and hides himself, by this, from the eye of an unbelieving world. But I have many questions to ask thee, Infidel, on this matter. Why was such a prudent man prepared for this occasion? Of the hundreds of men in power, even in the highest seats of power; how few of them possess such knowledge of human nature, as was displayed by this recorder of Ephesus? Not only did he display an uncommon knowledge of human nature, but the utmost address in managing the passions of the mob. He played his instrument so skilfully, that he hushed every passion which disturbed his purpose. Every topic that the utmost skill of a Demosthenes could employ in oratory, was employed in the extemporaneous effusion of the eloquence of the Ephesian magistrate. Had all his life been given to the study of rhetoric, he could not have selected his topics with more skill: had all his life been given to the practice of oratory, he could not have acquitted himself with more ability. Yet, after all, it was a speech that no Christian could imitate. Here, then, is the wisdom of God: the defender of Paul must be a heathen. He must sanction the religion of the people. This fitted him to appease them. Had the recorder become a convert to Paul, he could not have successfully defended his client. Here, then, is wisdom.

But there is another consideration. Tell me, Infidel, why was this idolatrous magistrate so intent upon saving Paul and his companions? With all his skill and address as an orator, he might have declined to use his talents in defence of the apostle. Why did not his liberality take the same turn with that of Gallio? Why did he concern himself about the matter? Why did he not refuse not only to decide in a religious question, but to keep the peace, when the quarrel was about religion? All, all was of Providence. Jesus fulfilled his promise to Paul, and quieted the mob at Ephesus as truly as he did the storm at sea. 'Peace, be still; and immediately there was a great calm.' His power over the minds of men is as great as over the winds.

In this fact, let us find a key to Providence, in the manner of delivering his people out of the hands of their enemies in every age. How many times are Christians defended and delivered by the hands of men as destitute of the knowledge of God as the very men who pursue them! Christians, when this takes place, fail not to give God the glory. Be not like the beast that knows not the Providence that preserves it from death. Be grateful even to the most wicked men on earth, when they are the means of preservation to you in the time of your danger or trouble. This is your duty, and never forget them in your prayers to God. But in the means of your deliverance, never forget the ultimate author of your deliverance.

125

Fall of Eutychus from a window in the third loft, during the preaching of Paul at Troas

Acts 20:9

' AND there sat in a window a certain young man named Eutychus, being fallen into a deep sleep: and as Paul was long preaching, he sunk down with sleep, and fell down from the third loft, and was taken up dead.' Have you ever seen anything providential in the fall of Eutychus? If not, you have never read this part of the Scriptures as the word of God. At least you have never seen what the Spirit of God here sets before your eyes. This fact is not recorded to gratify curiosity, or to excite interest by the relation of a surprising accident. It is not like a newspaper account of a young man falling in his sleep from the top of a night coach. This is the word of God, and it is profitable for our edification. The accident evidently happens for the purpose of confirming and comforting the disciples, as well as for the conviction of all who witnessed the miracle of the restoration to life. It was indeed a late hour, yet it was an interesting occasion, and though an individual might chance to be overcome with sleep, this could be the case with few. How did it happen that the only man who is said to be on that occasion overcome with sleep sat in so dangerous a situation? How many chances were on the other side? That this young man should sit in this window was as one to every individual of the crowd—one perhaps to thousands. Surely, then, there was the hand of Providence in his being in that situation. But when we have got him in his place, why was he not discovered in his sleep by some who sat near him, or at least had him in their view? It is strange that in such a situation no one took notice of him till he fell. But fall he must, and, therefore, all circumstances conspire to bring about the event. Paul was preaching, and the gospel must be confirmed by a most interesting miracle. This divine interposition was peculiarly adapted to give joy and consolation to the disciples. It was not only, like other miracles, proof of the gospel, but it relieved them from great distress, and comforted them by turning sorrow into joy. It gave much greater comfort than if the accident had not happened. 'And they brought the young man alive, and were not a little comforted.' There is more joy on a release from danger, than if danger had not made its appearance. The shepherd rejoices more over the lost sheep on its recovery, than over the whole flock that were not in danger. This, then, was a noble close to Paul's discourse at Troas.

Reader, you were not in the window at Troas, but you have had, it is likely, some escapes for your life. There are few individuals who cannot look back to some narrow escapes, and wonderful preservations. Ascribe all to Providence, and be confirmed in your belief of that ever-watchful care that the Ruler of the world has over all his creatures, but especially over his own peculiar people. Think also of the providential designs that your heavenly Father has, when he permits accidents to befall you. In one way or other it is for his own glory, and for your good. Is it no slight advantage to you to give you an occasion of gratitude to your protector, and of recognizing his hand in your deliverance?

And afflictive accidents teach a similar lesson to relatives when the object of their affection is removed by them. It was on this occasion necessary that Eutychus should be restored to life. But such accidents may be to death; and for the unspeakable advantage not only of the individuals to whom they happen, but also to the survivors. It may be overruled for a very general blessing on those connected. If we are called to glorify God by a very painful death, throughout eternity there will be no cause of regret; and others may be blessed by the occasion of our sufferings. More complete devotedness to God, and deadness to the world, with all its vanities, is a rich recompense for the acuteness of our distress in parting with beloved relatives. God's sovereignty is always to his people in wisdom and in love. This is the difference between sovereignty in God and sovereignty in man. We dread the sovereignty of man, because we have no security of its being exercised in mercy, or even in justice: we rejoice in the sovereignty of God, because we are sure it is always exercised for the good of his people. The missionary may sink with the ship that was to carry him to the place of his intended labours; but the sovereignty, through which we cannot see, may be both for the glory of God and the good of his servant, who is crowned with laurel before entering the field. A Christian may fall from his horse or from his feet, and die. And, as to Providence, is it not the same as if he had caught a fever or a cold, which issued in death? Let us, then, look to the Providence of our God by night and by day: let us see his hand in all our afflictions, and in all our deliverances.

126

Preservation of Paul from the Jews in the temple

Acts 21:31

ANOTHER escape for your life, Paul. Never were you in greater danger. The murderers have you in their hands, and they are in the very act of beating you to death. But you are saved by Providence, without a miracle. 'And as they went about to kill him, tidings came unto the chief captain of the band, that all Jerusalem was in an uproar. Who immediately took soldiers and centurions, and ran down unto them: and when they saw the chief captain and the soldiers, they left beating of Paul.' What a happy thing that tidings of the tumult were carried to the chief captain! But especially, how providential was it that the tidings reached him in time! The victim of vengeance might have been immolated before the arrival of the officers. And it was strange that such was not the fact. It would take some time to carry the tidings, and it would take some time to prepare the guard, and come to the place. Paul might have been killed a thousand times before the arrival of deliverance. The tumult must have commenced some considerable time before the mob drew Paul out of the temple to kill him, else he would have been killed long before the news had reached the officer. Here is the hand of Providence adjusting the deliverance to the danger, and putting the guard of deliverance in motion, so as to arrive at the critical moment the work of death was commenced; but Providence had a deliverer at the door. A few minutes longer, and a hundred thousand men could have done no service to Paul. How many times is murder prevented in a like providential manner! The accidental approach of others, or even the rustling of the leaves by the wind, may turn away the hand of the assassin.

What a blessing to the Christian is civil government! Even arbitrary and tyrannical governments are in general a protection to them from the assaults of illegal violence. God is the author of civil government; and he makes it in every country answer the purpose for which he has appointed it. True, it is often tyrannical, oppressive, and unjust; but it never is so, except when God designs to punish the nations. And if Christians know and perform their duty to the government under which Providence has placed them, they will usually find protection. But if it be the will of God that his people should suffer from the rulers of the nations, for the glory of his name, they may commit their safety to the Lord. If they suffer for his work, the Spirit of glory and of God resteth upon them. Let them never suffer for evil-doing. Let them be as strangers and pilgrims on the earth. They have before them a city that hath foundations, whose builder and maker is God.

127

Assault on Paul in the temple providentially afforded him an opportunity of defending himself, and preaching the gospel to persons of the first distinction

Acts 21

A CARELESS observer, unacquainted with the ways of God, would have judged the assault on Paul in the Temple, and his consequent imprisonment, to be unfortunate circumstances. Providence, he would think, was against the preacher and his new doctrine. But the truth was far otherwise. These things contributed to aid his cause. The chief captain had taken Paul for a noted disturber of the peace, and the imprisonment of the apostle afforded him an opportunity of setting the officer right on this subject. This was of great advantage. Rulers generally receive most unjust accounts of Christians from those who approach them; and personal intercourse is necessary to remove prejudice, and vindicate from false aspersions. No two characters could be more unlike than those of the persons who were confounded by the Roman tribune. The Egyptian was a man of blood, and the destruction of civil government: the apostle was a man of peace, and enjoined unlimited submission to the existing powers in all civil things. Such an impression, then, in the minds of those in authority must have been very injurious to the progress of the gospel; and Providence gave Paul this opportunity of removing it.

The seizure of Paul gave him also several opportunities of preaching the gospel to people of the first distinction in the country; many of whom were not likely in any other way to hear him. He was thereby enabled to defend himself, and, consequently, to commend the gospel before the highest councils of Jews and Gentiles. The Roman tribune gave him liberty to speak for himself; and, in doing so, he exhibits the gospel in the strongest manner. On the next day, Paul had an opportunity, through the command of the chief captain, to speak before the chief priests and all their council. Had he not been a prisoner, speaking in defence of his life, he could not have enjoyed the advantage of speaking to such an assembly. Providence took this way of gathering a congregation of the rulers of the earth to hear the ambassador of the Son of God. If they did not believe him, they shall at last be judged by his word; and the gospel is a sweet savour to God in those who perish by rejecting it, as well as in those who are saved by it.

Paul had another opportunity of preaching the gospel to the mighty, when he was accused by the orator Tertullus, with the high priest and elders of the Jews, before Felix the governor. Felix himself, in consequence of this, sent for Paul, and, with his wife Drusilla, heard him concerning the faith in Christ. Paul stood again in judgment before the governor Festus, when he was accused by the high priest and the chief of the Jews. Providentially also, Agrippa and Bernice came to Caesarea to salute Festus, and by this means Paul had another hearing before the most august personages, 'with the chief captains, and principal men of the city.' In this way, the gospel would excite great interest, and be heard by all ranks in the country. Were not such opportunities a rich recompense to Paul for all the hardships of this assault and imprisonment?

128

Paul sent to Rome in a providential way

Acts 23:11

PAUL expected to visit Rome, and God intended to send him there. But Paul's expectations and God's intentions, as to the manner of his conveyance to the seat of the empire of the world, were very different. Paul expected to go there of his own accord on some convenient opportunity. God intended to send him there as a prisoner. 'For God is my witness, whom I serve with my spirit in the gospel of his Son, that without ceasing I make mention of you always in my prayers; making request, if by any means now at length I might have a prosperous journey by the will of God to come unto you. For I long to see you, that I may impart unto you some spiritual gift, to the end ye may be established; that is, that I may be comforted together with you by the mutual faith both of you and me. Now I would not have you ignorant, brethren, that oftentimes I purposed to come unto you, (but was let hitherto,) that I might have some fruit among you also, even, as among other Gentiles. I am debtor both to the Greeks, and to the barbarians; both to the wise, and to the unwise. So, as much as in me is, I am ready to preach the gospel to you that are at Rome also.'—Rom. 1:9-15. Paul, you will go to Rome, but in far different circumstances from what you expect. 'Be of good cheer,' says God to Paul, when a prisoner, 'for as thou hast testified of me in Jerusalem, so must thou bear witness also at Rome.' Now, had a prize essay been announced on that occasion, on the best mode of sending Paul on this embassy, out of a hundred thousand competitors there would not be one who would have taken God's plan. All would have sent Paul to the seat of empire in a style worthy of the dignity of Christianity, and of its author. He would have had a numerous and magnificent retinue; and letters of recommendation to the most distinguished persons in the court; and, if possible, to the emperor himself. For such advantages Paul must be instructed to have some little complaisance to power, and to speak with moderation with respect to heathen idolatry. The superiority of the light of revelation he may be suffered to declare; but the broad condemnation of the religion of the emperor and his people would be unwise and intemperate. By prudent concessions and explanations, philosophers and statesmen may be brought over to the profession of the new religion. But to denounce damnation against all unbelievers would be harsh and uncharitable; and would raise every arm against the gospel.

But, Paul, your friends have no resources, and no means of affording you access to the distinguished men in Rome. What, then, says human wisdom? Why, if Paul cannot appear in pomp at Rome, let him attract notice by his singularity. Habit him with the cloak and staff of the philosopher. These are cheap but effectual means of securing honour. The tub of Diogenes drew the attention of Alexander the Great; and had the conqueror of the world been obliged to choose a second place, he would have chosen the tub of Diogenes.

But God took another way, and Paul was sent to preach the gospel in Rome, not as a friend of emperors, nor as a philosopher, but as a prisoner. And it is not difficult for those who are acquainted with God, to see that in this Providence the foolishness of God is wiser than men. Had Paul gone to Rome in any way that he could have been sent by his friends, he would not have had the same access to the emperor that he was permitted as a prisoner. Had Paul been a man even of the highest rank in society, or had he been the first of philosophers, or of orators, he might have preached the gospel in Rome for half a century without having an emperor for an auditor. He would have been looked upon as a crazy fanatic, or an interested impostor; and would have been so utterly despised by the court, that persons of distinction, and especially the emperor, would never think of hearing him. But, as a prisoner appealing to Caesar, Paul must be heard by Caesar. Thus, Caesar heard the gospel, and must be judged by it. Thus, the gospel would make a noise in Rome, so as to be heard, by almost every individual in the city; and the report of it would be propagated over the whole world. Even in our own free country a Christian suffering for the gospel, on any occasion, is the means of drawing attention to the gospel more than a man of chief distinction who is not persecuted. The poorest man standing for his life is an object of interest to all; and he will be heard in his own behalf. Neither the business nor the pleasures of Caesar could be allowed to prevent him from hearing the prisoner for the gospel of Christ. The bonds of the apostle, and the gospel through them, were noised over the whole world. This is one great end Providence has in view in all persecutions; and Christians should suffer with patience, when they consider that their sufferings are for the furtherance of the gospel. A Whitfield may, by his reproaches, be known to majesty; but a blaspheming Owen,[1] whose system overturns all order, law, and, decencies of society, is more likely to obtain an introduction to the presence of majesty.

Paul, then, must go to Rome as a prisoner, and every circumstance contributes to bring about the event. At the moment when God saw fit to send him, a most violent assault was made on him in the Temple; and for his rescue he was made a prisoner by the Roman tribune. But he was not hurried away immediately. Delays were providentially occasioned, in order that be might have an opportunity of defending himself, and preaching the gospel, before all the authorities in Judaea. For this purpose, again and again he is called to speak in the most august assemblies. And it is delightful to trace the hand of Providence, both holding him a prisoner, and preserving him from violence. He was in the very jaws of death; the Roman tribune is sent by Providence at the critical time to deliver him. He was commanded by the tribune to be examined by scourging. There is no need of this additional buffeting. Paul must go to Rome and be tried for his life. The interest of the gospel requires

[1] A reference to Robert Owen (1771–1858), Welsh social reformer and one of the founders of utopian socialism and the cooperative movement, is best known in Scotland for his pioneering reforms in the mill at New Lanark. — P.

this. But he has been often scourged; and Providence has no end to serve by his scourging on the present occasion. But how is this to be prevented? It is the order of the chief captain. Providence has this matter arranged many years ago, and Paul, though a Jew, was a Roman citizen,—an honour and privilege of great advantage, and which the tribune himself obtained only by high purchase. Let no Christian undervalue civil privileges, or decline to avail himself of them in the time of necessity. God is the author of them; as well as of other blessings. This privilege was valuable to Paul on the present occasion, and by his example, it is valuable to us. It shows us that Paul was not a fanatic, who wantonly exposed his life, or incurred sufferings unnecessarily. He would not willingly bear a single stripe, if it was not demanded by his Master. A man may as well whip his own back, as offer it to the whip of the persecutor; and he will have no more advantage from the one than from the other. God does not give a premium to ignorance and fanaticism.

Paul must go to Rome; therefore, he cannot be murdered, though he is a prisoner. Providence, therefore, watches over him, and guards him against all the plots of assassins. 'And when it was day, certain of the Jews banded together, and bound themselves under a curse, saying that they would neither eat nor drink till they had killed Paul. And there were more than forty which had made this conspiracy. And they came to the chief priests and elders, and said, We have bound ourselves under a great curse, that we will eat nothing until we have slain Paul. Now, therefore, ye with the council signify to the chief captain that he bring him down unto you to-morrow, as though you would enquire something more perfectly concerning him: and we, or ever he come near, are ready to kill him. And when Paul's sister's son heard of their lying in wait, he went and entered into the castle, and told Paul.' Why was it that the conspiracy was not kept secret? Why, especially, was it heard by Paul's sister's son? Why, this Providence disappointed the murderer. Paul did not show himself regardless of life, nor did he manifest that sort of trust in God which refuses to use the appointed means of safety.

He informed the tribune, and the tribune gave him such an escort to Felix that secured him from all the attempts of his enemies.

Paul stands before Felix, and a bribe would have procured his release. But Paul would not deliver himself in that way. Here we may see the Providence of God in the character of Felix. Had he been a just man, he would have released the prisoner. Had he not been a covetous man, he would have released him. He kept him from the hope of receiving money for his deliverance. In his behaviour also on going out of office, we may see the hand of Providence. Why did he not, then, set Paul at liberty? He could no longer entertain expectations of money. He retained him from a 'willingness to show the Jews a pleasure.' His love of popularity overcomes his sense of justice. In this, God's purpose was fulfilled in retaining Paul to send him as a prisoner to Rome. But why did not Felix go farther in courting the favour of the people? It would have been a greater pleasure to the Jews had he put Paul to death. Providence restrained him.

Paul stands also before Festus, and Festus also was 'willing to do the Jews a pleasure.' He asked Paul, then, if he was willing to go up to Jerusalem, and there be judged before him. Paul must go to Rome, and therefore Paul refuses to be judged by Festus. He appeals to Caesar. Here is the hand of Providence. Had it not been for this appeal, Paul in a short time would have been set at liberty. On another hearing before Agrippa he was declared innocent. 'Then said Agrippa unto Festus, This man might have been set at liberty, if he had not appealed unto Caesar.' Does not every child see here that it is Divine Providence that retained Paul a prisoner, in order that he might stand before the sovereign of the Roman world?

Paul must go to Rome; but Providence took care of his comforts, and raised him up friends even in those who were ignorant of his God. Julius the centurion, to whom Paul was delivered, treated Paul not only mercifully but politely. 'And Julius courteously entreated Paul, and gave him liberty to go unto his friends to refresh himself.' Yet Julius had no partiality to Paul as a Christian. When Paul warned them of the danger of the voyage, 'the centurion believed the master and the owner of the ship more than those things which were spoken by Paul.'

A remarkable feature in Providence here presents itself to our view. When God, by the mouth of his servant, had foretold the danger of the voyage, we might expect that the face of nature would have seconded the warning by frowning skies, and all the symptoms of an approaching storm. But this is not the wisdom of God. On the contrary, when Paul was not believed, Providence sent such symptoms of the weather, that a most prosperous voyage was anticipated. And when the south wind blew softly, supposing that they had obtained their purpose, loosing thence, they sailed close by Crete. Everything appeared favourable, and the prediction of Paul was considered false. And there is nothing more usual in the ways of Providence than this. The wicked man prospers often more than the righteous; and it is rashly concluded that God makes no distinction. Error is propagated and extensively received. It is concluded that God approves of the doctrine. Men hate the Scriptures, and God has formed them so that they can find specious cavils on which to ground the rejection of them. Moses gives an account of the creation: false science finds appearances which, in its judgment, contradict his obvious meaning; and Moses must either submit to explain, or to be held as an impostor. God, in his Providence, gives every opportunity to the infidel philosopher, and the theologian, who affects the honours of science, to manifest that they do not believe the Divine testimony. And for a time the south wind may blow softly, but the storm will come at last. 'But not long after there arose against it a tempestuous wind, called Euroclydon.' Lord, let me be found with those who, like Abraham, believe thy testimony in the face of all adverse appearances. I would not take the globe on which I stand, to force the account of its origin by the Holy Spirit through Moses, into an accordance with the dogmas of infidel science.

Paul must go to Rome as a prisoner, but why must there be a storm? Might it not have been confidently expected that the ship that carried the ambassador of the Son of God would have a prosperous voyage? Surely nothing but the gentle zephyrs will fill the sails. Not so. We must have a storm—a storm almost unexampled. This was for the glory of God: this was for the advantage and honour of the apostle. It afforded an opportunity to manifest God in a most powerful manner. By this God avowed that Paul was his servant, and that he was the only Lord of the universe. For such a purpose, then, Paul was to submit to very great hardships for a very long time. And so must all the Lord's people submit to whatever hardships, and dangers, and evils, the Lord shall see fit to expose them. Let them console themselves, then; no storm will arise which is not necessary for their good and the Lord's glory. If Paul was here called to great suffering, he was distinguished with signal honours. The Lord publicly owned him, and gave him the lives of all who sailed with him. Before the storm Paul was overlooked; now he is the principal personage on board, and all live on his word.

Paul must be saved, and all on board for his sake. But this is to be in the way of Providence, and not by miracle. The storm did not cease, as when Jesus said, 'Peace, be still.' It continued to rage, and the ship was a total wreck. The passengers were providentially saved, just as almost an every day's occurrence is witnessed on the seas. Some swam to shore, and some were saved on planks and broken pieces of the ship. Is not this a key to the Providences that occur in naval history? Are we not warranted from this to ascribe to Providence all the wonders of deliverances afforded to men at sea? A history of well authenticated deliverances from the perils of the ocean would be a most interesting work. Men do not see God in these things; but it is because they do not wish to see him. Is there anything in the occurrences of the shipwreck of Paul that is not occurring almost every day? Jehovah rules the world in its minutest concerns, as well as in affairs of greatest moment. Nothing is too great nor too little for his attention and care. They who do not love to retain him in their knowledge, remove him to a distance through the figment of his doing every thing, not by his own agency, but by general laws. A shipwreck in a storm is no way the work of the Lord, in their estimation, but as it is the result of original arrangement and adaptation of nature. This cursed philosophy is nothing but practical atheism, invented to hide God from his creatures.

But Paul, saved from the storm, is at the peril of death from the counsel of the soldiers. They wished to secure their prisoners by killing them. Paul, however, must not, cannot, fall. Providence secures his safety through the clemency of the centurion. Had he coincided with the judgment of the soldiers, Paul was a dead man. 'But the centurion, willing to save Paul, kept them from their purpose.' Thus Paul was saved providentially from slaughter, and all the prisoners were saved on his account. Wicked men often owe their safety to the mixture of their lot with that of the people of God. Had not Paul been one of the prisoners, the prisoners would all have been butchered by the cruel prudence of the soldiers.

Providence accompanies the apostle every step of his journey. For the sake of the servant of God, kindness and hospitality receive them as soon as they reach the shore. It might have been a desert island, or a coast at a distance from houses, at which they might have been wrecked. Their coming safe to land would in that case have been no safety. The inhabitants might have been inhospitable and cruel; and have either neglected them, or destroyed them for their property. In many places called Christian, the lives of the shipwrecked are not in safety. But Providence inclined the hearts of the barbarians to show kindness to Paul and the whole company. 'And the barbarous people showed us no little kindness: for they kindled a fire, and received us every one, because of the present rain, and because of the cold.' The God of Providence went before his servant, and opened the hearts of all to receive him with kindness. And cannot the missionaries who carry the gospel to barbarous nations witness that Providence disposes the barbarous people to show them no little kindness? And why should they not expect this? If they have Paul's gospel, they have as good reason to count on the presence of God in opening a way for them as Paul had himself.

But an apparently unfortunate accident now happens to Paul. He was assisting in gathering sticks and laying them on the fire, and a viper fastens on his hand. Why this occurrence? Why does the accident befall Paul, rather than any one of all the company? Is not this an adverse Providence? Does not this point him out as under the judgment of God? So thought the barbarians; and so would men think in general, as far as they see Providence. Philosophers, indeed, are better taught. They would see nothing in this but chance, as the operation of natural causes. But the barbarians, wiser than philosophers, though they misunderstood the language of Providence, recognized the thing as providential. It was providential, and turned out for the glory of God, and the advantage of the apostle. Providence took this way of introducing his ambassador with his credentials of office. And many things which at first appear to show that God is counteracting his servants, will ultimately turn out greatly for their honour and assistance. God may suffer vipers to fasten on their hands, while the crowd will look on the occasion as an indication of divine wrath; but when they shake off the reptiles without being injured, the cause of the Lord will be glorified.

The same Providence disposed the heart of the Roman governor, of the island to show kindness to Paul and his shipwrecked associates. Why was there at this time such a governor in the island? Why was he not a cruel and inhospitable man? He was placed there by the hand of Providence for this very occasion. God works through means, and his Providence plans and arranges all things to effect his purposes. 'In the same quarters were possessions of the chief man of the island, whose name was Publius; who received us, and lodged us three days courteously.'

But Providence was working by another dispensation to bring Paul into notice and favour. The father of Publius was at this time sick. Why this sickness at this particular time? Was it chance, or was it Providence? Look at the issue, and try to doubt this. The hand of God is in the fact. The man was sick, that God might honour his gospel and his servant, by his recovery. 'And it came to pass, that the father of Publius lay sick of a fever and of a bloody flux: to whom Paul entered in, and prayed, and laid his hands on him, and healed him.' The report of this spread over the island; and in this way the gospel would be spoken of by every mouth. 'So, when this was done, others, also, which had diseases in the island, came and were healed: who also honoured us with many honours; and when we departed, they loaded us with such things as were necessary.'

At last, Paul arrived at Rome; and though still a prisoner, his bonds were rendered as light as courtesy and kindness could make them. 'And when we came to Rome, the centurion delivered the prisoners to the captain of the guard: but Paul was suffered to dwell by himself with a soldier that kept him.' In this situation he was at liberty to discharge his office as an ambassador of Christ, and to converse privately and preach publicly to the Jews. Providence also ordered it that the Jews gave him a hearing, and were not shut up against him till they had heard the gospel; and God had called to the knowledge of the truth as many as were ordained to eternal life. Paul continued to enjoy such liberty in bondage, and went on in his labours without interruption. 'And Paul dwelt two whole years in his own hired house, and received all that came in unto him.' Thus did Providence carry Paul to Rome, and regulate everything concerning him with the minutest attention. The evil as well as the good that happened to the apostle was divinely directed, and no evil occurred out of which God did not bring ultimate good. The very evil was ordained for the sake of the good that was to come out of it.

129

Providential character of the standard of the Christian religion

IN GIVING a standard for the guidance of all ages in the doctrines, precepts, and ordinances of Christ, we would have naturally expected that all would have been drawn up in a formal, full, and precise system by the apostles. No such thing is found in the New Testament. All things are brought forward as circumstances called for; and they are taught in words, not in a regulated system. The epistles of the apostles contain the doctrines, precepts, and ordinances of the Christian religion as occasion demanded at the time; and all ages are left to find the truth by tracing their steps. Everything is brought forward in a way of Providence. This is admirable wisdom; this is the wisdom of God. It leaves a standard, while it apparently neglects a standard. While there is no formal symbol of divine truth, there is not a truth, nor duty, nor ordinance of Christ, which, in the words and scattered hints of Scripture, is not taught with sufficient evidence. Can there be a stronger demonstration of the divine original of the Scriptures? Surely this book cannot be a human production, when no man, learned or unlearned, would have followed the same plan.

The wisdom of God farther appears in this providential manner of revelation by hiding God from the wisdom of the wise, while he is seen by babes and sucklings, who renounce their own wisdom, and implicitly follow Christ. Is it not notorious that many learned men can find no standard in Scripture for many things that must be practised one way or other? Because there is no system or regulated symbol of worship, they think that they are, in many things, left to their own discretion. The epistles of the apostles were occasioned by the state and circumstances of the churches or individuals to which they are written. They are, therefore, as some think, mere *letters of business*, which are, indeed, in some measure, to guide us, but only by a *discriminating* application. Hence the never-ending variety in the ceremonial forms of worship under the Christian name, according to the different views of an enlightened and discriminating imitation of the first churches. Hence, in the wisdom of God, occasion was given for the rise and progress of the Man of Sin. That monster was predicted by the Spirit of inspiration, and will ultimately serve, with every thing else, to contribute to the exhibition of the divine glory. The Spirit of truth hath given a perfect standard; but, by the divine wisdom, the character of that standard is of such a nature, as to afford occasion of evasion to disaffection and human wisdom.

For the occasion of the full, and clear, and strong exhibitions of the doctrine of justification, for instance, we are indebted to the Jewish opposition. With immediate and especial reference to the Jews, Paul discusses this subject at large in his Epistle to the Romans. From this treasure the children of God enrich themselves with a never-ending increase of wealth. But, from the character of revelation to which I have referred, the enemies of justification, solely by faith in Jesus Christ, take occasion to invent evasions. Socinians, Arians, Arminians, with all the enemies of the pure gospel, tell us that Paul, as addressing Jewish error, must not be understood to mean the moral law, but the ceremonial law, or the judicial law; or that he meant not good works as conditions of justification on our part, but works of law as meritorious of pardon. In like manner, upon every other subject, enemies will find something to allege from the peculiar manner of revelation. Now, men would think this a defect in revelation; but in the Divine discovery of the will of God, it is a perfection. It manifests the disaffection of the heart of man to the things of God. It would really be a defect in human law; for human law is not to detect the state of the heart, but to regulate conduct only. The Divine law is to regulate the conduct in such a way as to discover the state of the heart. Such, then, is the wisdom of God in the providential way in which the standard of the Christian religion is regulated.

130

Hesitancy in receiving Paul by the church at Jerusalem

Acts 9:26

FAITH in Jesus Christ is the only bond of the union of Christians, and no questions ought ever to be put to any who seek admission among them, but such as are intended to ascertain this. To refuse any whom Christ has received, is as sinful as to receive those whom Christ has rejected. It is the very spirit of antichrist. Some may think that they discover zeal for the honour of Christ, when they insist on perfect conformity in order to fellowship. But like the Hebrews to whom Paul wrote, they need to be taught the first principles of the oracles of God. Accordingly, we find that when any, in the days of the apostles, confessed their faith in Christ, they were admitted among the disciples.

But this fact is misinterpreted by others, and is alleged to justify the admission even of Arians. Do they not, it is said, confess that Jesus Christ is the Son of God? No; they do not confess this. They confess it in words, not in meaning. And that true faith, as far as it can be ascertained, is required for a right of admission, is clear from the fact above referred to, with respect to the hesitancy of the church at Jerusalem, in relation to the reception of Paul. They did not take his mere confession, when they had cause of suspicion that his confession was feigned. He was received not simply on his confession, but on the recommendation of Barnabas.

What a providential thing, then, was it that Paul was stopped a moment at the door of the church at Jerusalem! Even an apostle was not received on his mere profession, when there was ground of suspicion. This providential occurrence, then, is the way in which Jesus Christ teaches us this part of his will. Instead of giving a general direction, with partial exceptions, he gives us the rule and the exceptions in the record of the practice of the first churches.

Let us never forget, in reading the Scriptures, that we are reading the oracles of God; and that every part of them is calculated to be useful. Let us ponder on them, and search them, as for hidden treasure, and we will not fail to be enriched with knowledge.

131
The incestuous man in the church at Corinth
1 Cor. 5

STRANGE! Is Jesus the ruler of his churches, and does he permit the occasion of such reproach to his cause? Why did he not prevent the admission of this man, of whom he must have been fully aware? Why did he not prevent him from falling into this sin, as he was really, from what afterwards appears, a true member of his body? Many wise purposes may be seen in this instance of the Divine sovereignty. Christ here shows us our own weakness. There is no sin to which we are constitutionally inclined, into which we could not fall, if we were not kept by the power of God through faith unto salvation. He here also shows us, that his churches are prone to neglect his laws, and to depart from his instructions. The Corinthians were already informed of their duty with respect to such offenders, else they could not have been blamed on this occasion. Hence we have the necessity for the continual care and watchfulness of Jesus over his churches. When Christians say, come and see my zeal for the Lord, they are not aware of their own weakness. No church of Christ could exist in purity for a single year, if left to the care of men, without the care of Christ. In this occurrence, also, Christ has given us a rule with respect to transgressors. Providence afforded this single example, to guide with respect to those who fall into sin in general. But there is still another purpose which this occurrence serves in the Providence of God. It gives occasion to the enemies of Christ and his cause to blaspheme. It draws forth an expression of that malignity with respect to God, which formerly existed in their hearts, but remained concealed till something presented itself that was calculated to give it utterance. This is still the case with respect to the conduct of David and Peter, and with respect to the misconduct of any of the Lord's people at present. It is in the wisdom of his sovereignty that God ordains such modes of detection of enmity to himself. Did they not hate God, instead of rejoicing in the fall of Christians, they would mourn for it. If the poorest Christian acts inconsistently with his character, it will be blazoned over the whole neighbourhood; and spoken of in circles, where, it might be thought, the name of the obscure individual could never find entrance. It is a relief to the guilty conscience. The ungodly are led to hope, that all profession is hypocrisy, and that there is no reality in the hopes and fears of Christians.

Christians, though in God's sovereignty he may afford such occasions for the manifestation of disaffection to his character and truth, yet it is your duty to avoid giving such offence. It must be that offences come, but woe unto that man by whom they come, David gave occasion to the enemies of the Lord to blaspheme, and on that account he was involved in trouble all his after-life.

132
Law-suits unbecoming between Christians
1 Cor. 6

BETWEEN the most upright men there may often be a difference of judgment with respect to matters of property. Hence occasions of dispute and litigation. Instances of this sort had occurred in the church at Corinth; and the brethren, instead of settling their differences by the arbitration of persons selected from their own members, had continued to appeal to the judgment of the courts of law. This was highly blamed by the apostle, as being injurious to the character of Christianity, and an insult to their own body. When a case has gone through every gradation of legal appeal, what have we but the judgment of men; and men who are certainly not more interested in doing justice to the parties, than arbitrators nominated from their brethren? No court can have so good an opportunity of examining and knowing the case. Their connection with the parties, and their local situation, give judges from among themselves every advantage. Can any court have so tender a concern for the credit and interests of both parties? True, indeed, there may be some important matters in question, which require a legal knowledge, beyond what may be possessed by any of the brethren. But when this is the case, there is nothing to prevent the brethren appointed to judge from taking proper legal advice on the point at issue. They will do this as effectually, and more cheaply, than both parties could do, and each to consult separately for himself. And when legal opinion is taken in this manner, there is no fear of excitement to legal appeal. Such a settlement of differences has every advantage, and is free of many serious disadvantages which lie against law-suits.

Hence we see the wisdom of Providence in ordaining the very faults of the Corinthian Christians to be for our learning. It was from their misconduct in this matter that occasion was given for the record of this law of Christ. And the law is contained in no other form than as a record of the reproof of the apostle. Consequently, to those not acquainted with the peculiar style of the divine wisdom in conveying the will of God this law lies hid. They read the transaction without perceiving a law binding on Christians in every age. They make no conscience of settling differences among Christians, about the things of this world, in the way pointed out by the apostle. This is one of the features of revelation, that is of so peculiar a cast that it proves the Scriptures to be from God. Instead of drawing up an article on the subject, with all the forms and minuteness of an act of Parliament, the Providence of the Lord supplied an example, and the Spirit of the Lord inspired the apostle to give a law indirectly by reproof. Innumerable examples of this nature may be found in the Scriptures.

Some, however, appear to stretch the law beyond its just extent, and regard it as unwarrantable in any case to appeal to law. They think that a Christian should rather lose his property than go to law about it. The law given by the apostle in this place has no such import. It forbids law-suits only when both parties are brethren in Christ. The opinion that a Christian should in no case appeal to law would, if acted on, soon strip believers of all their property, and endanger their lives. The cross of Christ is heavy enough; there is no occasion to carry a load of lumber along with it. Civil law, though not necessary among Christians, is to the Christian the greatest blessing. Without it he would soon be devoured by the innumerable sharks which lie about the ship which carries Christ and his people. To trust in Providence, without using the means which God has commanded and provided, is not faith but presumption. This is the snare in which the devil thought to take our Lord. Placing him on the pinnacle of the temple, he said, 'Cast thyself down, for it is written, He will give his angels charge concerning thee: and in their hands they shall bear thee up, lest at any time thou dash thy foot against a stone.' Here he sought to separate the end and the means to make Jesus look for safety without taking proper caution about his life. But he replied by another passage of Scripture, 'Thou shalt not tempt the Lord thy God.' If we look for the protection of Providence, we must avail ourselves of all the means of safety which Providence affords us.

133
Abuse of the Lord's Supper at Corinth
1 Cor. 11

THERE can be nothing more surprising than the fact placed before us in this passage. Could it be imagined that after the apostle had been so long with them, when they had for such a period enjoyed his personal labours, they should almost immediately fall into so gross an abuse of an ordinance of Christ? It is indeed so charged, that the apostle would not deign to call it the Lord's Supper. It was converted into a supper of their own. No man on earth would have anticipated such an event. And why did the Lord suffer this to take place? Does he not rule in his churches? He did it for a most important end. He knew how much men are prone to venerate antiquity, and foresaw the rise of the Man of Sin, whose throne rests on the authority of tradition and antiquity. In this example he totally discredits all reference to the authority even of his own churches planted by the apostles, except so far as it appears they were guided by the apostles. Instead of relying on the practice of the first four centuries, we cannot with safety rely on four days, or four hours. Did church history reach up to the very days of the apostles, giving us the fullest documents, in the most authentic records, there is no reliance to be placed on the result. The Bible, and the Bible alone, is the source of evidence of all things to be believed and practised by Christians. To keep us from being dashed to pieces on these

breakers, Divine Providence has set up, as on a tower, the church
of Corinth as a beacon. Had Scripture taken no notice of this fact,
and had church history recorded it as a fact without expressing an
opinion, what an example would we have had of the ancient observance of the Lord's Supper! We may bless God that his Providence
shipwrecked the Corinthian on these rocks, and that we still see the
spars and broken pieces of the vessel drifted by the surge. O yes,
sailor, breakers ahead; bear off to the open sea.

134
Collection in Greece for the poor saints at Jerusalem
1 Cor. 16

DIVINE Providence had reduced the church at Jerusalem to
great distress by poverty. This was peculiarly calculated to
cement the union between the Jewish and the Gentile brethren. It
served to soften the prejudice of the Jews, and to enliven the gratitude of the Gentiles for the gospel. But I refer to the fact principally
to observe, that the law of Christ, placed before us in this transaction, is seldom if ever observed. Christians in many places make the
most ample provision for the wants of the poor among themselves.
But there are few that take means to supply the destitution of brethren in different quarters of the globe. Some churches never think
of reaching their hand beyond those in immediate connection with
them. The churches of Greece contributed to the relief of the brethren in another quarter of the world. And this is quite as necessary
as the relief of those around. There may be many churches situated
in places where there are few or none rich, and while many are very
poor. Why, then, do churches suffer this law of Christ to lie in abey-

ance? In some places they seem to provide for the poor even beyond duty, while they never think of the poor of the Lord's people in other places. Brethren, these things ought not to be so. Christians in every place, and of every denomination, are brethren, and none of them should be allowed to want while others have abundance. There is no propriety in taking the poor out of their toils, nor of rendering their own industry unnecessary. All I plead for is, that the Lord's people ought to be provided for, wherever they are, and that the bounty of Christians should not be confined to their own locality.

What a richness is in the Scriptures! They are deficient on no point. Every possible occurrence will meet something to correspond to it. But the providential answers of revelation occasion many to overlook the things that are before their eyes.

135
Paul's cloak left at Troas
2 Tim. 4:13

'THE cloak that I left at Troas with Carpus, when thou comest, bring with thee, and the books, but especially the parchments.' Did Paul need any inspiration to inform him that he left his cloak with a certain person at Troas? Did he need inspiration to enable him to express this request to Timothy about the cloak? Is it not absurd, then, to suppose that every thing in Scripture is inspired, especially that all things are equally inspired? Human wisdom has reasoned in this way; and theories of inspiration have been invented to enable us to distinguish in Scripture between the things that are inspired and the things which need no inspiration, and to regulate the different kinds and degrees of inspiration which different things in Scripture require. The message about the cloak has been degraded from all kinds of inspiration, as a mere matter of worldly business, which admitted no interference of the Spirit of God.

But all such theories of inspiration directly contradict the testimony of the Holy Spirit, which attests that all Scripture is given by inspiration. The meaning of this testimony must be ascertained by grammar and the use of language—not by theory. To speak of settling the meaning and extent of inspiration by theory is as absurd as to call the verdict of a jury the theory of the jury. The men who have invented these theories, and those who adopt them, show themselves unacquainted with the fundamental laws which regulate the investigation of truth, and trespass against the philosophy of evidence, as well as against the testimony of the Spirit of God.

It did not, indeed, require inspiration to acquaint Paul that he had left a cloak with Carpus at Troas. It did not require inspiration to inform him that he now needed the cloak. But as his letter was the work of the Holy Spirit, such a message could not have found a place, except it was for the use of the people of God. It must convey some useful lesson, else it would not stand where it is. And do we not learn from it the humble circumstances of the apostle, and the attention that it was necessary for him to give to his worldly concerns even in small matters? We learn also the propriety and duty of attending to worldly concerns even in the most devoted men. The service of God is no cover for indolence, thoughtlessness, waste, or inattention. It shows us also that Paul did not set a value on exposing himself, without necessity, to cold or hardships. But, above all, this message appears to have been designed to manifest the petulance of human wisdom in the things of God. Paul providentially left his cloak at Troas, that occasion might be given for this message, in the words of the Holy Spirit. It is a gin and a snare to those who do not, like little children, submit implicitly to the testimony of Scripture. In the wisdom of God, the enmity of the human heart to the ways of God is detected. The truth revealed before the eyes, in this plan of revelation, lies hid from the wisdom of this world.

Accurate views of the Scripture doctrine of inspiration are of immense importance for the discovery of what the Scriptures contain. All theories which dispense with inspiration in some things, or modify it in others, tend to hide many things which the Scriptures reveal. What Dr. Thomas Brown, in his *Philosophy of the Human Mind,* says of these divisions of the mental phenomena, which he charges as leaving out some qualities which belong to it, is entirely applicable to this subject. The phenomena not included in the division, or which are included only by force, are likely to be overlooked. 'A new classification, therefore,' says he, 'which includes, in its generic characters, those neglected qualities, will, of course, draw to them attention which they could not otherwise have obtained; and the more various the views are which we take of the objects of any science, the juster, consequently, because the more equal, will be the estimate which we form of them. So truly is this the case, that I am convinced that no one has ever read over the mere terms of a new division in a science, however familiar the science may have been to him, without learning more than this new division itself, without being struck with some property or relation, the importance of which he now perceives most clearly, and which he is quite astonished that he should have overlooked so long before.' This observation is just, and profoundly philosophical. It applies to our subject as fully as to that of the philosopher. Those theorists that deny inspiration to some parts of Scripture, or which modify it, keep people from searching the Scriptures as the word of God, and from discovering much of the riches contained in them.

136

Timothy advised by Paul to take a little wine for the sake of his health

1 Tim. 5:23

'DRINK no longer water, but use a little wine for thy stomach's sake, and thine often infirmities.' This is another of the passages in which our wise men cannot see any necessity for inspiration. Paul, they think, might well give this direction from his own knowledge. Vain men, how long will you blaspheme! Does not God say, 'All Scripture is given by inspiration'? But as a dictate from the Spirit of God, has not this direction an importance that it could not have as a mere advice from man? It shows us that, even in the age of miracles, natural means were employed, and blessed by God, for the purpose to which he has adapted them. It shows us what fanaticism might, in its extravagance, deny, the lawfulness of the medical art. Have not persons been found, so far mistaking the will of God, as to allege that attention to medical advice is distrust in Providence? 'God is my physician,' some will exclaim, while they refuse the aid that Providence has provided. If God is our physician, we are here taught to look for a cure to our disorder from the means which he has in his Providence adapted to this end. If wine is useful for the stomach, surely God is the physician, who formed the stomach, and gave its qualities to the wine.

The infirmity of Timothy, then, has been overruled by Providence in its usual manner, to give occasion for a direction that gives instruction to every age.

In the frequent infirmities of Timothy which this direction brings before us, we see the usual Providence of God with regard to his people. To the gladiator the God of Providence gives herculean strength, while his best beloved servants are often oppressed with infirmities, and pained with ill health. The consideration of this is calculated to keep God's afflicted people from being stumbled by their afflictions.

137
Trophimus left sick at Miletum
2 Tim. 4:20

'TROPHIMUS have I left at Miletum sick.' Did you, Paul? And why did you leave him sick, when you possessed the power of working miracles? Why were you so profuse of your miracles in Melita, while you are so sparing of them among your best friends? For the very reason of showing that miracles are rather for the proof of the gospel, than for the private benefit even of the heirs of glory. God is sovereign in this as well as in everything else. Jesus healed the ear of the servant of the chief priest, while Paul did not heal his friend Trophimus. The apostles exercised their power, not by their own discretion or caprice, but by the suggestion of the Holy Spirit. This, then, is a providential fact, the record of which, though to human wisdom trifling, yet is of great importance to the children of God. They are not to expect that they will be always free from sickness, or that their sickness will always be soon dismissed. They have reason to trust that God will always be with them, and will turn everything to good for them. But they must submit to him as a sovereign who gives no account of his matters.

138

Angels created to minister to the heirs of salvation

Heb. 1:14

FOR what purpose were the angels created? What purpose
do they serve? The answer to the last question will afford an
answer to the first. Paul tells us what is the occupation of the angels.
'Are they not all ministering spirits, sent forth to minister for them
who shall be heirs of salvation?' Now, whatever is the office of
angels, for that office were they created. Their peculiar work is no
after-thought in the Creator, but was in the contemplation of their
Creator in their creation. 'Known unto God are all his works from
the beginning of the world.' The office for which he designed the
angels was provided for before the creation of man. Nurses and all
attendants are in readiness for the heir apparent to a throne before
his birth. In like manner, before the birth of the heirs of salvation,
the angels were in waiting, ready to minister to them. What a view
does this thought give of the dignity of the Christian! Grovelling
superstition is ready to fall down at the feet of the angels to worship
them: the meanest of the people of God have angels as their attendants! We may estimate the glory of those waited on by the glory of
the attendants. What must be the dignity of the heirs of salvation,
if, even in their fallen state, the angels of God were created to be
their ministers! As Christians are one with Christ, they are worthy
of attendants so dignified. In no other point of view are they worthy
of this. In all other lights the thing is incongruous. But as Christians
are one with him who is one with God, all created dignities are
under their feet. In this view it was worthy of the wisdom of Divine
Providence to create innumerable hosts of powerful spirits, to wait
on the heirs of salvation before the creation of human nature.

Their very name shows that they were destined in their creation to the office of ministering to the heirs of salvation. The word *angel* signifies *messenger*, as they were to be the messengers of God in deeds of kindness to his children, as well as of vengeance against their enemies. What a wonderful thought, that God should employ his mighty spirits of light to wait on Lazarus, covered with sores, and sitting as a beggar at the way side! Two hosts of them appeared to Jacob on the eve of his approach to Esau, and a whole mountain was filled with them, under the appearance of horses and chariots around the prophet and his servant.

139
Christ the Sun of Righteousness
Rev. 12:1

THE resemblances that are found between things in nature are of great importance, not merely for the enlivening of human speech, but for the illustration of truth. The Spirit of God in revelation avails himself of this advantage, and freely employs figurative language. All adaptation to an end, however accidental it may appear, must have been known to the Author of nature. No relation can be new or unknown to him. Among the figures employed to represent the Lord Jesus Christ, there are some, the adaptation of which to their end is so striking, so wonderful, and so various, that the likeness cannot be supposed to be accidental. The Creator, it would appear, in giving its constitution to the natural object, had an eye to the spiritual; and the pattern on the mount takes its construction from the true heaven of God. The sun, for instance, is so wonderful a figure of Christ, and the correspondence of the figure with the thing represented is so strong and varied, that nothing but design in the Creator of the figure could secure its adaptation. Light and darkness are adapted to represent the knowledge of God manifested in Jesus Christ, as opposed to the natural blindness and ignorance of fallen man. The sun in the firmament of heaven is a bright image of the Sun of Righteousness announced by the prophet Malachi. How wonderful is the coincidence between the sun enlightening the world, and Jesus Christ, the Sun of Righteousness, enlightening all nations by his gradual progress! The nineteenth psalm, representing Christ enlightening the world, finds everything in the course of the sun. And can it be supposed that the provident Creator had no eye to this in forming the sun, and in giving its peculiar nature to light? He is no philosopher who thinks so. Adaptation proves design. In the symbolic language of the book of Revelation, Jesus is represented as the sun, while the moon and the stars in different points of view represent his people. He is the light of the world. They also are the light of the world. The light which they receive from him they reflect on others. Indeed, it is quite evident, that great and glorious as is the work of creation, it is only as a stage for the performance of a more glorious work of redemption.

The glories of creation are only a figure of the Redeemer, as they are all his own work. All creation came into existence for the sake of displaying the glory of Christ and his church. If astronomy is well founded in the most extravagant of her conceptions as to the extent of creation, it is so much more added to the extent of the dominion of the heirs of salvation. Go on, then, you men of science, go on in your discoveries of new worlds! You are mere surveyors of estates which belong to the heirs of salvation.

Also available from The Banner of Truth Trust:

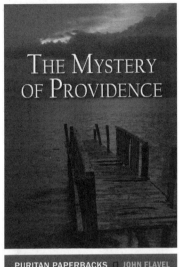

PURITAN PAPERBACKS ☐ JOHN FLAVEL

The Mystery of Providence
John Flavel

It should be a delight and pleasure to us to discern how God works all things in the world for his own glory and his people's good. But it should be an even greater pleasure to observe the particular designs of providence in our own lives. 'O what a world of rarities,' says the Puritan John Flavel (1628-91), 'are to be found in providence. . . with profound wisdom, infinite tenderness and incessant vigilance it has managed all that concerns us from first to last.'

'My life seemed like a jigsaw of many pieces. It was not until I read John Flavel's The Mystery of Providence *that I realised there was a divine purpose holding every part together and providing the plan.'*

[Derek Eagles in EVANGELICAL TIMES]

ISBN 978-0-85151-104-7 paperback 224pp.

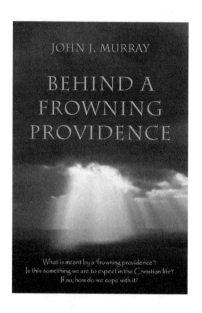

Behind a Frowning Providence
John J. Murray

John J. Murray writes out of his years of experience as a Christian minister and counsellor, using the wisdom of God's Word to give guidance and direction. But *Behind a Frowning Providence* also bears the marks of a precious stone, quarried from the deep and dark places of the author's own experience of pain and sorrow. It speaks to the mind, giving wise counsel; it also speaks to the heart, and brings a message of encouragement which points to the way of true peace.

'A *wonderful booklet for afflicted saints.*' [NEW HORIZONS]

ISBN 978-0-85151-572-4 booklet 30pp.

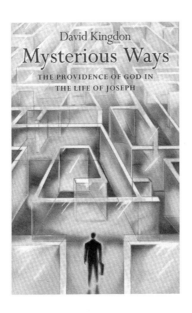

Mysterious Ways:
The Providence of God in the Life of Joseph
David Kingdon

With great insight and pastoral wisdom, David Kingdon helps us to apply lessons from the life of Joseph to our own lives. He shows that God's people are not lost in a meaningless maze, but are safe in the hands of a loving Father. However 'mysterious' his ways seem at present, he has purposed good for his people, and will 'make it plain' in his own time. Even now, he is teaching us lessons which could be learned in no other way.

'Kingdon combines the ability to understand the text of Scripture with the sensitive heart of a pastor well prepared to be our friend and guide in this area of spiritual experience.'

[SINCLAIR B. FERGUSON *in the Foreword*]

ISBN 978-0-85151-871-8   paperback   112pp.

All Things For Good
Thomas Watson

First published in 1663 (under the title *A Divine Cordial*), the year
after Watson and some two thousand other ministers were ejected
from the Church of England and exposed to hardship and suffering,
All Things For Good contains the rich exposition of a man who lived
when only faith in God's Word could lead him to such confidence.
Thomas Watson's exposition is always simple, illuminating and rich
in practical application. He explains that both the best and the worst
experiences work for the good of God's people. He carefully analyses
what it means to be someone who 'loves God' and is 'called according to his purpose'. *All Things For Good* provides the biblical answer
to the contemporary question; Why do bad things happen to good
people?

ISBN 978-0-85151-478-9   paperback   128pp.

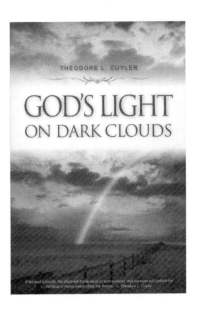

God's Light on Dark Clouds
Theodore L. Cuyler

It has been said that 2 Corinthians 1:4 deserves to be written in letters of gold, for it is one of the hardest and noblest works in all Christianity to be able to bring divine comfort to others in trouble; and yet by sufferings God fits and prepares his people for this noble and difficult service. Theodore L. Cuyler was thus divinely fitted for the great task of comforting God's suffering people. Fourteen years after losing two of his children in their infancy, this one-time pastor of Lafayette Avenue Presbyterian Church, Brooklyn, New York, lost a daughter at the age of twenty-one. In the pain-filled months following this deeply felt bereavement he penned the short chapters that make up this little book. A bestseller when first published in 1882, its pages offer hope for the desponding, consolation for the bereaved, and light for those in darkness.

ISBN 978-1-84871-023-8 paperback 144pp.